Financing Healthcare in China

China's current social medical insurance system has nominally covered more than 95 per cent of the 1.4 billion population in China and is moving towards the ambitious goal of universal health insurance coverage. Challenges posed by a rapidly ageing population, an inherently discriminatory design of the health insurance system, the disorder of the drug distribution system and an immature legal system constrain the Chinese government from realizing its goal of universal health insurance coverage in the long run.

This book uses a refined version of historical institutionalism to critically examine China's pathway to universal health insurance coverage since the mid-1980s. It pays crucial attention to the processes of transforming China's healthcare financing system into the basic social medical insurance system alongside rapid socio-economic changes.

Financing Healthcare in China will interest researchers and government and think-tank officials interested in the state of healthcare reforms in China. Healthcare specialists outside of East Asia may also be interested in its general study of healthcare in developing countries. Scholars and students interested in the healthcare field will also find this useful.

Sabrina Ching Yuen Luk is Associate Professor at the Faculty of Management and Economics, Kunming University of Science and Technology, China.

Routledge Studies in the Sociology of Health and Illness

Available titles include

Institutionalizing Assisted Reproductive Technologies
The Role of Science, Professionalism and Regulatory Control
Alexander Styhre and Rebecka Arman

Assisted Reproductive Technologies in the Global South and North
Issues, Challenges and the Future
Edited by Virginie Rozée and Sayeed Unisa

Socio-economics of Personalized Medicine in Asia
Shirley Sun

Financing Healthcare in China
Towards universal health insurance
Sabrina Ching Yuen Luk

Forthcoming titles

Vaginal Examination in Labour
Challenging contemporary practice
Mary Stewart

Transnationalising Reproduction
Third Party Conception in a Globalised World
Edited by Roisin Ryan Flood and Jenny Gunnarsson Payne

The Social Determinants of Male Health
John MacDonald

Fathering Children with Autism
Needs, Practices and Service Use
Carol Potter

Financing Healthcare in China

Towards universal health insurance

Sabrina Ching Yuen Luk

Routledge
Taylor & Francis Group

LONDON AND NEW YORK

First published 2017
by Routledge

2 Park Square, Milton Park, Abingdon, Oxfordshire OX14 4RN
52 Vanderbilt Avenue, New York, NY 10017

Routledge is an imprint of the Taylor & Francis Group, an informa business

First issued in paperback 2019

British Library Cataloguing in Publication Data
A catalogue record for this book is available from the British Library

Library of Congress Cataloging-in-Publication Data
Names: Luk, Sabrina Ching Yuen, author.
Title: Financing healthcare in China : towards universal health
  insurance / by Sabrina Ching Yuen Luk.
Description: Abingdon, Oxon ; New York : Routledge, 2017. | Series:
  Routledge Studies in the Sociology of Health and Illness | Includes
  bibliographical references and index.
Identifiers: LCCN 2016011362 | ISBN 9781138844391 (hardback) |
  ISBN 9781315516295 (ebook)
Subjects: | MESH: Healthcare Financing | Health Care Reform—
  history | Insurance, Health—history | Universal Coverage | China
Classification: LCC RA410.55.C6 | NLM WA 11 JC6 | DDC 362.1068/
  10951—dc23
LC record available at https://lccn.loc.gov/2016011362

ISBN: 978-1-138-84439-1 (hbk)
ISBN: 978-0-367-37463-1 (pbk)

Typeset in Galliard
by Apex CoVantage, LLC

Dedicated to my father (Roger Luk) and my mother (Sandy Chu) for their support and unconditional love

To the memory of my godfather (Wing Lin Leung)

Contents

List of tables   viii
Acknowledgements   ix
Preface   x
List of abbreviations   xi

1 Achieving universal health coverage through a
   multi-layered social health insurance system   1

2 Population ageing and epidemiologic transitions in China   11

3 Health care system in the pre-reform era   27

4 Four phases of health insurance reform   43

5 A multi-layered health insurance system: composition,
   models and characteristics   56

6 Problems in the current multi-layered social health
   insurance system   71

7 Ways to ensure the financial sustainability of health
   insurance systems   90

Bibliography   107
Index   133

Tables

2.1 The proportion of population aged 65 and above to the total
     number of population in China in 2000   15
2.2 The proportion of population aged 65 and above to the total
     number of population in China in 2010   16
2.3 The proportion of population aged 60 and above to the total
     number of population in urban and rural areas in China in
     1982, 2000 and 2010   17
2.4 The five leading causes of death in urban areas, 1990–2012   21
2.5 The five leading causes of death in rural areas, 1990–2012   22
2.6 Crude mortality rate of major cause of death in urban areas,
     1990–2012   23
2.7 Crude mortality rate of major cause of death in rural areas,
     1990–2012   23
4.1 Health insurance related regulation/guiding opinions in China   46

Acknowledgements

This book is the result of two years' hard work. The arguments of this book have been developed mainly from primary research using a combination of documentary sources, archival records and semi-structured interviews. I owe a particular debt of gratitude to the informants of this study who generously spent their valuable time and sincerely shared with me their expertise and thoughts but who cannot be named.

Writing this book has been an intellectually stimulating journey. I am extremely grateful to Professor Peter Preston for his unwavering support and encouragement all along the way. I would also like to express my deepest gratitude to my parents and elder brother for being the anchor of my soul and the pillar of my strength. This book is testimony to their unconditional love and support throughout my prolonged pursuit of knowledge.

I hope the book conveys some of my enthusiasm for health care and political science.

Preface

Health insurance reform in China has been explored and examined in many studies. But the processes of health insurance reform and forces that shape the reform trajectory have not been understood completely. In order to fill this research gap, this book adopts a refined version of historical institutionalism to track and analyze the process of health insurance reform since the mid-1980s and examine a complex interplay of forces that lead to China's transformation from a free health care system to a multi-layered social health insurance system.

Health care itself is a complex issue and a political controversy. The reason why health care reform keeps rising to the top of the political agenda is that health care involves lots of competing values and competing interests. In China, health care is a hot topic. However, it is also a sensitive topic. The reason is that any in-depth investigation will unavoidably touch upon some sensitive issues. In this book, the author will touch upon some sensitive issues such as the disorder of the drug distribution system, fake hospitalization, health insurance fraud, 'black clinics' and the problem of 'feeding hospitals by selling drugs' (*yi yao yang yi*) when examining health insurance reforms. Some of the issues or problems are unique to China, but some are not. All these problems are closely related to the current social health insurance system and they are central to the institutional analysis.

The author hopes that this book can provide some valuable insights into some of the key issues of health insurance reform in China.

Abbreviations

ACFTU	All-China Federation of Trade Unions
BCG	bacille Calmette-Guérin
BMI	Basic Medical Insurance
BMIFURR	Basic Medical Insurance for Urban and Rural Residents
CIRC	China Insurance Regulatory Commission
CCP	Chinese Communist Party
CHA	Cooperative Health Agency
CMS	cooperative medical system
CLPRC	Criminal Law of the People's Republic of China
CIIS	Critical Illness Insurance Scheme
DPT	diphtheria-tetanus-pertussis vaccine
EPI	Expanded Programme on Immunization
GHS	Government-Funded Health Care Scheme
GDP	Gross Domestic Product
HPPC	Health Preservation Pharmaceutical Cooperative
HIG	Human Tetanus Immunoglobulin
IMR	Infant Mortality Rate
IFB	Insurance Fraud Bureau
KDD	Knowledge Discovery in Databases
LIS	Labor Insurance Scheme
MFCUs	Medicaid Fraud Control Units
MFA	Medical Financial Assistance
MSA	Medical Savings Account
MFSF	Medicare Fraud Strike Force
MOA	Ministry of Agriculture
MCA	Ministry of Civil Affairs
MOF	Ministry of Finance
MOH	Ministry of Health
MOL	Ministry of Labor
MOLSS	Ministry of Labor and Social Security
NDRC	National Development and Reform Commission
NRCMS	New Rural Cooperative Medical System
NCDs	non-communicable diseases

OPV	oral polio vaccine
OTC	over-the-counter
PRC	People's Republic of China
RMB	Renminbi
SILPRC	Social Insurance Law of the People's Republic of China
SPF	social pooling fund
SOEs	state-owned enterprises
SID	supply induced demand
TFR	total fertility rate
US	United States
UHC	universal health coverage
UEBMI	Urban Employee Basic Medical Insurance
URBMI	Urban Resident Basic Medical Insurance
WHO	World Health Organization

1 Achieving universal health coverage through a multi-layered social health insurance system

Introduction

Universal health coverage (UHC) is at the top of the global health agenda and 'now an ambition for all nations at all stages of development' (World Health Organization 2013a: 5). Rapidly ageing populations, rising medical costs and financial constraints on public budgets have driven governments in both developed and developing countries to explore ways that can provide affordable health care for their people. In 2005, all member states of the World Health Organization (WHO) made the commitment to achieve UHC (World Health Organization 2013a: xi), which was 'a collective expression of the belief that all people should have access to the health services they need without risk of financial ruin or impoverishment' (World Health Organization 2013a: xi). The commitment also expressed 'concern for equity and for honouring everyone's right to health' (World Health Organization 2013a: 5). At present, people in many countries are still denied access to health care because of insufficient financial means. Meanwhile, large numbers of people fall into poverty or fall back into poverty every year due to their inability to pay for health care. The lack of access to affordable health care unavoidably leads to deficits in health and wellbeing of people. In particular, low-income people worry about getting sick or injured because they are far less likely to receive diagnosis and treatment. The lack of access to affordable health care is also detrimental to economic development that requires a healthy and productive workforce. For many years, the affordability of health care has become a great concern for governments and their people worldwide. Governments are under great pressure to find appropriate financing strategies that can guarantee adequate and affordable health care for all people, regardless of their circumstances. They strive to achieve UHC by experimenting with different approaches and translating their plans into action.

However, achieving UHC is never an easy task. A country's transition to UHC can take years, even decades (World Health Organization 2005) because there are lots of hurdles to overcome. Due to the enormous cross-national differences, there is neither a single logic of reform nor a one-size-fits-all reform model to achieve UHC. Successful experience in one country is not easily transferable to another country. It is unwise or even dangerous for a country to blindly copy another country's reform model without careful consideration of its reality of development. Health care itself is a complex issue. It is a subject of debate and political controversy. The reason why health care reform keeps rising to the top of the political agenda is that health care involves lots of competing values and competing interests. Some will gain from reform, but some will lose. Besides, reform does not guarantee success. It may not be able to address fundamental problems. It may even create new, unanticipated problems that must be evaluated and addressed by the government. To achieve UHC definitely requires ongoing reform processes, strong political will and long-term commitment.

China's three decades of health insurance reforms

In China, health care financing reform began in the mid-1980s when the collapse of the entire health care financing regime caused by China's transformation to market economy forced the government to find new ways to finance health care. Until now, the reform has undergone four phases: the exploration phase (1984–92); the experimental phase (1993–7); the implementation phase (1998–2001); and the extension phase (2002 to present). After years of substantial efforts, the government has established a multi-layered social health insurance system to provide different segments of the population with financial protection against the costs of illness. The multi-layered health insurance system consists of the Urban Employee Basic Medical Insurance (UEBMI), the New Rural Cooperative Medical System (NRCMS), Urban Resident Basic Medical Insurance (URBMI) and the Critical Illness Insurance Scheme (CIIS). Medical Financial Assistance (MFA) System was also established to subsidize people with financial hardship to participate in the URBMI or the NRCMS. Together, these social medical insurance schemes have covered more than 95 per cent of the China's population (Qian 2013: 334). However, there is still much to be done before achieving a real sense of UHC.

According to WHO, moving toward UHC is to expand coverage in three ways: (i) the breadth of coverage; (ii) the depth of coverage; and (iii) the height of coverage (World Health Organization 2008: 25–6). The breadth of coverage refers to 'the proportion of the population that enjoys social health protection' (World Health Organization 2008: 25). The depth of coverage refers to 'the range of essential services that are necessary to address people's health needs effectively' (World Health Organization 2008: 26). The height of coverage refers to 'the portion of health-care costs covered through pooling and pre-payment mechanisms' (World Health Organization 2008: 26). While the current social medical insurance schemes achieve a 95 per cent breadth of coverage, they still lag behind in terms of the depth and the height of coverage. Due to its compulsory nature, the UEBMI is the most dominant medical insurance scheme with the largest number of participants in the nation. It offers comprehensive coverage to both inpatient and outpatient medical expenses. The rest of the medical insurance schemes are voluntary in nature and only provide partial coverage for the insured. Such disparities result in high out-of-pocket medical expenses faced by the insured.

Health insurance system: inherently discriminatory in design

In fact, deep inequality and wide disparity in treatment among the insured popu-lation is attributed to the design of the social health insurance system that is inherently discriminatory in nature. The multi-layered social health insurance system is similar to a feudal system in ancient China, dividing people into differ-ent ranks. It privileges retired cadres, old Red Army and disabled revolutionary soldiers by letting them enjoy free health care with their medical expenses paid by the basic medical insurance fund. Due to the ideas of Confucianism, retirees do not need to pay any insurance premium, but can enjoy higher reimbursement levels than incumbent employees. Urban employees enjoy better insurance cover-age than non-working urban population and rural households. Given the limited availability of financial resources to finance health care of 1.4 billion people, it is understandable that providing equal treatment for every person seems to be an impossible task. Equity, universality, efficiency, cost containment, responsiveness and comprehensiveness are some of the desirable qualities in health care (Fierl-beck 2011: 3). But there is always a trade-off when it comes to the attainment of these qualities. The more the government moves to secure one of these qualities, the more it can undermine one or several other qualities (Fierlbeck 2011). In China, the government can only guarantee the provision of basic medical treat-ment rather than equal treatment across insurance programs at this stage.

Due to the logic of segregating one group of people from others, the multi-layered social health insurance system does not have a single national risk pool but fragmented risk pools. Risk pools are fragmented in two ways. First, different types of health insurance schemes have their own risk pools. Since health insur-ance schemes vary in terms of revenue base and coverage, there is no integration or transfer between risk pools. Second, social health insurance funds are collected and managed by local governments in the areas under their jurisdiction. There are also no transfers between risk pools across regions. Consequently, fragmented risk pools increase uncertainty associated with health care expenditures and lead to an ineffective transfer and redistribution of financial resources from healthy individuals to the sick.

The disorder of the drug distribution system

While the inherently discriminatory design of the health insurance system acts as an impediment to achieve UHC, the disorder of the drug distribution sys-tem also poses as an ongoing challenge for moving towards UHC. Since the economic reform and opening up in the late 1970s, the government has lifted its control on drug prices, leading to a drastic increase in drug prices. The centralized drug distribution system was abandoned and the number of drug manufacturers and distributors increased rapidly (Luk 2015: 48–9). In order to survive in this competitive environment, drug manufacturers recruited pharma-ceutical sales representatives to promote and sell pharmaceutical products (Luk 2015: 48). Pharmaceutical sales representatives who wanted to meet sales target used rebates – commonly known as 'kickbacks' – to lure health care providers and physicians to purchase and prescribe their drugs (Luk 2015: 48–9). The collusion among drug manufacturers, drug distributors, health care providers and doctors for the sake of earning more profits led to skyrocketing drug prices (Luk 2015: 41). Their collusion was so strong that even the government's drug price control policy in the later stage failed to deliver any noticeable results. Drug expenses constituted the largest proportion of medical expenses in China. Many people who were insured had to pay high out-of-pocket drug expenses because doctors' prescriptions of expensive, imported drugs could not be reimbursed by the basic medical insurance (Luk 2014: 72).

The deeply flawed hospital system

Meanwhile, the deeply flawed hospital system is another reason why achieving UHC is difficult. Since the 1980s, the government's retreat from financing health care has substantially decreased subsidies for the public hospitals (Duckett 2011; Luk 2015). Public hospitals that were given financial autonomy to charge for their services began to run like for-profit organizations (Luk 2015: 49). Doctors who would receive performance bonuses were incentivized to prescribe unnecessary drugs or provide unnecessary medical tests and treatment. The problem of physician-induced demand and the problem of 'feeding hospitals by selling drugs' (*yi yao yang yi*) have become very serious. The self-funding interests of public hospitals weakened their social responsibilities (The World Bank 2010: 6) while 'the profit-seeking interests of doctors hurt the interests of patients' (Luk 2015: 50). Without an effective mechanism to restrain supply-side moral hazard, health care expenditures continued to increase. As a result, people had to bear heavy financial burdens for meeting their medical needs, regardless of whether they were covered by medical insurance.

An immature legal system

An immature legal system also limits the government's capability to achieve UHC. Since the implementation of basic medical insurance schemes, China has experienced a rapid increase in health insurance fraud that is committed by health care providers, medical staff and dishonest patients. It led to a substantial amount of health insurance fund draining away. Due to the immature legal system, China does not have state law that specifically targets health care fraud and abuse. Social Insurance Law of the People's Republic of China (SILPRC) and Criminal Law of the People's Republic of China (CLPRC) are the only existing laws applicable to health insurance fraud. But they are too vague to adequately address health care fraud. In particular, penalties for those in violation of SILPRC seem to be too mild and do not produce a strong deterrent effect, letting fraudsters continue to take advantage of the inadequacy of the existing legal system. If health insurance fraud cannot be combatted effectively, the sustainability of the health insurance fund will become questionable.

In sum, the inherently discriminatory nature of the multi-layered social health insurance system, together with the disorder of the drug distribution system, the deeply flawed hospital system and an immature legal system, have no doubt impeded the pace of achieving UHC. These problems are intimately connected with each other and they are central to institutional analysis. However, there are no easy answers to these problems and they cannot be solved overnight. Having said that, however, real progress can still be made if there is strong political will and long-term commitment. At present, the situation of 'difficult to see a doctor, expensive to see a doctor' (*kan bing nan, kan bin gui*) is still widespread in China (Chan *et al.* 2012: 113). It continues to be a normal part of daily life for ordinary people. Unreasonably high drug prices decrease patients' trust in doctors. In recent years, high drug prices or medical expenditures have led to increasing disputes between doctors and patients and even become one of the main causes of violent attack against doctors. The tense doctor–patient relationship and patients' violence against doctors are warning signs in health care that require the government to take action before the situation further deteriorates. When President Xi Jinping became a new generation of party leader, he had the goal of providing affordable and accessible health care for all Chinese people (Luk 2015: 42). It is important to realize and hold up the promise of providing accessible and affordable health care, especially when China has been experiencing unprecedented growth in the older populations and its older populations are facing the problem of 'growing old before getting rich'. Increasing medical needs and health care costs associated with ageing population have compelled the government to pay more attention to maintain sustainability of health insurance fund. There is a pressing need for the government to accomplish the goal of UHC in order to cope with the challenges brought by the ageing population.

Analytical foundation: refined theory of historical institutionalism

This book tracks and analyzes the process of health insurance reforms in China since the mid-1980s and critically examines the complex interplay of forces that shape health insurance reforms over time. It also examines the problems in the current health insurance system and suggests practical ways to maintain a sustainable health insurance system. It adopts the refined theory of historical institutionalism, which was developed by the author in her book entitled *Health Insurance Reforms in Asia* (2014), to identify forces that lead to China's transformation from a free health care system to a multi-layered social health insurance system.

The traditional version of historical institutionalism emphasizes the importance of political institutions and policy legacies in structuring the strategic behavior and interactions of political actors during the policy-making process (Skocpol 1992; Hall and Taylor 1996; Immergut 1998; Thelen 1999). It 'see[s] institutions as formal or informal procedures, routines, norms, and conventions in the organizational structure of the polity or the political economy' (Amenta and Ramsey 2010: 16). It 'centres on the concept of path dependence' (Thelen

2003), which refers to the dynamics of increasing returns and self-reinforcing processes with the potential for a lock-in of a specific trajectory (Pierson and Skocpol 2002; Amenta and Ramsey 2010). Subsequent policy development tends to continue along the same path regardless of the advantages of the alternatives (Peters 1999). Historical institutionalism is 'a useful and compelling approach to explain institutionalism stability, policy continuities within countries and different policy trajectories across countries over time' (Luk 2014: 10). However, its power to explain institutional and policy change is limited. Although the notions of 'punctuated equilibrium' (Krasner 1984), 'conjunctures' (Wilsford 1994) and 'accidental logics' (Tuohy 1999) are introduced to the theory of historical institutionalism, they have several drawbacks that limit the power to explain institutional and policy change. The notion of 'punctuated equilibrium' is basically flawed because simply relying on external shock to explain change leads to institutional change becoming purely a product of fate (Steinmo 2008). The notion of 'conjunctures', which refers to 'the fleeting comings together of a number of diverse elements into a new, single combination' (Wilsford 1994: 257) is also problematic because the definition of 'conjuncture' is 'too vague and lacks a coherent theoretical underpinning' (Luk 2014: 11). It is hard to understand 'what the diverse elements are and what the composition of these diverse elements should be in order to bring about path change' (Luk 2014: 11). There is also a lack of a common set of criteria to measure when and how a conjuncture is powerful enough to bring about path change (Luk 2014: 11). As to the notion of 'accidental logic', it 'downplays the role of political institutions during the policy process' (Luk 2014: 12) by arguing that a mixture of factors can be 'salient at particular moments for shaping policy outcome' (Luk 2014: 12). Previous studies show that the traditional version of historical institutionalism has limited power to explain institutional change.

The refined theory of historical institutionalism is different from the traditional version of historical institutionalism in a sense that it identifies three sources of changes and offers new insight that institutional or policy change can be understood as an outcome shaped by the dynamic interaction of these three sources of change with political institutions and policy legacies (Luk 2014: 12). It brings the roles of environmental triggers, actors and ideas in to explain institutional change without abandoning the core assumptions that political institutions and policy feedback effects remain key influences on policy outcomes (Luk 2014: 16).

The first source of change is environmental trigger. Institutions are open systems and hence they are not immune to environmental pressure. Environmental trigger refers to international or domestic environmental pressure that can affect the way an institution operates and its access to resources. Based on the work of Cortell and Peterson (1999), international environmental triggers refer to war, geopolitical conflict, changing balance of power, macroeconomic change, international treaties, technological changes, dislocation and shocks while domestic environmental triggers refer to civil war, revolution, change of government, economic change, demographic change, social movement and social conflict (Cortell and Peterson 1999: 185). Environmental trigger, alone or in combination, can 'open

windows of opportunity for policy makers to make institutional change possible'
(Luk 2014: 13). But political institutions are not passive recipients of environmental
pressures (Aldrich 1979: 144). They 'can either reinforce or offset the effects of
environmental pressures, which in turn facilitate or inhibit change' (Luk 2014: 16).

The second source of change is policy actors. Policy actors refer to leaders,
policy makers and government officials. They function as bridges between the
political institution and the broader environment and are the agents of change
(Luk 2014: 13). Political institutions play a determinant role in distributing
power among policy actors and affect their willingness to act on a window of
opportunity and implement reform strategies (Cortell and Peterson 1999;
Galperin 2004). The subject position a policy actor occupies provides him/her a
legitimated identity that facilitates access to resources (e.g. capital and skills) and
the exertion of power over the field at a particular time (Luk 2014: 13–14).
Nevertheless, for policy actors to break with existing rules and champion and dif-
fuse new practices, they need ideas to help them do so.

Being the third source of change, ideas are 'notions which link norms and
values to practical action' (Alaszewski and Brown 2012: 208) and help policy
makers make sense of their world (Béland and Wadden 2012). There are three
types of ideas: programmatic ideas, policy paradigms and societal beliefs (Hwang
2006: 17). Programmatic ideas are cognitive in nature. They are technical and
professional ideas that can prescribe a precise course of policy action (Campbell 1998: 386). For example, fiscal or monetary instruments are adjusted by
policy makers to achieve macroeconomic goals (Campbell 1998: 28). Policy
paradigms are also cognitive in nature. They refer to a framework of ideas and
standards such as the principles of neoclassical economics that 'specifies policy
goals, [and] the kind of policy instruments that can be used to achieve such goals'
(Luk 2014: 15). Societal beliefs are normative in nature. They are broad-based
attitudes and normative assumptions about what is moral or socially appropriate
(Campbell 1998, 2002), which constrain 'the normative range of solutions that
policy makers view as politically acceptable and legitimate' (Luk 2014: 15).

Ideas can play three important roles. First, they enable policy makers to legiti-
mize institutional or policy change by associating their policy decisions and
actions with commonly held assumptions, norms and values (Alaszewski and
Brown 2012: 188–208). Second, ideas bound the rationality of decision making and prioritize certain concerns of policy makers over others (Alaszewski and
Brown 2012: 192–208). Third, ideas help policy makers 'strategically craft frames
to make policies politically plausible and acceptable' (Luk 2014: 14). Ideological
framing helps justify the need of policy makers to reform and bring about institutional and policy change (Campbell 2002; Béland and Wadden 2012). 'Ideas are
important source of actors' preferences and of their decisions to exploit windows
of opportunity' (Luk 2014: 15).

Policy change 'has a strong ideational component' (Béland and Wadden
2012: 8). There are conditions under which new ideas rise to political prominence
and policy makers trade old ideas for new ones. New ideas rise to political prominence when there is dissatisfaction with the inadequacy of existing belief structures

(Berman 2001: 234). Old ideas are 'delegitimized when they are perceived to fail for some reason' (Campbell 2002: 33). They produce negative feedback effects such as negative socio-economic consequences that undermine the fiscal, political or social sustainability of existing policy (Weaver 2010). When old ideas are delegitimized, it opens up 'a political space into which new ideas can be inserted' (Berman 2001: 234). New ideas must be championed by policy makers who have power and resources to win support and enable the new idea to get a better or more respectful hearing (Berman 2001: 235). Besides, new ideas must fit with existing institutional structures, correspond to the needs of a particular situation better than old ideas, or are more responsive to particular policy problems in order to gain wide acceptance (Berman 2001: 236). But new ideas can be filtered by political institutions (Luk 2014: 17). Political institutions define channels in which new ideas can be absorbed, integrated or translated into policy (Thelen and Steinmo 1992).

The refined theory of historical institutionalism shows that bringing the roles of environmental triggers, actors and ideas in to explain institutional change would not downplay the role of political institutions. Conversely, the role of political institutions becomes more distinct when these three sources of change are integrated into the theory. It is because political institutions can reinforce or offset the effects of environmental pressures (Welch and Wong 1998); affect the way policy makers define their goals, policy preferences and strategies based on their institutional position, responsibilities and relationships with others (Thelen and Steinmo 1992; Hall and Taylor 1996; Immergut 1998); and define the channels in which ideas can be absorbed and translated into policy.

Methodology and data collection

This book adopts an interpretive case study approach in order to obtain in-depth, multi-faceted investigation of health insurance reform in China since the mid-1980s. It uses the refined theory of historical institutionalism as a unifying logic and the basis of case interpretation to examine the developmental trajectory of health insurance reform over time and the complex interplay of forces that shape the ongoing reform process. It collects data through multiple sources in order to offer insights and give a rich and holistic account of the development of health insurance reform in China. To achieve data triangulation, this book collects data from semi-structured interviews, documents and archival records. Semi-structured interviews with government officials, civil servants, nurses, scholars and ordinary citizens were conducted in Shanghai and Kunming in order to 'compensate for both the lack and limitations of documentary evidence' (Tansey 2007: 767). They could also provide the most updated information about health insurance reform and help the author gather rich details about the thoughts and attitudes of different people. Documents which included books, journal articles, government publications and newspaper articles were obtained through open channels such as university libraries, research centres and the Internet. Many Chinese publications, government publications and newspaper articles were used in this study to explain issues related to health insurance reform. Some of these materials have never appeared in previous Western studies. Archival records such as statistical yearbooks and population censuses were used to provide useful figures from decades past that could not be accurately obtained from interviews. Coding is used to analyze data of this study.

Central argument

Health insurance reform in China has been explored and examined in many studies. But the processes of health insurance reform and forces that shape the developmental trajectory of health insurance reform have not been understood completely. In order to fill this research gap, this book adopts the refined theory of historical institutionalism to track and analyze the process of health insurance reform over time and demonstrate how the complex relationships and interaction among political institutions, policy legacy, environmental triggers, actors and ideas produce a specific reform trajectory and outcome. The central argument of this book is that China's health insurance reform is a political process revealing an intricate interplay of power relationships and diverse interests. Health insurance reform is a political controversy that involves competing values and competing interests. Competing interests among ministries and the autonomy of local governments affect the development of health insurance reform. Besides, health insurance reform is an ongoing process responding to changing circumstances such as China's transformation to market economy, rapid ageing population and epidemiologic transitions. The basic medical insurance system that was originally established to provide medical coverage for urban employees had been gradually extended to cover rural households and the non-working urban population. Three decades of health insurance reforms show that China was able to exit from the old policy path of providing free health care due to three sources of change. The combined forces of the new Party leader and his government, China's transformation to market economy, Deng Xiaoping's endorsement of new ideas opened windows of opportunity for the implementation of a new social health insurance system combined with individual medical savings account (MSA) and a social pooling fund (SPF). Once the social health insurance system was established, it provided increasing returns and self-reinforcing processes that resulted in a lock-in of a development trajectory based on implementing different health insurance schemes tailored for different segments of the population. Health insurance reform in the latter stage revolved around the ideas of individual MSA and the SPF. As a result, a multi-layered health insurance system was established in China. This book argues that the role of political institutions remains the most influential element in explaining health insurance reform and its outcomes.

Chapter outline

The remainder of this book is structured as follows: Chapter 2 provides a detailed account of demographic and epidemiologic transitions in China since 1949. Chapter 3 critically examines the health care system established during

Mao Zedong's era. It provides important historical and institutional background necessary for understanding the development of health insurance reforms in the later stage. Chapter 4 critically examines four phases of health insurance reform since the mid-1980s and identifies the complex interplay of forces that shape the reform trajectory. Chapter 5 gives a detailed account of the current health insurance schemes and the models that were adopted by local governments when implementing health insurance reform. Chapter 6 examines problems in the current multi-layered health insurance system and explains why these problems act as impediments to achieve UHC. Chapter 7 provides constructive and pragmatic ways that can ensure the sustainability of social health insurance system and achieve UHC in future.

2 Population ageing and epidemiologic transitions in China

Introduction

Since 1949, China has undergone enormous demographic and epidemiologic transformations. Demographically, China has become one of the world's fastest ageing countries and has the world's largest ageing population. Epidemiologically, China has shifted from carrying a heavy burden of infectious diseases to chronic, non-communicable diseases (NCDs). Since 2010, cancer has become the leading cause of death in China. The combined forces of population ageing and epidemiologic transition to NCDs have imposed heavy financial pressure on both the government and citizens. There is a pressing need for the government to ensure a sustainable health care financing system and affordable care for its people. This chapter gives a detailed account of demographic and epidemiologic transformations in China since 1949, and identifies and examines reasons causing such transformation. It also examines the implications of population ageing and epidemiological transitions for health financing.

Population ageing

Over the past 67 years, China has undergone enormous demographic transformation. At present, China is the most populous country in the world. It has approximately 1.38 billion people, representing 19 per cent of the world's population (United Nations 2015: 1). Population in China has been ageing at an unprecedented speed and scale over time. Population ageing in China has five characteristics.

Ageing at an unprecedented speed

First, China is one of the world's fastest ageing countries (Beijing Evening News 2015). In 1999, China met the United Nation's definition of an 'ageing society', with persons aged 65 and above making up more than 7 per cent of its total population. It took China only 40 years to become an ageing society while it took the United Kingdom, the United States (US) and the Nordic countries more than 100 years to do so (Cai et al. 2012: 12). Since 2000, the speed of population ageing in China has surpassed that of the world (Chen and Chan 2011: 63). While it took the world 60 years (1950–2010) to experience a 3 per cent increase in the ratio of those aged 60 and above, it took China only 10 years (2000–10) to experience a 3.8 per cent increase in the ratio of those aged 60 and above (Zhang W. 2012).

Ageing at an unprecedented scale

Second, China has the world's largest ageing population (Beijing Evening News 2015). Using data from *China's Aging Statistics Compendium, 1953–2009* and *Tabulation on the 2010 Population Census of the People's Republic of China (Book I)*, the author calculated the number of elderly population aged 60 years and over and the proportion of elderly population aged 60 years and over to the total population in China. The result indicated that the number of elderly population and the proportion of elderly population to the total population have increased over the past 60 years. In 1953, the number of elderly population aged 60 years and over was about 41.5 million, which accounted for 7.3 per cent of the total population. In 1982, the number of elderly population 60 years and over rose to about 76.6 million, which accounted for 7.6 per cent of the total population. From 2000 to 2010, the number of elderly population aged 60 years and over rose from about 129.9 million to 177.5 million, which respectively accounted for 10.5 per cent and 13.3 per cent of the total population. By the end of 2014, China's population aged 60 years and over reached 212 million, accounting for 15.5 per cent of the total population (Xinhua News 2015a). In 2013, China had the world's largest number of oldest-old group aged 80 years or over, which were 23 million persons (United Nations 2013: 32). The total number of old-est-old group has currently reached 24 million (Beijing Evening News 2015). The increase in the proportion of elderly population to the total population was related to rapid fertility decline and increased life expectancy.

Rapid fertility decline was reflected in a decrease in the total fertility rate (TFR) over time. TFR refers to the average number of children born to a woman over her lifetime. In 1949, the TFR was an average of 6.14 births per woman (White 2006: 44). During the period of Great Leap Forward (1958–61), the TFR precipitously dropped from an average of 5.68 births per woman in 1958 to an average of 3.29 births per woman in 1961 due to the devastating famine and economic dislocation (White 2006: 43–4). The TFR rebounded to an average of 7.5 births per woman in 1963 (White 2006: 51) but dropped quickly during the Cultural Revolution decade (1966–76) due to the integration of an increasingly aggressive birth control program into the economic planning process (White 2006: 57–60). The TFR dropped from an average of 6.26 births per woman in 1966 to 3.24 births per woman in 1976 (White 2006: 44). The TFR has continued to drop further since the one-child policy was officially enforced in 1980 to curb fast population growth that was 'said to pose a serious threat to economic development and environmental sustainability' (Yan 2006: 3). It dropped from an average of 2.63 births per woman in 1981 to 2.01 births per woman in 1991 (White 2006: 44), which was below the replacement level of 2.1 births per woman. The demographic effects of below replacement fertility on a country accelerated population ageing process and population decline because couples, on average, did not produce enough children to replace themselves. Since the early 1990s, the TFR has been below the replacement level. In July 2015, the National Health and Family Commission of the People's Republic of China announced in a press conference that the TFR in China was somewhere between 1.5 and 1.65 per cent (Xinhua News 2015b).

Increased life expectancy was another reason for China to have a higher proportion of elderly population. In 1949, the average life expectancy in China was only 35 years of age (Xinhua News 2004). In 1960, the average life expectancy rose to 43.46 years of age (Zhang and Zhang 2012). In 1970, the average life expectancy became 63 years of age (Tulchinsky and Varavikova 2014: 708). From 1982 to 1990, the average life expectancy slightly increased from 67.77 years of age to 68.55 years of age (National Bureau of Statistics of China 2013a: 101). From 2000 to 2010, the average life expectancy increased from 71.4 years of age to 74.83 years of age (National Bureau of Statistics of China 2013a: 101). In 2012, the average life expectancy reached 75 years of age (World Health Organization 2014: 60). According to *World Health Statistics 2015*, the average life expectancy was 74 years of age for men and 77 years of age for women (World Health Organization 2015: 44). With rapid fertility decline and increased life expectancy, 'future cohorts of elderly can expect to have smaller numbers of living children – and fewer sources of familial support' (Chinese Academy of Social Sciences *et al.* 2011: 7).

Geographical differences in the proportion of elderly population

Third, there were differences in the proportion of elderly population among provinces, municipalities and autonomous regions due to geographical differences in socio-economic development. Since the 1950s, Eastern coastal regions of China have had a higher level of ageing than Western regions of China. Besides, Eastern coastal regions of China have aged faster than Western regions of China. The study of Liu S. (1997), which ranked Chinese provinces from top to bottom by the proportion of elderly population aged 65 years and over in the first four population censuses of China (1953–90), showed that most of the provinces in Eastern China had higher proportions of elderly population than provinces in Western China. In 1953, Shandong and Hebei provinces in Eastern China, which respectively had 6.31 per cent and 6.24 per cent of elderly population aged 65 years and over, ranked first and second while Gansu and Qinghai in Western China, which respectively had 3.09 per cent and 2.82 per cent of elderly population aged 65 years and over, ranked twenty fifth and twenty sixth (Liu S. 1997: 34). In 1982, Shanghai (7.42 per cent), Zhejiang (5.76 per cent), Hebei (5.67 per cent), Beijing (5.65 per cent) and Shangdong (5.62 per cent) in Eastern China were the Top Five Municipalities/Provinces having high proportion of elderly population aged 65 and above (Liu S. 1997: 34). In 1990, municipalities and provinces in Eastern China were still the Top Five Places having high proportion of elderly population aged 65 and above. They were Shanghai (9.38 per cent), Zhejiang (6.83 per cent), Jiangsu (6.79 per cent), Tianjin (6.46 per cent) and Beijing (6.35 per cent) (Liu S. 1997: 34). Liu S. (1997) argued that municipalities or provinces having a high level of ageing were due to having very low TFR.

Using the data obtained from the *2000 Population Census of China*, the author calculated the proportion of elderly population aged 65 years and over by provinces and ranked the provinces from top to bottom. The result indicated that the Top Five Places having high proportion of elderly population were similar to the results in 1990. Shanghai (11.46 per cent), Zhejiang (8.92 per cent) and Jiangsu (8.84 per cent) were still the Top Three places having high proportion of elderly population while Beijing (8.42 per cent) and Tianjin (8.41 per cent) respectively ranked fourth and fifth this time (Table 2.1).

However, the situation became quite different when it came to 2010. Table 2.2 illustrates the author's calculation using data from the *2010 Population Census of the People's Republic of China*. The result indicated that there was a huge difference in the Top Five Places having a high proportion of elderly population aged 65 and above. Some of the provinces in Western and central China had a higher proportion of elderly population. Chongqing (11.72 per cent) and Sichuan (10.95 per cent) in Western China ranked first and second this time, which was followed by Jiangsu (10.88 per cent), Liaoning (10.31 per cent) in Eastern China and Anhui (10.23 per cent) in central China. Chongqing and Sichuan were two of the largest labor-exporting provinces in China. These two provinces had striking labor export with young, working-age labor force exploring employment opportunities in other provinces while leaving old aged parents at home, which resulted in having higher proportion of elderly population. Anhui Province had higher proportion of elderly population because of the generation of baby boomers born in the 1950s joining the ranks of China's older population (Anhui Ageing Commission Office 2008).

Besides, Table 2.2 indicated that, in 2010, 26 places (four municipalities, two autonomous regions and 20 provinces) in China had become an ageing society, with population aged 65 and above making up more than 7 per cent of its total population. Only Guangdong, Xinjiang, Ningxia, Qinghai and Tibet provinces were not ageing societies. Guangdong Province had the largest number of floating population 'who live and work in areas other than their registered address' (World Health Organization 2013b: 3). According to the *2010 Population Census of the People's Republic of China*, the number of floating population in Guangdong was about 21.5 million (Population Census Office and Department of Population and Employment Statistics 2012a: 490). And 85.77 per cent (about 18.4 million) of the floating population went to Guangdong Province due to working and doing businesses in the place (Population Census Office and Department of Population and Employment Statistics 2012a: 622). The floating population is young and belongs to the working-age population, thereby decreasing the proportion of elderly population. According to *Report on China's Migrant Population Development 2015*, the proportion of work-age population aged between 15 and 59 accounted for 78 per cent of the total number of floating population in China in 2014 (Southern Metropolis Daily 2015). Xinjiang, Ningxia, Qinghai and Tibet were ranked in the bottom four in terms of the proportion of elderly population aged 65 years and over. Their proportions of elderly population aged 65 years and over were very low, which respectively accounted for only 6.48 per cent, 6.39 per cent, 6.30 per cent and 5.09 per cent. They shared the common characteristics of being remote provinces located in the northwest and western part of China with less developed economies. Besides, these four provinces implemented a second-child permit policy for peasants (Scharping 2003: 104) and granted 'privileges for even higher birth orders for some groups of their population' (Scharping 2003: 104). This can explain why the proportion of elderly population aged 65 years and over remained low in these places.

Appendix

Table 2.1 The proportion of population aged 65 and above to the total number of population in China in 2000

Province/Municipality/ Autonomous Region	Total population*	Number of population Aged 65+**	Proportion of population aged 65+ to the total number of population**	Ranking
Beijing	13,569,194	1,142,864	8.42%	4
Tianjin	9,848,731	828,413	8.41%	5
Hebei	66,684,419	4,699,148	7.05%	14
Shanxi	32,471,242	2,055,048	6.33%	18
Inner Mongolia	23,323,347	1,284,647	5.51%	26
Liaoning	41,824,412	3,297,206	7.88%	8
Jilin	26,802,191	1,619,759	6.04%	23
Heilongjiang	36,237,576	2,015,344	5.56%	25
Shanghai	16,407,734	1,880,316	11.46%	1
Jiangsu	73,043,577	6,458,388	8.84%	3
Zhejiang	45,930,651	4,098,584	8.92%	2
Anhui	58,999,948	4,479,972	7.59%	9
Fujian	34,097,947	2,279,642	6.69%	16
Jiangxi	40,397,598	2,532,328	6.27%	19
Shandong	89,971,789	7,308,473	8.12%	6
Henan	91,236,854	6,482,364	7.10%	13
Hubei	59,508,870	3,818,701	6.42%	17
Hunan	63,274,173	4,726,550	7.47%	11
Guangdong	85,225,007	5,259,948	6.17%	20
Guangxi	43,854,538	3,202,960	7.30%	12
Hainan	7,559,035	509,531	6.74%	15
Chongqing	30,512,763	2,445,382	8.01%	7
Sichuan	82,348,296	6,229,433	7.56%	10
Guizhou	35,247,695	2,102,966	5.97%	24
Yunnan	42,360,089	2,580,293	6.09%	22
Tibet	2,616,329	124,282	4.75%	28
Shaanxi	35,365,072	2,175,962	6.15%	21
Gansu	25,124,282	1,307,498	5.20%	27
Qinghai	4,822,963	220,039	4.56%	30
Ningxia	5,486,393	245,501	4.47%	31
Xinjiang	18,459,511	862,480	4.67%	29

Note: *The data are obtained from *Tabulation on the 2000 Population Census of the People's Republic of China (Book I)*, China Statistics Press, p. 134.**This is the author's calculation using data from *Tabulation on the 2000 Population Census of the People's Republic of China (Book I)*, China Statistics Press, pp. 141–4.

Table 2.2 The proportion of population aged 65 and above to the total number of population in China in 2010

Province/ Municipality/ Autonomous Region	Total population*	Number of population Aged 65+**	Proportion of population aged 65+ to the total number of population**	Ranking
Beijing	19,612,368	1,708,852	8.71%	13
Tianjin	12,938,693	1,102,388	8.52%	15
Hebei	71,854,210	5,919,738	8.24%	19
Shanxi	35,712,101	2,705,259	7.58%	25
Inner Mongolia	24,706,291	1,868,177	7.56%	26
Liaoning	43,746,323	4,509,441	10.31%	4
Jilin	27,452,815	2,301,838	8.38%	16
Heilongjiang	38,313,991	3,173,314	8.28%	18
Shanghai	23,019,196	2,331,313	10.13%	6
Jiangsu	78,660,941	8,558,646	10.88%	3
Zhejiang	54,426,891	5,081,675	9.34%	9
Anhui	59,500,468	6,084,548	10.23%	5
Fujian	36,894,217	2,912,130	7.89%	22
Jiangxi	44,567,797	3,388,301	7.60%	24
Shandong	95,792,719	9,429,686	9.84%	7
Henan	94,029,939	7,859,344	8.36%	17
Hubei	57,237,727	5,201,894	9.09%	11
Hunan	65,700,762	6,419,361	9.77%	8
Guangdong	104,320,459	7,086,150	6.79%	27
Guangxi	46,023,761	4,252,921	9.24%	10
Hainan	8,671,485	699,682	8.07%	21
Chongqing	28,846,170	3,381,468	11.72%	1
Sichuan	80,417,528	8,805,507	10.95%	2
Guizhou	34,748,556	3,026,181	8.71%	12
Yunnan	45,966,766	3,505,474	7.63%	23
Tibet	3,002,165	152,908	5.09%	31
Shaanxi	37,327,379	3,183,837	8.53%	14
Gansu	25,575,263	2,105,575	8.23%	20
Qinghai	5,626,723	354,684	6.30%	30
Ningxia	6,301,350	402,787	6.39%	29
Xinjiang	21,815,815	1,414,079	6.48%	28

Note: *The data are obtained from *Tabulation on the 2010 Population Census of the People's Republic of China (Book I)*, China Statistics Press, p. 115.**This is the author's calculation using data from *Tabulation on the 2010 Population Census of the People's Republic of China (Book I)*, China Statistics Press, pp. 120–2.

Urban–rural differences in the proportion of elderly population

Fourth, there were urban–rural differences in the proportion of elderly population in China. Ageing was faster in rural areas than urban areas. From 1982 to 2010, rural areas had a higher proportion of population aged 60 years and over than urban areas. Table 2.3 illustrates the author's calculation using data from the 1982, 2000 and 2010 Population Census of China. It showed that

Table 2.3 The proportion of population aged 60 and above to the total number of population in urban and rural areas in China in 1982, 2000 and 2010

	1982		2000		2010	
	Urban	*Rural*	*Urban*	*Rural*	*Urban*	*Rural*
(a) No. of population aged 60+	10,702,060	61,977,195	29,420,070	85,568,096	46,313,673	99,303,297
(b) Proportion	7.37%	7.77%	10.05%	10.92%	11.47%	14.98%

Note: (a) and (b) are the author's calculation according to the data obtained from *1982 Population Census of China*, Beijing: The Statistical Publishing House; pp. 284–93, 304–13; *Tabulation on the 2000 Population Census of the People's Republic of China (Book I)*, Beijing: China Statistics Press, pp. 145–55, 167–77; and *Tabulation on the 2010 Population Census of the People's Republic of China (Book I)*, Beijing: China Statistics Press, pp. 123–30, 139–46.

in 1982, the proportion of elderly population aged 60 years and over was 7.77 per cent in rural areas and 7.37 per cent in urban areas. The rural–urban difference in the proportion of elderly population was only 0.4 per cent. However, the urban–rural differences in the proportion of elderly population has widened over the past three decades. In 2010, the proportion of the elderly population aged 60 years and over rose to 14.98 per cent in rural areas while that of urban areas rose to 11.47 per cent. The rural–urban difference in the proportion of the elderly population was 3.51 per cent.

The reason why rural areas have higher proportions of elderly population than urban areas needs more explanation. Rural areas had higher fertility rates than urban areas because Chinese population with rural or agricultural household registration status could give birth to more than one child. In 2010, the TFR was 1.44 in rural areas but 0.88 in urban areas (China Economic Herald 2012). According to the *2010 Population Census of China*, the number of births in rural areas was two times more than the number of births in urban areas. In 2010, the number of births in rural areas was 650,170 while the number of births in urban areas was only 315,041 (Population Census Office and Department of Population and Employment Statistics 2012b: 2027–33). However, 'a large-scale migration of younger workers from rural to urban areas' (Liu J. 2014: 305) for more and better job opportunities in non-agricultural fields resulted in accelerating population ageing in rural areas.

The phenomenon of "Getting old before getting rich"

Fifth, China is getting old before getting rich (*wei fu xian lao*). This is a situation when population is ageing rapidly while the economy is still in development. Most industrialized countries got rich first before getting old (*xian fu hou lao*). 'In most industrialized countries, population ageing went hand-in-hand with economic growth in a gradual and natural manner' (Yan 2006: 6). But China had relatively low Gross Domestic Product (GDP) per capita compared to its Asia counterparts such as Singapore, Japan and South Korea that also encountered an ageing population (Zhang M. 2012). According to the data of the World Bank, the GDP per capita in China in 2014 was less than US$10,000 while the GDP per capita in Singapore, Japan and South Korea were respectively about US$56,000, US$36,000 and US$28,000 (The World Bank 2015). These Asian countries 'can confront their ageing demography with the accumulated wealth of having become rich first' (Johnston 2012) while China fails to do so. Since the 1980s, old-age dependency ratio has increased. It increased from 8.0 per cent in 1982 to 8.3 per cent in 1990, 9.9 per cent in 2000, 11.9 per cent in 2010 and 13.1 per cent in 2013 (National Bureau of Statistics of the People's Republic of China 2014a). Rising old-age dependency ratio has put pressure on economic growth, the health care system and the social security system.

Meanwhile, the number of working-age population aged between 15 and 59 years old had decreased for three consecutive years. According to *Statistical Reports on National Economic and Social Development*, the number of working-age population decreased from 940.72 million in 2011 to 937.27 million in 2012, to 919.54 million in 2013 and to 915.83 million in 2014 (National Bureau of Statistics of the People's Republic of China 2012, 2013b, 2014a, 2015). The shrinking working-age population has three consequences. First, China faces the problem of labor shortage. It will increase the bargaining power of workers for higher wages and better benefits. This will drive up labor costs. Second, the shrinking working-age population is 'eroding the manufacturing and export competitiveness that helped fuel China's 30-year expansion' (South China Morning Post 2015). Demographic dividend, which refers to a period of accelerated economic growth resulting from a growing number of the working-age population and a relatively low ratio of young and elderly dependents, is declining in China. China's demographic dividend is quantity-oriented rather than quality-oriented (Zhang M. 2012). The declining demographic dividend was one of the main reasons for China having a 7.4 per cent of GDP growth in 2014, which failed to meet the official target of 7.5 per cent in 2014 and was the slowest since 1990 (Liu B. 2015). Third, the shrinking population may lead to working people having less household savings because 'they need to support larger cohorts of elderly family members' (Organisation for Economic Co-operation and Development 2015: 28).

Epidemiologic transitions

A shift from infectious diseases to non-communicable diseases

When the People's Republic of China (PRC) was established in October 1949, it was an impoverished and unhealthy country. It carried a heavy burden of infectious diseases due to years of warfare, poor sanitary conditions with polluted water supplies (Banister 1987: 50) and the 'absence of modern medical resources and trained manpower' (Lampton 1977: 14). It had high death rate and high disease rate. In 1949, the death rate was 20 per cent (Department of Comprehensive Statistics of National Bureau of Statistics 2005: 6). The infant mortality rate was approximately 200 deaths per 1,000 live births, which was considerably higher than even India's at the same time (Lampton 1977: 14). Maternal mortality was 1,500 per 100,000 births in 1949 (Tulchinsky and Varavikova 2014: 708). There was a lack of comprehensive statistics of death rates from infectious diseases in the early years of the PRC. The available data obtained from previous studies can only 'be interpreted as an approximation rather than a precise series of assertions' (Lampton 1974: 2). But it shows that China was plagued by communicable diseases of various kinds. In 1950, the disease mortality rate for tuberculosis was 230 deaths per 100,000 people, dysentery was 216 deaths per 100,000 people, smallpox was 207 deaths per 100,000 people, typhoid and typhus was 204 deaths per 100,000 people, cholera was 165 deaths per 100,000 people, and diphtheria was 155 deaths per 100,000 people (The China Health Care Study Group 1974: 54). In 1955, it was estimated that at least 10.5 million people were infected with schistosomiasis (Lampton 1974: 3). 'Venereal disease was exceptionally common, with prevalence rates of 3 to 5 percent in the cities' (Lampton 1977: 14).

The government's early effort to promote public health through mass campaigns, vector control, vaccination, health education and proper human waste disposal succeeded in eliminating or reducing incidence of infectious deceases, apart from reducing the infant mortality rate (China Health Care Study Group 1974; Lampton 1977; Hipgrave 2011). In 1959, the infant mortality rate had declined to 70 deaths per 1,000 live births (Lampton 1977: 15). By 1960, contagious diseases such as cholera, plague and smallpox were virtually eliminated (Lampton 1977: 15). In 1959, the mortality rate for tuberculosis reduced to 49 deaths per 100,000 people, with the incidence rate dropping to 1 per cent (The China Health Care Study Group 1974: 64). There was also a reduction of the schistosomiasis and malaria incidence rate (Lampton 1977: 15). By the 1970s, the infant mortality rate (IMR) had further declined to 60 deaths per 1,000 live births (Lampton 1977: 15). IMR fell further from 36.4 per 1,000 live births in 1995 to 19.0 per 1,000 live births in 2005 and 13.1 per 1,000 live births in 2010 (National Bureau of Statistics of the People's Republic of China 2013a: 767). It fell to 9.5 per 1,000 live births in 2013 (Xinhua News 2015c). By 1980, life expectancy in China was 67 years, which 'exceeded that of most nations of similar gross domestic product per capita by seven years and that of many middle-income nations' (Hipgrave 2011: 225). People's health and wellbeing were greatly improved.

Since the policy of reform and opening up in the late 1970s, China has experienced strong economic growth. It made remarkable progress in agricultural production (World Bank 1997: 2), transportation, scientific and technological fields. Urbanization brought about 'more physically undemanding jobs in the service sector and increased use of automated transportation' (Cheng 2009: 107). The living standards of the Chinese people were significantly improved. People had higher disposable income and better consumption ability. Their lifestyle, food consumption behavior and nutritional status changed. 'Chinese households [had] a marked increase in ownership of motorized vehicles, televisions, and computers' (Cheng 2009: 106). People became less physically active when there was better transportation and physically undemanding pastimes. Meanwhile, the combined forces of 'liberalization of food production controls and the introduction of a free market for food and food products' (Du *et al.* 2007a: 432) led to changes in dietary patterns and the acceleration of nutrition transition. 'Intake of animal foods increased slowly before 1979 and more quickly after the economic reforms occurred' (Du *et al.* 2007a: 431). The study of Du *et al.* (2007b), which analyzed data from China Health and Nutrition Survey (1989–97), found that the consumption of animal foods was strongly related to increased income. People with higher income were more likely to consume animal foods (Du *et al.* 2007b: 269). The dietary structure of the Chinese people shifted from the consumption of grain products and starchy roots to the consumption of 'high-energy density, high-fat and low-fiber diets' (Du *et al.* 2007b: 271). The consumption of saturated fat and cholesterol also increased (Zhai *et al.* 2007: 870). Lack of exercise and the high-fat, low-carbohydrate diet led to 'a rising epidemic of over-weight and obesity among adults and adolescents, as well as widespread diet-related, non-communicable diseases' (Cheng 2009: 103). According to *China Statistical Yearbook 1986*, the leading causes of death in urban areas in 1985 were heart disease (23.39 per cent), cerebrovascular disease (20.98 per cent) and cancer (20.32 per cent) (National Bureau of Statistics of the People's Republic of China 1986: 797). In rural areas, the leading causes of death in 1985 were heart disease (25.47 per cent), cerebrovascular disease (15.57 per cent), cancer (15.17 per cent) and respiratory disease (12.25 per cent) (National Bureau of Statistics of the People's Republic of China 1986: 797).

Leading causes of death for urban and rural population 1990–2012

Since the 1980s, chronic and non-communicable diseases (NCDs) have replaced infectious disease as the main causes of death in urban and rural China. For the period 1990–2012, the four leading causes of death in urban and rural areas were cancer, heart disease, cerebrovascular disease and respiratory disease (Ministry of Health 2012a; National Bureau of Statistics of the People's Republic of China 2013a). However, the ranking, death rate and crude mortality rate of these diseases in urban areas are different from that of in rural areas. In urban areas, the leading cause of death in 1990 was cancer (21.88 per cent), which was followed by cerebrovascular disease (20.83 per cent), heart disease (15.81 per cent) and respiratory disease (15.76 per cent) (Ministry of Health 2012a: 267) (Table 2.4). In rural areas, the leading cause of death in 1990 was respiratory disease (24.82 per cent), which was followed by cancer (17.47 per cent), cerebrovascular disease (16.16 per cent) and heart disease (10.82) (Ministry of Health 2012a: 282) (Table 2.5).

Table 2.4 The five leading causes of death in urban areas, 1990–2012

Disease	1990		2000		2010		2012	
	ranking	Death rate (%)	ranking	Death rate (%)	ranking	Death rate (%)	ranking	Death Rate (%)
Cancer	1	21.88	1	24.38	1	26.33	1	26.81
Cerebro-vascular disease	2	20.83	2	21.28	3	20.23	3	19.61
Heart disease	3	15.81	3	17.74	2	20.88	2	21.45
Respiratory disease	4	15.76	4	13.29	4	11.04	4	12.32

Source: Data of 1990, 2000 and 2010 come from Ministry of Health (2012a) *China Health Statistics Yearbook 2012*, pp. 267–9; Data of 2012 comes from National Bureau of Statistics of the People's Republic of China (2013a) China Statistical Yearbook 2013, p. 765.

Table 2.5 The five leading causes of death in rural areas, 1990–2012

Disease	1990		2000		2010		2012	
	ranking	Death rate (%)	ranking	Death rate (%)	ranking	Death rate (%)	ranking	Death Rate (%)
Respiratory disease	1	24.82	1	23.11	4	14.15	4	15.75
Cancer	2	17.47	3	18.30	2	23.11	1	22.96
Cerebro-vascular disease	3	16.16	2	18.73	1	23.37	2	20.61
Heart disease	4	10.82	4	11.94	3	17.86	3	18.11

Source: Data of 1990, 2000 and 2010 come from Ministry of Health (2012a) China Health Statistics Yearbook 2012, pp. 282–4; Data of 2012 comes from National Bureau of Statistics of the People's Republic of China (2013a) China Statistical Yearbook 2013, p. 766.

In urban areas, the leading cause of death in 2012 was cancer (26.81 per cent), which was followed by heart disease (21.45 per cent), cerebrovascular disease (19.61 per cent) and respiratory disease (12.32 per cent) (National Bureau of Statistics of the People's Republic of China 2013a: 765) (Table 2.4). In rural areas, the leading cause of death in 2012 was cancer (22.96 per cent), which was followed by cerebrovascular disease (20.61 per cent), heart disease (18.11 per cent) and respiratory disease (15.75 per cent) (National Bureau of Statistics of the People's Republic of China 2013a: 766) (Table 2.5). Health statistics of 2012 showed that cancer had become the No.1 killer in both urban and rural areas. But the death rate of cancer in 2012 was higher in urban areas than in rural areas. Health statistics of 2012 also showed that respiratory disease was ranked number four in the leading cause of death in both urban and rural areas. But the death rate of respiratory disease in 2012 was higher in rural areas than in urban areas.

In urban areas, the crude mortality rate for cancer increased from 128.03 deaths per 100,000 people in 1990 to 164.51 deaths per 100,000 people in 2012 (Ministry of Health 2012a: 267; National Bureau of Statistics of the People's Republic of China 2013a: 765). The crude mortality rate for heart disease substantially increased from 92.53 deaths per 100,000 people in 1990 to 131.64 deaths per 100,000 people in 2012 (Ministry of Health 2012a: 267; National Bureau of Statistics of the People's Republic of China 2013a: 765). Meanwhile, the crude mortality rate for cerebrovascular disease slightly decreased from 121.84 deaths per 100,000 people in 1990 to 120.33 deaths per 100,000 people in 2012 (Ministry of Health 2012a: 267; National Bureau of Statistics of the People's Republic of China 2013a: 765). The crude mortality rate for respiratory disease also decreased from 92.18 deaths per 100,000 people in 1990 to 75.59 deaths per 100,000 people in 2012 (Ministry of Health 2012a: 267; National Bureau of Statistics of the People's Republic of China 2013a: 765) (Table 2.6).

Table 2.6 Crude mortality rate of major cause of death in urban areas, 1990–2012

	1990 (1/100,000)	2000 (1/100,000)	2010 (1/100,000)	2012 (1/100,000)
Cancer	128.03	146.61	162.87	164.51
Heart disease	92.53	106.65	129.19	131.64
Cerebrovascular disease	121.84	127.96	125.15	120.33
Respiratory disease	92.18	79.92	68.32	75.59

Source: Data of 1990, 2000 and 2010 come from Ministry of Health (2012a) China Health Statistics Yearbook 2012, pp. 267–9; Data of 2012 comes from National Bureau of Statistics of the People's Republic of China (2013a) China Statistical Yearbook 2013, p. 765.

Table 2.7 Crude mortality rate of major cause of death in rural areas, 1990–2012

	1990 (1/100,000)	2000 (1/100,000)	2010 (1/100,000)	2012 (1/100,000)
Cancer	112.36	112.57	144.11	151.47
Heart disease	69.60	73.43	111.34	119.50
Cerebrovascular disease	103.93	115.20	145.71	135.95
Respiratory disease	159.67	142.16	88.25	103.90

Source: Data of 1990, 2000 and 2010 come from Ministry of Health (2012a) China Health Statistics Yearbook 2012, pp. 282–4; Data of 2012 comes from National Bureau of Statistics of the People's Republic of China (2013a) China Statistical Yearbook 2013, p. 766.

In rural areas, the crude mortality rate for cancer substantially increased from 112.36 deaths per 100,000 people in 1990 to 151.47 deaths per 100,000 people in 2012 (Ministry of Health 2012a: 282; National Bureau of Statistics of the People's Republic of China 2013a: 766). The crude mortality rate for heart disease also substantially increased from 69.60 deaths per 100,000 people in 1990 to 119.50 deaths per 100,000 people in 2012 (Ministry of Health 2012a: 282; National Bureau of Statistics of the People's Republic of China 2013a: 766). The crude mortality rate for cerebrovascular disease increased from 103.93 deaths per 100,000 people in 1990 to 135.95 deaths per 100,000 people in 2012 (Ministry of Health 2012a: 282; National Bureau of Statistics of the People's Republic of China 2013a: 766). Meanwhile, crude mortality rates for respiratory disease decreased from 159.67 deaths per 100,000 people in 1990 to 103.90 deaths per 100,000 people in 2012 (Ministry of Health 2012a: 282; National Bureau of Statistics of the People's Republic of China 2013a: 766) (Table 2.7).

Health statistics of 2012 showed that the crude mortality rate for cancer was higher in urban areas than in rural areas. The crude mortality rate for heart disease was also higher in urban areas than in rural areas. On the contrary, crude mortality rate for cerebrovascular disease was higher in rural areas than in urban areas. The crude mortality rate for respiratory disease was also higher in rural areas than in urban areas.

Leading causes of death from cancer

With increasing incidence and mortality, cancer since 2010 has become the leading cause of death in China (Chen *et al.* 2016). According to the World Cancer Report 2014, China accounted for about 22 per cent of global new cancer cases and about 27 per cent of global cancer deaths (Liu Z. 2014). In February 2015, World Health Organization (WHO) warned that '[t]he growth of cancer in China is ferocious' (ABC News 2015 February 4) and 'the country accounts for one-fourth of global deaths from various forms of the disease' (Liu X. 2015). The Chinese government has collected cancer-related data for a few decades. But until the early 1990s, 'cancer' was still a strange word to most ordinary people (Liu J. 2014). 'As a key chronic disease, cancer is much more expensive in diagnosis, treatment and care than acute infectious diseases' (Shen 2014: 148). The National Health Service Survey in 2003 showed that cancer had the highest economic costs of RMB 86.85 billion, which accounted for about 7 per cent of the total economic cost of diseases (Zhao *et al.* 2010: 282). According to *China Health and Family Planning Yearbook 2013*, the three leading causes of death from cancers for the period 1973–5 were those of the stomach, esophagus and liver (National Health and Family Planning Commission 2013). For the period 1990–2, the three leading causes of death from cancers were those of the stomach, liver and lung (National Health and Family Planning Commission 2013). For the period 2004–5, the three leading causes of death from cancers were those of the lung, liver and stomach (National Health and Family Planning Commission 2013). In 2015, the five leading causes of death from cancers were those of the lung and bronchus, stomach, liver, esophagus and colorectum, which accounted for about 75 per cent of all cancer deaths (Chen *et al.* 2016: 5).

In ranking cancer cases in 1990–2, stomach cancer had the highest crude mortality of 25.16/100,000, which was followed by liver cancer (20.37/100,000), lung cancer (17.54/100,000), esophageal cancer (17.38/100,000) and colorectal cancer (5.3/100,000) (Ministry of Health 2012a: 253). In 2004–5, lung cancer had the highest crude mortality (30.83/100,000), which was followed by liver cancer (26.26/100,000), stomach cancer (24.71/100,000), esophageal cancer (15.21/100,000) and colorectal cancer (7.25/100,000) (Ministry of Health 2012a: 253). Chinese Cancer Registry Annual Report 2012, which was jointly issued by the National Central Cancer Registry and Disease Prevention and Control Bureau of Ministry of Health to publicly release cancer figures for the first time, stated that 'every minute, six people were diagnosed with cancer in China' (Xinhua News 2013). It showed that in 2009, lung cancer remained the leading cause of cancer-related mortality, which had the crude mortality of 45.57/100,000 (Chen *et al.* 2013: 18). It was followed by liver cancer (26.04/100,000), stomach cancer (25.88/100,000), esophageal cancer

(16.77/100,000) and colorectal cancer (14.23/100,000) (Chen *et al.* 2013: 18). The cancer mortality increased drastically after 50 years old and reached its peak after 85 years old (Chen *et al.* 2013: 12). 'Urban areas had higher cancer mortality of 181.86/100,000 than that of rural areas (177.83/100,000)' (Chen *et al.* 2013: 12). In 2011, lung cancer, liver cancer, stomach cancer, esophageal cancer and colorectal cancer were still the top five cancer mortality, which respectively had a crude mortality of 39.27/100,000, 23.93/100,000, 22.08/100,000, 15.25/100,000 and 11.11/100,000 (Chen *et al.* 2015: 9). The cancer mortality increased drastically after 45 years old and reached its peak after 85 years old (Chen *et al.* 2015: 5). Health statistics of cancer show that the 'disease burden of cancer is increasing' (Chen *et al.* 2015: 2).

There are a number of risk factors for cancer. But lifestyle-related risk factors and environmental risk factors play a major role in several common types of cancer in China. The Director of the Lung Cancer Treatment Centre in Beijing said that lung cancer was associated with 'smoking, long-term exposure to air pollution and occupational exposure to carcinogens' (Li J. 2014). '[S]econd-hand smoke was also reported to moderately increase the risk of lung cancer incidence and mortality' (Shen 2014: 158). Stomach cancer is associated with unhealthy dietary habits, which include 'regular consumption of fried or grilled food, consumption of high-salt, high-fat and spicy food and drinking strong Boiled brick-tea' (Yan *et al.* 2014: 10486). In fact, China accounts for more than 40 per cent of global new gastric cancer cases (Bu and Ji 2013: 1). '[N]umerous case-control studies in China suggest a positive association between a high intake of preserved fish and vegetables and gastric cancer risk' (Lin *et al.* 2011: 4421). High mortality of gastric cancer was found in rural areas with underdeveloped socio-economic conditions, 'especially in Gansu, Henan, Hebei, Shanxi and Shaanxi Provinces in the middle-western part of China' (Yang 2006: 17). Colorectal cancer 'is primarily a cancer of the older population and risk for it increases with age' (Li and Gu 2005: 4686). It was also associated with long-term exposure to a high-fat, high-protein, low-fiber diet, mental stress and a lack of physical activity (China News of Medicine 2015). As regards liver and esophageal cancers, they were 'related largely to conditions of relatively less development' (Wang *et al.* 2012: 131). Liver cancer is associated with hepatitis B and C viral infections, exposure to aflatoxin, alcohol consumption and cigarette smoking (Fan *et al.* 2013: 7251).

Implications of population ageing and epidemiological transitions for health financing

It is undeniable that '[p]opulation ageing is a triumph of civilization and medical science' (Chinese Academy of Social Sciences *et al.* 2011: 5). But 'it also raises critical issues for countries, states, and families related to economic growth, economic security in old age, [and] health care' (Chinese Academy of Social Sciences *et al.* 2011: 5). China's demographic shift towards an ageing society inevitably places greater demands on the health care system and puts a strain on health care finance because older people have heavier disease burdens and greater medical needs than younger people. In general, the elderly population has much higher medical expenditures than other segments of the population. Besides, among the elderly population, average medical expenditures of the 'oldest-old' and that of the 'old-old' are higher than that of the 'young-old'. For example, average medical expenditures was Renminbi (RMB) 3689.8 for the 'oldest-old' aged 80 years or over, RMB 3,873.2 for the 'old-old' aged 70 to 79 years and RMB 2139.9 for the 'young-old' aged 60 to 69 years in 2005 (Zhang and Guo 2010: 179). However, the elderly population has fewer sources of income when they retire. Even though some of the elderly people manage to remain in the labor force, the amount of salary they receive is usually lower than that of working-age adults. According to Jin (2014), about 90 per cent of the elderly population relied on pensions as their main source of income, the average amount of which was RMB 2532.8 per month. Only 5.2 per cent of the elderly population relied on financial assistance from their children as the main source of income (Jin 2014). Heavy medical expenditures definitely impose financial burden on the elderly population and their families.

Meanwhile, epidemiological transitions from infectious diseases to chronic, NCDs 'posit challenges for allocating resources for formal care and social intervention such as public expenditures on healthcare' (Higo and Williamson 2011: 121). It is because NCDs 'involve different challenges, skills and approaches: often very long term – even lifelong – care and treatment' (Anderson 2012: 40). They 'can impose costs on governments that are high in absolute and relative terms, especially as a disease progresses or becomes chronic' (Anderson 2012: 3). 'Estimates of the lost output attributable to NCDs amount to trillions of dollars a year' (Ebrahim *et al.* 2013: e1001377). And 'the costs of simple effective interventions are measured in millions of dollars' (Ebrahim *et al.* 2013: e1001377). NCDs also impose heavy financial burdens to patients and their families because NCDs usually require prolonged medical treatment and care and lead to patients losing their working ability. Recently, NCDs 'have become an emerging pandemic globally with disproportionately higher rates in developing countries' (Islam *et al.* 2014: 81). But compared to their developed counterparts, developing countries have fewer resources and less time to efficiently respond to NCDs (Anderson 2012: 2). Hence, there is a pressing need for developing countries like China to formulate policies and provide proper health care facilities and services to treat and prevent NCDs. In the aspect of health care finance, it is crucial for the government to improve access to medical insurance and establish a health care financing system that can ensure affordable and sustainable health care for its people in the long run.

3 Health care system in the pre-reform era

Introduction

The Chinese Communist Party (CCP) under the leadership of Mao Zedong undertook the immediate task to rebuild the nation after the end of Second Sino-Japanese War (1937–45) and civil war (1947–9). It made health a priority and regarded the health care system as a major pillar of state socialism (Gu 2001: 197). This chapter provides important historical context necessary for understanding health insurance reform in China by examining the development and characteristics of public health system, health care delivery and financing systems in urban and rural areas during Mao's era (1949–76). It also examines how the centrally planned health care system was shaped by the complex interplay of forces, namely institutions, historical legacy, interests and ideologies. It shows that the development of health care carried political, ideological and diplomatic significance in the pre-reform era.

Background and context

The CCP won the civil war and founded the People's Republic of China (PRC) on 1 October 1949 under the leadership of Mao Zedong. When the PRC was established, it was a very unhealthy and impoverished country with high death rates and high disease rates. Its 'health indicators [were] at the lowest level compared with other countries at a comparable level of development' (Ma and Sood 2008: 5). The vast majority of Chinese people sickened and died due to years of internal and external warfare, 'gross inadequacy and unavailability of modern health workers and medical facilities' (Sidel and Sidel 1979: 157), and 'the cycle of poverty, disease and disability' (Sidel and Sidel 1979: 158). Against this background, Mao noted that his immediate tasks were to consolidate his new regime, reconstruct the ruined economy and promote health. During Mao's era, the development of health care carried political, ideological and diplomatic significance. Politically, the development of health care was regarded by Mao as a key component of state building. Ideologically, the development of health care was heavily shaped by socialist and communist ideologies. Diplomatically, the development of urban and rural health care was directly impacted by changes in Sino-Soviet relations. Sino-Soviet alliance contributed to the development of urban health care in the 1950s while Sino-Soviet split led to a major shift towards the development of rural health care in the 1960s.

The 'PRC's birth coincided with the Cold War' (Arnold and Wiener 2012: 133), which was marked by intense and hostile superpower rivalry between the United States (US) and the Soviet Union shortly after the Second World War. This led to Mao putting forward a new theory of 'two camps'. According to Mao, the world was divided into two irreconcilable camps: the socialist camp led by the Soviet Union and the capitalist camp led by the US (Larus 2012: 376; Zhang P. 2014: 89). Due to the hostility of the US towards the newly founded PRC and 'the possibility of military intervention from imperialist countries' (Chen 1994: 65), Mao leaned to the side of the Soviet Union. The conclusion of the Sino-Soviet Treaty of Peace, Friendship and Mutual Assistance on 14 February 1950 marked the beginning of the Sino-Soviet alliance. Over the next few years, 'learning from the Soviet Union was at the heart of [the PRC's] official propaganda work' (Yu 2005: 1). China adopted the Leninist political system and Soviet-style command economy (Marsh 2005: 34). It obtained the urgently needed technical and financial assistance from the Soviet Union to develop its economy.

Following Leninist political system and organizational principles, China adopted a 'highly centralized political power structure concentrated within a one-party state' (Saich 2004: 28). The CCP was the only ruling party by the constitution (Yu 2008: 264). It had the exclusive right to control 'the nation's political, economic and social goals and policies' (Loh and Yip 2004: 164). As an organization, the CCP is centralist, pyramidal and hierarchical in nature (Wang 2002: 70). Power was highly concentrated in the hands of the top party leaders. The CCP penetrated all levels of government from provinces, cities, counties to townships (Luk 2015: 45). It adopted the interlocking system of party personnel and organizational structures to control and direct the government bureaucracy (Loh and Yip 2004: 165). 'Leading party cadres at various levels concurrently occupied the highest posts in local government institutions' (Luk 2015: 45). Party cells were established within government institutions to oversee all activities (Luk 2015: 45) and led the work of the government from within (Zheng 2004: 5). The CCP also penetrated every corner of society (Zheng 2004: 9) by replacing the traditional social network that was formed by blood, kinship and geographical proximity with mass organizations led by the party (Guo 2013: 206). It monopolized and coercively redistributed all 'resources, employment, location of living, and opportunities for mobility and career advancement' (Guo 2013: 206). The CCP's tight control over society ensured political compliance among domestic populations. Under the highly centralized political system, Mao enjoyed absolute authority and gained unchallenged command of the CCP (Zheng 2004; Luk 2015). Voices from non-state actors and the public were so weak that any open criticism of the CCP and its policy was deemed risky (Luk 2014: 59).

Following the Soviet model of economic development, China adopted a centrally planned economy. The centrally planned economy 'was characterized by the public ownership of all productive resources and the [central government's] direct and indirect control over nearly all economic activities' (Hsu 1989: 130). The government nationalized all private capital and property (Birn *et al.* 2009: 603). Private enterprises were sold to the state or were converted into joint public–private enterprises under state control (Zhang X. 2014: 4). 'Industry and commerce [also] became totally controlled by publicly owned enterprises' (Li 1991: 10). 'Enterprises did not function as independent economic units but as organizations subordinate to the central planning body' (Hsu 1989: 130). The central planning body would 'set production goals' (Morrison 2015: 2), and 'decide on the products to be produced and direct lower-level enterprises to produce those goods' (Zheng 2004: 10). Besides, it controlled every aspect of enterprises' operation, 'including the method of production, the hiring and firing of workers, the procurement of equipment and material inputs, and the level of output' (Hsu 1989: 130). Any rewards 'were to be distributed according to the value that the state ascribed to the service performed' (Zheng 2004: 14). In urban areas, 'all organizations where people worked were generally classified as *danwei*, which literally meant work unit' (Luk 2014: 39). Work units functioned as an economic institution that guaranteed permanent employment known as the 'iron rice bowl' and as a welfare delivery institution that provided employees with comprehensive benefits from housing, social security, health care to subsidies for meals, transportation and haircuts (Luk 2014: 39). They also served the purpose of political control because the dependency of employees on the work units for livelihood and welfare benefits could guarantee political compliance and allegiance (Luk 2014: 40).

The adoption of a highly centralized political system gave the central government considerable leverage over the development of health care system and the formulation and implementation of health care policy (Chen and Bunge 1989; Luk 2014). A top-down, command-and-control system of governance allowed top party leaders to formulate health care policy behind closed doors and face little or no opposition. Meanwhile, the centrally planned economy created a national, centrally planned health care system that the government played a major role in providing and financing health care.

The idea of health care

During Mao's era, the development of health care was shaped by the socialist and communist ideologies that 'emphasized public ownership and welfare, mass-based collectivism and egalitarianism' (Chen 2001: 456). Due to manpower and resource scarcities, the development of health care was also shaped by the legacy of the Red Army's base area medicine that was developed in the 1930s and 1940s (Lampton 1977: 11). It was a guerrilla medical tradition that 'placed emphasis on prevention, on the use of paramedics with little formal training, and on mass mobilization' (Lampton 1977: 11). Mao, who favored 'the subordination of professional knowledge to revolutionary ideals' (Scheid and Lei 2014: 249), greatly promoted the legacy of base area medicine when carrying out public health work and developing rural health care. In fact, the idea of prevention or preventive medicine resonated well with the Chinese medical tradition, which saw medicine as 'the art of maintaining health, not curing disease' (Lampton 1977: 3).

The CCP under the leadership of Mao Zedong made health a priority (Bloom 2005: 25). This could be substantiated by its adoption of the Common Program of the Chinese People's Political Consultative Conference on 29 September 1949, which was a provisional constitution that emphasized the importance of promoting public health and medical work and protecting the health of mothers, infants and children (XinhuaNet 2011). Health care 'was seen as an integral component of the communist system and important to the development of a collective Maoist Chinese identity' (Daemmrich 2013: 448). To ensure a healthy labor force and to mobilize enthusiasm of the people in nation-building became the core in the development of health care (Hu 2013: 87). After undertaking 'a critical appraisal of available resources in the health care sector' (Scheid 2002: 67), the government formulated four guiding principles of health care policy, which were announced at the First National Health Conference in Beijing in August 1950:

1   Medicine should serve the needs of the workers, peasants and soldiers;
2   preventive medicine should take precedence over curative medicine;
3   traditional Chinese medicine should be united with Western medicine; and
4   health work should be carried out through mass movements (Kraus 1982: 24; Wong and Chiu 1997: 77).

These four guiding principles were used to meet the basic medical needs of the Chinese population by making the best use of available resources, such as medical personnel, materials and mobilized free labor (Wong and Chiu 1997: 77). But '[h]ow these principles were to be translated into practice was not specified' (Scheid and Lei 2014: 249). Consequently, concrete policies were shaped by the combining forces of politics and ideology (Scheid 2002: 68).

Public health system

Public health was regarded by the Chinese government 'not only as an obligation of the state to the citizens, but also as a vital requirement to economic development and national defense' (Bu 2014: 118). During Mao's era, a preventive approach was adopted in public health to compensate for a lack of hospitals, trained physicians and medical personnel. Efforts for preventing and controlling communicable diseases included establishing the former Soviet Union model of public health system, implementing public health education, mass vaccination programmes and patriotic health campaigns.

First, '[d]ue to close ties with the Soviet Union, China introduced a comprehensive public health system based on the Soviet model' (Bangdiwala *et al.* 2011: 208). Epidemic prevention stations were established all over the country as technical centers for preventing, controlling and monitoring infectious diseases (Liu Y. 2009: 37). The number of epidemic prevention stations 'grew slowly between 1950 and 1955, [but] multiplied fourfold between 1955 and

1957' (Banister 1987: 52). By 1957, 1,626 epidemic prevention stations were established at the provincial, prefectural and county levels (Huang 2013: 27). Besides, China established 'more specialized centres for the control of specific diseases (such as malaria, plague, schistosomiasis, leishmaniasis and brucellosis)' (Hipgrave 2011: 225). Compared to the mobile Epidemic Prevention General Team established by the Ministry of Health (MOH) in 1950 to control parasitic and communicable diseases in Northeast, East and Southern China (Huang 2013: 27), both epidemic prevention stations and specialized centers were more organized, systematic and efficient in controlling and preventing communicable diseases.

Second, public health education was carried out as 'the key to preventive work' (China Health Study Group 1974: 59). Through the use of radio, films, dramas and printing media (China Health Study Group 1974: 59), the Chinese government raised the general public's consciousness for personal hygiene and improving sanitation of public places. In particular, 'visual materials were used extensively in the health education movement to achieve immediate impact among the illiterate and the literate alike' (Bu 2014: 123). For example, magazines, picture books, wall bulletins and health posters were effective 'to explain abstract concepts of disease and complicated ideas of science in direct, concrete and vivid images' (Bu 2014: 123). In particular, public-health posters 'were an integral part of the mass political and public-health campaigns of those movements to enforce conformity, test loyalty, and designate enemies' (Hanson 2008: 1457). These posters were conductive to informing, mobilizing, instructing the masses, and were a useful medium to educate the public in what kind of behavior or thought was correct and wrong (International Institute of Social History 2008: 1). The poster messages could be 'passed on in an almost subconscious manner' (International Institute of Social History 2008: 3).

Third, mass vaccination programmes were carried out to significantly reduce the death caused by infectious diseases such as smallpox. Health personnel paid house-to-house visits to persuade people to receive vaccinations that were provided by the government free of charge (China Health Study Group 1974: 59). Between 1950 and 1952, about 512 million people were vaccinated against smallpox (Banister 1987: 55). 'The last outbreak of smallpox in China was in Yunnan province in 1960' (Banister 1987: 55). Besides, diphtheria vaccinations were given to urban population in 1951 and children in 1957 (Banister 1987: 55). Also, by the end of 1958, 10.5 million Chinese children had received tuberculosis vaccinations (Banister 1987: 56). Preventive vaccination that was initiated in Shanghai and Beijing in 1955 became popular in China in 1958 (Zhang *et al.* 2002: 133). In the 1960s, there was gradual implementation of 'bacilli Calmette-Guérin (BCG) [vaccine], oral polio vaccine (OPV), diphtheria-tetanus-pertussis vaccine (DPT) and measles vaccine' (Liu Y. 2010: 375). In the 1970s, there was on-the-spot vaccination every spring and winter (Liu Y. 2010: 375). 'In 1978, the Expanded Programme on Immunization (EPI) was established' (Liu Y. 2010: 375). Decades of preventive vaccination greatly reduced the burden of illness from the relevant infectious diseases and the mortality from such diseases.

Fourth, public health campaigns were implemented to 'improve health for the socialist reconstruction of modern China' (Bu 2014: 119). 'Building on the patriotic sentiments of the people during the Korean War [1950–1953]' (China Health Study Group 1974: 55), the Chinese government implemented the first patriotic health campaigns, which required all community members to kill 'the "four pests" – rats, flies, mosquitoes and sparrows – and urged the cleaning up of village water supplies' (China Health Study Group 1974: 55). In the following decades, the practice of combining health campaigns with mass movements was extended to remove trash and filth, animal and insect vectors, build or repair public latrines, clean one's residence, working place and the adjoining streets (China Health Study Group 1974: 58–60). Household representatives and health workers were appointed to carry out constant supervision and ensure that community members followed directives, joined the mass campaigns and fulfilled their duties as citizens (China Health Study Group 1974: 60). The patriotic health campaigns served an important purpose of 'turn[ing] the masses from passive recipients of medicine and health care into active fighters against diseases and masters of their own health' (Bu 2014: 120). They also helped 'create a public culture infused with the distinct values of Chinese socialism and national pride' (Bu 2014: 130).

After three decades of efforts in promoting public health, 'China was already undergoing the epidemiologic transition, years ahead of other nations of similar economic status' (Hipgrave 2011: 224). 'In 1973–75 only 7 percent of the reported deaths were due to infectious diseases' (Banister 1992: 202). 'Tuberculosis, reported as the leading cause of death in 1957, by the mid-1970s had become the eighth leading cause of death' (Banister 1992: 202). The fulminating infectious diseases 'such as smallpox, cholera, plague, recurrent fever, typhus, and kala azar (or visceral leishmaniasis), have been eradicated or effectively controlled' (Lee 2004: 328). Through EPI, infectious diseases such as 'poliomyelitis, diphtheria, pertussis (whooping cough) and measles have [also] been controlled' (Lee 2004: 328). But infectious intestinal diseases such as dysentery and hepatitis were not eliminated (Banister 1987: 64). Dysentery and hepatitis were transmitted by contaminated food and drinking water. These two diseases could not be quickly controlled because it was difficult to provide pure food and water nationwide (Banister 1987: 64–5).

Health care delivery system

In 1949, China had scarce medical manpower and resources. The 'minimal resources for Western medicine, both doctors and hospitals, were concentrated in the cities' (Sidel and Sidel 1979: 158). The number of hospitals was less than 600 (China Health Study Group 1974: 36). The hopeless doctor to population ratios of one doctor for every 25,000 to 50,000 persons (Lampton 1977: 14) led to poor access to health care and poor quality of care. In 1949, the hospital bed to population ratio was 2.26: 1,000 in Shanghai and 2.11: 1,000 in Canton (Lampton 1977: 14), which was inconceivable against the ratio of one hospital bed for every 200 to 500 people in rich countries (Sidel and Sidel 1979: 158).

Improved health care was crucial for social and economic development (Cohen *et al.* 1996: S224–5). Since the health care system was regarded as 'a major pillar of state socialism' (Gu 2001: 197), the Chinese government strived to make health care accessible to the majority of the population (Luk 2014: 43). 'Mao's objective of equality was embedded in the provision of health care' (Lo 2015: 66). The implementation of the household registration (*hukou*) system, which classified people as a rural or an urban resident, created a dual social structure in China (Guo 2013: 207). In order to meet the health care needs of the urban and rural population, the government respectively established a three-tiered medical institution network in urban and rural areas. The establishment of a three-tiered medical institution network did not require the government to start from scratch because hospitals already existed prior to 1949. The first step to establish the three-tiered medical institution network was nationalizing hospitals that 'were previously run by foreign medical missionaries or privately run by local elites and businessmen' (Luk 2014: 41). All the hospitals became non-profit work units (Gu 2001: 201) and were put under the control of the MOH, which was established on 1 November 1949 and was organized based on a model provided by the MOH of the Soviet Union (Rosenthal and Pongor 1987: 79). The subordinate bureaus of the MOH supervised hospitals at provincial, municipal, district and county levels (Luk 2014: 40–1). Hospital employees were recruited by the MOH (Duckett 2011: 22) and 'were fully paid by the state according to standard salary scales regulated by the central government' (Luk 2014: 41). Prices for medical services and drugs were set below actual costs by the Central Pricing Commission so as to make health care financially affordable.

Three-tiered medical institution network in urban areas

Due to scarce resources in health care and the adoption of the Soviet model of economic development that emphasized heavy industry, the development of health care and the allocation of health resources had a strong urban bias. The first Five-Year Plan of the MOH stated that priority must be given to improve the health and medical services in urban areas (Rosenthal and Pongor 1987: 79–80) because the state-directed growth of heavy industry relied on a large amount of healthy workforce. In urban areas, the three-tiered health care system was established in the early 1950s. Each tier of the health care system was different in scale. Each tier provided different kinds of medical service and it had different target groups (Dong 2003; Luk 2014).

The first tier consisted of street-level hospitals, workplace clinics and street health stations. It acted as a healthcare 'safety net', providing primary and preventive care for residents, employees and retirees within the relevant community and enterprises. A workplace clinic was established in almost every enterprise, government institution and school to provide very basic curative and preventive services (Tang and Meng 2004: 18). The clinics were small and were 'staffed by secondary-school trained Western-style and Chinese doctors, and sometimes only by minimally trained paramedics or by nurses' (Cheng 1991: 10). The street health stations were staffed by auxiliary staff to provide emergency treatment and carry out health propaganda work for an entire neighbourhood (China Health Study Group 1974: 38). Their staff also 'visit[ed] homes to look after the infirm and to record the general state of a family's health and the dates of inoculations' (China Health Study Group 1974: 38). The second tier was district-level hospitals and enterprise-level hospitals, providing both outpatient and inpatient services for enterprise workers and their dependents, and patients from neighbourhoods within their assigned areas (Cheng 1991: 10). By 1965, about 1,500 hospitals had been built by military organizations and the mining, railways and telecommunications sectors (Tang and Meng 2004: 18). The third tier consisted of municipal hospitals and university-affiliated hospitals, which were staffed by highly trained Western-style physicians and equipped with better medical facilities. It provided patients with specialist care and complex treatments (Luk 2014: 42). It also conducted medical research and provided medical training (Cheung and Gu 2004: 39). The third tier performed a supervisory role over the second tier while the second tier performed a supervisory role over the first tier (Cheung and Gu 2004). For decades, the three-tiered health care system 'provided an efficient framework for referring patients for care in the most appropriate setting' (Dong 2003: 225).

Due to the government's bias toward urban health care development in the 1950s, 'little was done in rural health other than construction of a few county hospitals and clinics and the dispatch of mobile units to distant areas' (Chen and Bunge 1989: 196). There was the shortage of health personnel in rural areas. By 1957, only 22,000 out of 79,000 college-trained physicians practiced in rural areas (Huang 2013: 34). There was also a shortage of drugs and equipment in rural areas. It was because most of the health resources were used to meet the increasing urban demand for health care, which was caused by rising employment and a growing incidence of workplace injuries in urban areas (Huang 2013: 38). The rural majority had inadequate access to basic health services (Tang and Meng 2004: 19), 'especially [those] in inaccessible remote and mountainous areas' (Hu 2013: 142). However, the deterioration of the Sino-Soviet relationship and Mao's 'unfulfilled and important obligations to the rural masses who had made the revolution a success' (Rosenthal and Greiner 1987: 6) led to the focus of health care development shifting to the rural areas in the mid-1960s.

During the 1950s, the development of the health sector in urban areas mainly followed the model imported from the Soviet Union (Tang and Meng 2004: 19). Mao linked the widening urban–rural gap in health care to the Soviet model that favored the urban-based, capital-intensive and Western-style health care system (Huang 2013: 38–9). Hence, the deterioration of the Sino-Soviet relationship opened a window of opportunity for Mao to 'purge the Soviet influence in the health sector' (Huang 2013: 39) and made a radical shift in the development of health care system. The deterioration of the Sino-Soviet relationship originated in a dispute over ideology in 1956 when Mao criticized Stalin's successor Nikita Khrushchev for betraying Marxism and turning 'revisionist'. Mao regarded Khrushchev's political campaign of de-Stalinization, which condemned Stalin for his 'cult of personality' style of leadership and his tyrannical policies, as an attack on his style of leadership that undermined his legitimacy. He was also discontent with Khrushchev's new foreign policy that 'favoured a peaceful co-existence with the United States and undermined the Sino-Soviet alliance' (Hong and Lu 2013: 31). The Sino-Soviet relationship got worse further when Khrushchev denounced Mao's Great Leap Forward (1958–60) campaign as 'economically unsound and dangerously fanatical' (Larus 2012: 85) and 'abruptly cancelled almost all Soviet technical assistance to China and withdrew some 1,400 Soviet advisers and experts' (Gelman 1980: 622). In 1960, the Sino-Soviet alliance officially came to an end and the Soviet Union became the opponent of China after the security and territorial disputes in the 1958 Taiwan Strait Crisis and the Sino-Indian border issue of 1959.

Internally, the relationship between Mao and the MOH had always been tense since the founding of the PRC because Mao criticized the MOH for its sectarianism as reflected in its negative attitude toward Chinese medicine and its indifferent attitude toward the rural medical needs (Hu 2013: 142). But the tension between Mao and the MOH reached a new height in 1965 when Mao's 'June 26 Directive' sharply criticized the MOH for its medical elitism and being 'the Ministry of Urban Health' (Huang 2013: 41) or 'the Ministry of Health for Urban Lords' (Hu 2013: 142). Following the June 26 Directive, Mao replaced elite medical professionals in the MOH with leftist revolutionaries who had little or no medical experience and radically shifted the focus of medical and health work to the countryside. Hence, the rural health care development carried political and revolutionary significance.

Three-tiered medical institution network in rural areas

In rural areas, the three-tiered health care system was established between the mid-1960s and mid-1980s (Daemmrich 2013). It was built from the bottom upward (Chen and Bunge 1989) and was financed and administered locally (Chow 2004: 139). Through a policy of graduated responsibility, health personnel at each tier were assigned with different responsibilities (Chen and Bung 1989: 194), in accordance with 'marked differences in the degree of technical training among personnel at each level' (Chen and Bunge 1989: 194). 'No one was expected or permitted to undertake tasks beyond one's technical capability' (Chen and Bunge 1989: 194). Those who received the least training worked in the villages, those who received better training worked at the intermediate level and those who received the best training worked at the county level (Chen and Bunge 1989: 194). Health personnel at each tier 'respected the superior knowledge and skill of those of higher grade' (Chen and Bunge 1989: 194). 'The marked difference in the technical competency of those in charge at each level ensured control of quality' (Chen and Bunge 1989: 194).

The three-tiered health care system 'was founded on the institutions of collectivized agriculture set up from the mid-1950s' (Duckett 2011: 26). The first tier was the production brigade health stations, which was the lowest rural health units providing preventive and primary care (Wong and Chiu 1997: 77–8). They were 'staffed by two to three barefoot doctors' (Cheng 1991: 10). Barefoot doctors were peasants chosen by their work comrades to receive rudimentary health training that ranged from one month to three months or lasted for six months (Rosenthal and Greiner 1987: 10–11). They only 'worked about one-third of their time in the fields, and attended to health work for the rest' (Hillier and Zheng 1994: 98). The barefoot doctor policy was announced by Mao on the eve of the Cultural Revolution in June 1965 to 'deal with the continuing shortage of physicians for China's vast rural population' (Rosenthal and Greiner 1987: 5) and 'bring minimal health care within reach of the poorest rural communities' (Becker 2000: 225). Barefoot doctor was 'a new health provider category' (Rosenthal and Greiner 1987: 6) that 'reflected an unusual medical concept combining some of the functions of doctor, nurse, and sanitation engineer' (Rosenthal and Greiner 1987: 9). Barefoot doctors took charge of first aid work (Chen and Bunge 1989: 195), treating minor ailments, 'environmental sanitation, rehabilitative care for discharged patients' (Rosenthal and Greiner 1987: 9), 'systematic immunization for preschoolers and sporadic seasonal programs for the entire population' (Rosenthal and Greiner 1987: 9), 'health education through the patriotic health campaigns' (Rosenthal and Greiner 1987: 10), 'maternal and child health, and family planning' (Cheng 1991: 10). They referred seriously ill patients, emergency or more complex cases to the second tier of commune health centers (Daemmrich 2013).

In fact, the barefoot doctor system was established to popularize rural health care through an economic and effective means (Wei 2013: 263). But the operation of this system depended on the economic level of a commune and its production brigades, which was closely tied to the annual agricultural output (Rosenthal and Greiner 1987: 10). Communes that were poorer and located in more remote areas were less able to support the barefoot doctor system (Rosenthal and Greiner 1987: 9). For decades, barefoot doctors brought 'modern health services to previously underserved communities' (Fischer 2012: 180). '[A]s a result of their skills, barefoot doctors enjoyed higher political and economic status in their community' (Wei 2013: 264). They did not receive wages like other levels of medical workers but were paid in work points like the agricultural workers (Rosenthal and Greiner 1987: 9). Their work points were equivalent to that of the local Party Secretary (Wei 2013: 264). '[S]ome barefoot doctors could earn 10 times more than a commune farmer in their communities' (Wei 2013: 264). By the mid-1970s, the first tier had more than one million barefoot doctors (Daemmrich 2013).

The second tier was commune health centers having an outpatient clinic and containing 10 to 30 beds (Chow 2004: 139). They were staffed by one or two trained junior doctors (Daemmrich 2013) who were 'graduates of middle-level medical schools and practitioners of traditional herbal medicine' (Cheng 1991: 10). Junior doctors took charge of diagnostic responsibilities, performing sterilization and abortions, supervising the barefoot doctors and organizing in-service training for the treatment of complex cases (Cheng 1991: 10).

The third tier was county hospitals providing curative care and training doctors in commune health centers (Duckett 2011: 27). They were 'equipped with an operating room, x-ray and laboratory facilities, and some in-patient beds' (Cheng 1991: 10). They were 'staffed mostly by graduate physicians trained in either Western or traditional herbal medicine' (Cheng 1991: 10). The three-tiered health care system in rural areas 'used an integrated system with a formal bottom-up referral process for patients' (Lo 2015: 66). It 'allowed not only for effective collaboration of all levels but also for careful supervision up and down the line' (Chen and Bunge 1989: 194).

Health care financing system

In order to move towards socialism, the government implemented new labor policies that 'centred on universal lifelong employment and a comprehensive welfare package for urban worker' (Traub-Merz 2011: 3). The provision of a comprehensive, employment-based welfare benefits 'were regarded as a social wage that was necessary to compensate for low wages' (Luk 2014: 39). In the aspect of health care, the government provided two types of free health care programs for urban employees: the Labor Insurance Scheme (LIS) and the Government-Funded Health Care Scheme (GHS).

Labor Insurance Scheme (LIS)

In February 1951, the LIS was formally established after the Government Administration Council had promulgated *Regulation Regarding Labor Insurance in the People's Republic of China*. It was a constituent part of a comprehensive social security package that also included benefits for the disabled, occupationally injured employees, pensioners, expectant and nursing mothers (Government Administration Council 1951). Initially, the LIS mainly covered employees in factories that were owned or managed by the state with more than 100 employees and those in railway industry, shipping industry, post and telecommunications industry. In 1953, the LIS was extended to cover employees in capital construction units of factories, mines and transport enterprises and state-owned construction enterprises. Collectively owned enterprises were also required to adopt the LIS in order to finance health care of their employees (Liu *et al.* 2004: 39; Tang and Meng 2004: 24). After nationalization, private enterprises were replaced by state-owned enterprises (SOEs). A growing number of urban employees became eligible for the LIS. By 1956, the LIS covered '94 per cent of urban employees in the enterprise sector' (Gu 2001: 200).

Although the term 'insurance' was used to describe the scheme, the LIS was not a health insurance scheme in the real sense because it did not have any premium contributions and did not have any insurance institutions to manage the scheme (Luk 2014: 5). The LIS was originally financed by employers who had to contribute an amount that was equivalent to 3 per cent of the payroll to the labor insurance fund (Government Administration Council 1951). While 70 per cent of the labor insurance fund was managed by grassroots trade unions, the rest of it was administered by the All-China Federation of Trade Unions (ACFTU), which was 'hierarchically organized and incorporated into the Party-state body' (Gu 2000: 81) and 'functioned as Leninist "transmission belts" in the totalitarian system of political social control' (Gu 2000: 82). Having trade unions to manage the labor insurance fund allowed risk sharing among enterprises (Pearson 1995: 94). In 1953, employers had to contribute 5 to 7 per cent of the payroll to finance the LIS, depending on the nature of the industry (Shi 2003: 16). In the midst of the Cultural Revolution, the ACFTU in 1967 'was formally dissolved, and virtually all enterprises ceased to function' (Naughton 1997: 177). Each individual enterprise became responsible for administering the LIS. Risk pooling no longer existed. Individual enterprises had to pay the medical expenses of their employees through the employee welfare funds that were 'retained as a certain portion of the total salary outlays' (Liu *et al.* 2004: 39). In 1969, individual enterprises were required by the Ministry of Finance (MOF) to draw 11 per cent of the payroll to establish the employee welfare funds by combing welfare funds (2.5 per cent), bonus funds (3 per cent) and medical funds all together (5.5 per cent) (Shi 2003: 16). The employee welfare funds were treated as part of the enterprises' operating expenses (Pearson 1995: 94). Being subject to soft budget constraints, however, enterprises that were struggled financially to pay the outstanding medical bills would receive financial support from the government.

Initially, the LIS provided medical coverage for eligible employees and their direct dependents. It covered all the fees for diagnosis, treatment, general medicines, surgery and hospitalization of eligible employees. Eligible employees only needed to pay expensive medicines, meals and travel expenses on their own. Their direct dependents could consult the Chinese medicine practitioners or Western doctors free of charge, with the LIS covering one-half of any fees for general medicines and surgery (Government Administration Council 1951). But they needed to pay the fees for expensive medicines, meals during hospitalization and transportation on their own. In April 1966, the Ministry of Labour and the ACFTU jointly issued the *Circular on Several Questions Concerning the Improvement of the Labour Health Insurance System* (hereafter the 1966 Circular), which required eligible employees to bear more medical expenses. The 1966 Circular stated that employers would bear the fees for expensive medicines while eligible employees had to pay registration fees, fees for home visit, nutrients and tonics on their own (The Ministry of Labour and the ACFTU 1966). It also stated that direct dependents of eligible employees had to pay the fees for registration, examination and laboratory tests on their own apart from paying one-half of the fees for medicines and surgery (The Ministry of Labour and the ACFTU 1966).

Government-Funded Health Care Scheme (GHS)

As regards the GHS, it initially began in 1951 as a pilot experiment in certain communist revolutionary base areas and certain ethnic-minority areas (Government Administration Council 1952). In July 1952, the GHS was formally established in urban China after the Government Administration Council had promulgated the *Directive Regarding the Precaution to Implement the Government-Funded Health Care Scheme for Personnel of the People's Governments, Parties, Organizations and Institutions at Various Levels in the Nation.* It mainly covered government officials, employees in trade unions, youth leagues and women's leagues, personnel in cultural, educational, health and economic institutions and disabled military personnel (Government Administration Council 1952). In January 1953, the GHS was extended to cover cadres, university and college students after the MOH had issued *Several Provisions on the Government-Funded Health Care Scheme* (Liu H. Q. 2013). In 1956, the GHS was further extended to cover retired employees of the state and government institutions (Liu H. Q. 2013). The GHS 'was directly financed by each level of the government through the state budget' (Luk 2014: 41). The per capita GHS budget was set by the central government and was allocated to each level of government through the MOF (Luk 2014: 41). The per capita GHS budget rose from Renminbi (RMB) 18 in 1952 to RMB 25 in 1962 (Li 2009: 37). The GHS covered both inpatient and outpatient expenses for diagnosis, treatment, general medicines, surgery and hospitalization of eligible persons (Government Administration Council 1952). Eligible persons only needed to pay meals and travel expenses on their own.

Cooperative Medical System (CMS)

In rural areas, health care was covered by the cooperative medical system (CMS). The embryonic stage of the CMS could be traced back to the period of Second Sino-Japanese War when Health Preservation Pharmaceutical Cooperative (HPPC) and Cooperative Health Agency (CHA) were established in the communist-base areas (Cao 2006: 134). The establishment of HPPC and CHA were a response to an appeal made by Mao in a conference held in January 1939 that the essence of health work should be applied in the course of ethnic revolution (Zhang Q. A. 2001: 58). Mao said in the conference that health officials should overcome financial and material difficulties to help the sick and injured recover (Zhang Q. A. 2001: 57). HPPC was first established under the government leadership of the Shaan-Gan-Ning Border Region in 1939 (Zhang X. X. 2015a). It took the form of shareholding system (Zhang X. X. 2015a). Each corporate or individual that made payment for stocks and complied with the memorandum of HPPC would become a shareholder of HPPC after approval by the board of directors (Zhang X. X. 2015a). Each shareholder had to purchase at least one share that was worth RMB 10 (Zhang X. X. 2015a). But there was no limit for the maximum number of shares to be purchased. HPPC was a business entity for the trading of medicinal materials as well as a health care organization (Zhang X. X. 2015a). It not only provided medical treatment, but also manufactured and sold drugs (Cao 2006: 134). It used the profit from the trading of medicinal materials as the source of finance to promote the development of Chinese medicine business (Zhang X. X. 2015a). HPPC was staffed by Chinese medicine practitioners who would pay home visits to seriously ill patients (Cao 2006: 134). Drugs were sold at a low price to patients and were delivered to disaster victims free of charge (Cao 2006: 134). HPPC was never closed. It was open 24 hours a day, 7 days a week (Zhang X. X. 2015a). Its branches were established in more than 20 places, including Yan'an, Yanchuan County and Qingjian County (Zhang X. X. 2015a).

CHA was first established in Yan'an under the government leadership in 1944 due to the prevalence of typhoid and relapsing fever (Cao 2006: 134–5; Li 2009: 55). These two communicable diseases killed more than 240 people, 897 livestock (including cows, pigs, sheep, horses, donkeys and mules) and 6,757 chickens (Zhang X. X. 2015b). Meanwhile, the establishment of CHA was also a campaign against superstitions and witch doctors (Zhang X. X. 2015b). The Yan'an government commissioned a commercial sales agency called the Mass Cooperative to establish CHA. CHA was mainly funded by the Mass Cooperative and HPPC, but individual and group shares were also absorbed (Li 2009: 55). The government supported CHA by sending Chinese medicinal materials as gifts, which were worth more than RMB 1 million (Zhang X. X. 2015b). CHA adopted the policy of 'cooperation between traditional Chinese medicine and Western medicine and medical treatment for both human and animals' (Li 2009: 55). Hence, it contained three outpatient clinics – Chinese medicine outpatient clinic, Western medicine outpatient clinic and veterinary outpatient clinic – and a pharmacy that sold both traditional Chinese medicine and Western medicine (Zhang X. X. 2015b). Until the end of July 1944, a total of 1,813 patients visited the Western medicine outpatient clinic and a total of 1,798 patients visited the Chinese medicine outpatient clinic (Zhang X. X. 2015b). By 1946, a total of 43 CHA were established (Cao 2006: 135). In sum, HPPC and CHA provided basic medical services to rural populations during the period of Second Sino-Japanese War.

After the establishment of the PRC, the government focused on developing health care in urban areas. Prior to 1955, the vast majority of the rural population had poor access to health care. Besides, they could not afford to see a doctor because fee-for-service payment was the dominant form of health care financing. In 1950, rural peasants in the northeast provinces established a batch of medical cooperatives based on the spirit of mutual aid. These medical cooperatives were financed by the masses. In Rehe and Songjiang Provinces, some peasants who had no money used their grain, eggs and potatoes as investment to set up medical cooperatives (Cao 2006: 135). The medical cooperative as a system gradually took shape following the development of agricultural cooperativization movement in the mid-1950s. In 1955, the collective health care financing system established in Mishan village, Gaoping County, Shanxi, received a lot of attention from the government (Wang 2009: 375). Its main sources of finance came from the annual 'health care fee' contributed by individual peasants, 15 to 20 per cent of the public welfare funds contributed by the agricultural production cooperative and drug charges contributed by doctors (Cao 2006: 136; Wang 2009: 375). Peasants who had paid the annual 'health care fee' could enjoy free preventive health care services and were exempt from paying fees for registration, home visits and surgery (Cao 2006: 136). 'With the approval of the State Council, the Ministry of Health began to disseminate the Mishan experiences'

(Wang 2009: 375). Subsequently, the collective health care financing system was established in Hubei, Henan and Guizhou (Li 2009: 56). In November 1959, the CMS was formally established when the MOH mentioned the phrase 'cooperative medical system' for the first time in a central government document and agreed that the CMS was a more appropriate form of health care financing system in rural China (Wang 2009: 376–7). But it was not until the period of the Cultural Revolution (1966–76) that the CMS grew rapidly.

The CMS was a low-cost prepayment system (Liu D. 2013: 30–1). It varied across regions in terms of management, contribution and medical coverage. It 'might be run by a brigade, a commune, or by both' (Wang 2009: 381). It was 'not legally mandatory, but in communes and brigades that adopted the system, participation was compulsory' (Wang 2009: 380). It was financed by three parties: individuals, collectives and the government. In general, each brigade or commune member contributed RMB 1 to 5 as an annual fee to the cooperative medical fund, depending on the economic status of the local community (Liu D. 2013: 31). This amount was matched by a similar contribution from brigade and commune welfare funds. Subsidies were given by the higher level of government 'for the purpose of compensating health workers and purchasing medical equipment' (Liu D. 2013: 31). The cooperative medical fund was used to pay for 'medicines, a portion of hospital costs, equipment and barefoot doctors' workpoint remuneration' (Hillier 1983: 109). But medical coverage enjoyed by CMS participants differed, depending on the economic conditions of the regions. In general, there were three types of medical coverage: (i) receiving treatment and medicine at the brigade health station or commune clinic free of charge; (ii) receiving treatment free of charge but paying medicine out of pocket; and (iii) exempting part of the drug costs but paying charges for examination and hospitalization (Shi 2003: 47). In some places, participants with major illnesses had to pay 20 to 50 per cent of medical expenses on their own if they received treatment at a county or provincial hospital (Wilenski 1976). By the end of 1971, the CMS had more than 500 million participants and had been implemented in 70 per cent of the brigades (Huang 2013: 45).

In sum, the establishment of the three-tiered medical institution network in urban and rural areas greatly improved the accessibility of health services and ensured a healthy and productive workforce that was essential to the process of nation building and economic and social development. The provision of free health care programs for urban employees alleviated the financial burden caused by illnesses while the establishment of a low-cost prepayment system in rural areas made health care more affordable to the rural majority. The centrally planned health care system greatly improved the health status of the Chinese people, 'leading to an increase in average life expectancy, a decrease in infant mortality and a decrease in the prevalence of infectious diseases' (Luk 2014: 43). Infant mortality rate (IMR) drastically fell from 200 per 1,000 live births prior to 1949 (National Population and Family Planning Commission 2012: 513) to 47.0 per 1,000 live births in 1973–5 (National Population and Family Planning Commission 2012: 513).

Conclusion

The historical review shows that the development of a centrally planned health care delivery and financing system in urban and rural areas in the pre-reform era was shaped by a complex interplay of forces, namely institutions, historical legacy, interests and ideologies. The development of health care delivery and financing is a political process revealing an intricate interplay of power relationships and diverse interests. The highly centralized political system gave the government considerable leverage to formulate health care policy and develop the health care system without any political opposition. Mao's endorsement of the socialist and communist ideologies led to the establishment of a state-run health care system that was characterized by three-tiered medical institution networks in urban and rural areas, free health care programs in urban areas and a low-cost prepayment system in rural areas. The historical legacy of the Red Army's base area medicine drove Mao to emphasize prevention and mass mobilization when developing health care. The early development of health care system with a strong urban bias was due to China's close and good relations with the Soviet Union. The radical shift towards the development of rural health care in the 1960s was caused by the tense relationship between Mao and the MOH and the Sino-Soviet split. To conclude, the development of health care carried political, ideological and diplomatic significance in the pre-reform era.

4 Four phases of health insurance reform

Introduction

Since the mid-1980s, the Chinese government has implemented health insurance reforms with the aim of replacing the free health care system with a new contributory health insurance system. The reforms have been implemented in a gradual and peaceful manner. They have gone through four phases: the exploration phase (1984–92); the experimental phase (1993–7); the implementation phase (1998–2001); and the extension phases (2002 to present). After almost three decades of effort, a multi-layered health insurance system has been established to provide financial protection against illnesses for different segments of the population. The multi-layered health insurance system consists of the Urban Employee Basic Medical Insurance (UEBMI), the New Rural Cooperative Medical System (NRCMS), Urban Resident Basic Medical Insurance (URBMI) and the Critical Illness Insurance Scheme (CIIS). The UEBMI is the biggest health insurance scheme in China and the only compulsory health insurance scheme in the nation. The rest of the schemes are voluntary in nature and only provide partial coverage for the insured.

The subsequent three sections of this chapter respectively examine the background and context of health insurance reform in the 1980s, four phases of health insurance reform and the complex interplay of forces that shape the phases of health insurance reform over time.

Background and context

Health insurance reform began in the mid-1980s when the Chinese government tried to fix the health care system that was plagued by a substantial rise in health care costs and poor quality of medical care. The free health care system encouraged both patients and health care providers to overuse medical resources. Patients who were entitled to the Labor Insurance Scheme (LIS) and the Government-Funded Health Care Scheme (GHS) lacked cost consciousness. Since their medical expenses were paid by their work units or the government, they did not confront the real cost of medical care and were inclined to over-utilize medical services. Meanwhile, health care providers relied on over-prescription and unnecessary medical tests and treatments to gain more revenues because prices of medical services and drugs were set below actual costs during Mao's era and health care providers failed to get compensation from the government (Li 2009: 39; Zheng 2009: 260). The problems of demand-side and supply-side moral hazard were very serious, leading to over-consumption of health care and waste of drugs.

Meanwhile, the situation was further complicated by China's transformation from a centrally planned economy to a market economy. Deng Xiaoping, who was the successor to Mao, came to power in 1978. His immediate tasks were to rebuild the ruined economy caused by the Cultural Revolution (1966–76) and consolidated his authority by improving the living standards of people and the delivery of the economic goods (Luk 2014: 64). 'He denounced Mao's egalitarianism as a dangerous nation that retarded economic growth while embracing the ideas of marketization and efficiency' (Luk 2015: 48). He transformed China to a market economy through reform and opening-up policies in the late 1970s. Market replaced government in allocating and distributing resources. Economic responsibility and material incentives were emphasized to stimulate more productive labor. Enterprises were given economic autonomy to decide upon capital allocation and utilization, production, personnel management (recruitment, promotion, dismissal), salaries (Luk 2014: 65) and became solely responsible for their own profits and losses (Hsü 2000: 850). Various forms of enterprise emerged and prospered, such as state-owned enterprises (SOEs), collective enterprises, joint venture and sole proprietorship. China's transition to a market economy due to the country's leadership change and the endorsement of new economic ideas and principles adversely affected the free health care system.

Under the market economy, the pursuit of economic growth became the paramount objective of the political leaders, which inevitably marginalized the importance of social policy issues (Huang 2013: 13). Health care became subordinate to economic development. The government retreated from health care financing (Duckett 2011). The central government granted discretionary spending power to local governments through fiscal decentralization. Since the growth of Gross Domestic Product (GDP) served 'as a yardstick by which to measure local government performance' (Huang 2013: 13), local governments were not enthusiastic about investing in health care. They 'moved towards a cost recovery policy in hospital financing that significantly reduced subsidies to hospitals' (Luk 2014: 64). 'Government subsidies decreased and accounted for only about 10 per cent of average public hospital revenues' (Luk 2015: 49). Meanwhile, local governments granted financial autonomy to public hospitals to 'charge for their services and to sell drugs at a profit' (The World Bank 2010: vii). A bonus payment system was also introduced to public hospitals to reward high-achieving doctors (Henderson 1989). The performance of doctors was directly linked to the revenues they generated through service provision and drug prescription (Liu and Mills 2005). Both public hospitals and doctors had strong incentives to 'earn more revenue through different sources and to charge patients substantially greater than the actual cost' (Luk 2014: 64). Public hospitals began to run like for-profit organizations (Luk 2015: 49). Supplier-induced demand (SID) or physician induced demand became prevalent and serious (Luk 2014). It was common for doctors to aggressively prescribe expensive and unnecessary drugs and provide unnecessary medical treatment for the sake of earning more revenue for hospitals and receiving more bonuses (Tian *et al.* 2011). The problem of SID led to drastic increase in health care expenditures.

Rising health care expenditures, coupled with a drastic increase in the number of the GHS and LIS participants, resulted in imposing unbearable financial burdens on the government and enterprises. For the GHS, the number of participants rose from 4 million in 1953 to 14.29 million in 1979 and 21.28 million in 1985 (Zheng 2009: 260). The overall GHS expenditure rose from about Renminbi (RMB) 100 million in 1953 to RMB 570 million in 1979 to about RMB 1.54 billion in 1985 (Zheng 2009: 260). The average per capita medical expenses of GHS participants rose from RMB 26.25 in 1953 to RMB 39.9 in 1979 and RMB 72.57 in 1985 (Zheng 2009: 260). As to LIS, the overall expenditure rose from RMB 2.73 billion in 1978 to RMB 3.64 billion in 1980 and 6.47 billion in 1985 (Zheng 2009: 260). The average per capita medical expenses of LIS participants rose from RMB 36.1 in 1978 to RMB 44.3 in 1980 and RMB 65.1 in 1985 (Zheng 2009: 260). Since the economic reform, enterprises have become responsible for paying the medical expenses of their employees. Rapid increase in health care expenditures drained away a substantial amount of profits earned by enterprises (Luk 2014: 65). When enterprises became financially incapable of paying employees' medical expenses, many employees became 'uninsured' or 'underinsured' (Luk 2014: 65). This problem was particularly serious in SOEs (Luk 2014: 65). Meanwhile, local governments also had difficulty in paying medical expenses of GHS participants due to a continuous drain on government revenue. The insufficient financial support from the enterprises and the government led to the collapse of the LIS and GHS. There was a pressing need for the government to reduce health care costs and ensure that health care dollars could be spent in the most productive way.

In rural areas, the CMS also collapsed between 1982 and 1984 due to the dismantling of communes (Duckett 2011: 59). Under the economic reform, the transition of rural areas from agricultural collectives to the household responsibility system weakened the local collective's ability to gather cooperative funds for health care spending (Duckett 2011: 59). Meanwhile, the CMS, which was 'closely associated with Mao himself and the Cultural Revolution' (Duckett 2011: 72), did not get support from the central government during Deng's era because the new leadership 'had little commitment to a policy associated with the Cultural Revolution' (Duckett 2011: 60). Inadequate financial support resulted in the collapse of the CMS and many rural people ended up paying out-of-pocket medical expenses. In 1996, 'it was revealed that 90 per cent of the peasants [were] not covered by any form of health insurance' (Becker 2000: 227). 'Starting in 1984, the emphasis of economic structural reform shifted from rural to urban areas' (China Development Research Foundation 2013: 14). For this reason, the problem of substantially increased health care costs in urban areas became a priority for the government to address. The rapid increase in health care expenditure caused by free health care severely weakened the financial capability and competitiveness of enterprises (Luk 2014: 65) The free health care system became an impediment to implement economic reform further. This compelled the central government to reform the free health care system in urban areas first.

Four phases of health insurance reform

Health insurance reforms have been implemented in a gradual and peaceful manner. They have gone through four phases: the exploration phase (1984–92); the experimental phase (1993–7); the implementation phase (1998–2001); and the extension phases (2002 to present). Table 4.1 contains health insurance related regulation, guiding opinions or decisions issued by the Chinese authorities since the mid-1980s.

Table 4.1 Health insurance related regulation/guiding opinions in China

Year	Health insurance related regulation/guiding opinions
1984	Notice on Further Strengthening the Management of Government Insurance Scheme
1988	Considerations on the Reform of the Employee Health Insurance System (Draft)
1989	The Notification of the Key Points of 1989 Economic Reform
1989	Management Measures for the Government-Funded Health Care Scheme
1994	Opinions on the Trial of Health Care System Reform for Urban Employees
1996	Opinions on Expanding the Number of Pilot Cities for Reform of the Medical Insurance System for Employees
1997	Decision Concerning Health Reform and Development
1998	The Decision of the State Council Concerning the Establishment of the Urban Employee Basic Medical Insurance
2000	Notice on Issuing the National Basic Medical Insurance Drug Catalogue
2002	Notice on Strengthening the Management of Medical Savings Account of the Basic Medical Insurance Scheme for Urban Employees
2002	Decision on Further Strengthening Rural Health Work
2003	Opinions on Establishing the New Rural Cooperative Medical System
2006	Notice on Accelerating Pilot Work of the New Rural Cooperative Medical System
2007	Guiding Opinions on Piloting Basic Medical Insurance for Urban Residents
2008	Guiding Opinions on Including University Students in the Pilot Basic Medical Insurance for Urban Residents
2009	The Opinions of the Central Committee of the Communist Party of China and the State Council on Deepening Health Care System Reform
2009	The Guiding Opinions on Further Strengthening the Management of the Basic Medical Insurance Fund
2009	Opinions on Basic Medical Insurance Settlement Service for Medical Expenses Incurred outside Home Territory
2012	Guiding Opinions on the Launch of the Work on Critical Illness Insurance for Urban and Rural Residents
2014	The Notification of Accelerating the Implementation of the Critical Illness Insurance Scheme for Urban and Rural Residents
2014	Guiding Opinions on Further Improving Basic Medical Insurance Settlement Service for Medical Expenses Incurred outside Home Territory

The exploration phase (1984–92)

For the period of 1984–92, local governments were encouraged to experiment with different solutions to reduce medical expenditures in the areas under their jurisdiction. It was hoped that medical expenditures could be reduced by restraining provider and consumer moral hazard. In April 1985, the Ministry of Health (MOH) issued *Report Concerning a Number of Policy Issues Connected with the Health Service Reforms*, which encouraged local governments to reform charging system in hospitals through conducting exploratory experimentation (Ministry of Health 1985). Local governments were encouraged to raise charges or formulate charging standards for different types of wards, medical services, new medical equipment and new medical treatment according to their needs and local circumstances (Ministry of Health 1985). Reforming the charging system aimed at reducing consumer moral hazard in health care. Patients being insured would become more cost conscious when they were asked to bear part of their financial costs of treatment at the point of consumption. In March 1988, Research Group on Health Care Reform headed by the MOH was formed to examine issues related to reforming the LIS and GHS. It was a trans-departmental research group involving representatives from the MOH, the Ministry of Finance (MOF), the Ministry of Labor (MOL), the State Commission for Restructuring Economic Systems, State Pharmaceutical Bureau, the Organization Department of the Central Committee of China, All China Federation of Trade Unions and the People's Insurance Company of China (Luk 2014: 61). In July 1988, the Research Group drafted a proposal, which recommended that medical costs of the LIS should be borne jointly by employers and employees while medical costs of the GHS should be borne jointly by individuals and public finance (Li 2009: 42). In March 1989, Dandong, Siping, Huangshi and Zhuzhou were chosen as the pilot cities to carry out health financing reform experiments (Li 2009; Luk 2014). In May 1992, the Health System Reform Group under the leadership of the State Council was formed to conduct a comprehensive study on reforming the LIS and GHS and examine the effectiveness of health financing reform experiments carried out in the pilot cities (The State Council 1992).

The initial health care financing reform mainly contained three approaches: co-payment; financial contracting with work units; and financial contracting with hospitals (Gu 2001: 209). Co-payment referred to a payment paid by the insured when receiving the medical service. For example, the Shanghai municipal government implemented a co-payment scheme in selected enterprise units and selected districts, which required LIS and GHS beneficiaries to pay 10 per cent of the outpatient charges out-of-pocket (Luk 2014: 47). Financial contracting with work units was an approach in which the government appropriated certain amounts of health care funds to work units for paying the medical expenses of their employees (Gu 2001: 209). Work units had to cover any health care spending beyond the contracted amount on their own (Gu 2001: 209). As regards financial contracting with hospitals, it referred to an approach in which work units signed contracts with hospitals and hospitals, after receiving a year-round budget from work units, took full responsibility for the health care of the work units' employees (Gu 2001: 209). However, the initial health care financing reform was piecemeal and incremental in nature. It was limited to certain funding adjustments without involving any institutional transformation of the existing free health care system (Luk 2014: 47). Many local governments 'demonstrated little political determination to implement the health reforms' (Gu 2001: 209). The initial reform was far from effective to reduce medical expenditures.

The experimental phase (1993–7)

The second phase of health insurance reform began in 1993 when the Third Plenary Session of the 14th Central Committee of the Communist Party of China clearly stated that health insurance for urban employees should be borne jointly by employers and employees and a new insurance system that combined individual medical savings accounts (MSA) and the social pooling fund (SPF) should be established (Li 2009: 42). In April 1994, the State Commission for Restructuring the Economic Systems, together with the MOF, the MOL and the MOH, issued *Opinions on the Trial of Health Care System Reform for Urban Employees* (hereafter the 1994 Opinions), which specified the model, details and design of a new health insurance system. According to the 1994 Opinions, a new health insurance system combining individual MSA and SPF would be established and urban employers and employees were required to enroll in the new health insurance scheme and make premium contributions to such scheme (The State Commission for Restructuring the Economic Systems *et al.* 1994).

In 1995, the cities of Zhenjiang in Jiangsu Province and Jiujiang in Jiangxi Province were selected by the central government to implement this pilot medical insurance model. Following the central government guidelines, health insurance models in Zhenjiang and Jiujiang were in line with the principles of individual responsibility and solidarity and they shared many common features in terms of coverage, sources of finance, funding structure and payment structure. For this reason, the pilot medical insurance model came to be known as the two-*jiang* model. 'The health insurance schemes of Zhenjiang and Jiujiang were successful, and valuable lessons could be drawn from their experiences' (Wong *et al.* 2006: 17). In May 1996, the two-*jiang* model was extended to '57 cities in 27 provinces, autonomous regions and provincially ranked municipalities across the country' (Gu 2001: 209). But local governments were given considerable room to modify the two-*jiang* model according to their needs and socio-economic conditions (Luk 2014: 47). In January 1997, the Central Committee of the Communist Party of China and the State Council issued the *Decision Concerning Health Reform and Development*, which called for further extension of the two-*jiang* model in order to provide basic medical protection for all urban employees (The Central Committee of the Communist Party of China and the State Council 1997).

The implementation phase (1998–2001)

The third phase of health insurance reform officially began in December 1998 when the State Council promulgated a landmark decree known as the *Decision of the State Council Concerning the Establishment of the Urban Employee Basic Medical Insurance* (hereafter the 1998 Decree) (The State Council 1998). According to the 1998 Decree, a compulsory scheme known as the Urban Employee Basic Medical Insurance (UEBMI) would be implemented nationwide. The UEBMI required the participation of all urban work units in both the public and private sectors and their employees. Premium contribution was shared by work units and their employees. Retired employees could also join the UEBMI without paying any insurance premium. The contribution rate for work units, at the minimum, had to be at the level of 6 per cent of an employee's total wage bill (The State Council 1998). The contribution rate for employees, at the minimum, had to be at the level of 2 per cent of an employee's total wage bill (The State Council 1998). The Basic Medical Insurance fund (hereafter the BMI fund) was formed by an individual MSA and a SPF. Premium contribution was split into an MSA that covered insured employees' general outpatient and emergency medical expenses, and prescribed drug charges, and a SPF that covered inpatient charges (including inpatient observation in emergency rooms). The SPF covered inpatient charges that were above the payment threshold and below the ceiling, with the remainder paid by the individual MSA or out-of-pocket payment. Ministry of Labor and Social Security (MOLSS) was established to formulate basic guidelines, standards, and policies for implementing medical insurance schemes and exercise insurance supervision. Local governments were given discretion to determine and adjust contribution rate, payment threshold, ceiling and reimbursement ratio of the BMI in accordance with socio-economic conditions.

A medical insurance card was issued to the insured employees for seeking medical treatment at designated medical institutions or buying medicines at designated drug stores. The card stored the identity card number, name, gender, consumption patterns and transferred account payment of an insured employee (Interview 10SH1). In May 2000, the *National Basic Medical Insurance Drug Formulary List* (hereafter the Drug Formulary) was issued by the government to ensure equitable access by patients to cost-effective drugs. The Drug Formulary listed Western medicines and Chinese proprietary medicines that were eligible for full or partial reimbursement by the BMI. These medicines were essential medicines that were clinically effective, safe, convenient to use and reasonably priced. 'National, provincial, and local authorities ha[d] their own responsibilities in the formulary-making and implementing process' (Ngorsuraches *et al.* 2012: S123).

The extension phase (2002 to present)

The fourth phase of health insurance reform has begun since 2002 when the government introduced different types of medical insurance schemes for different segments of the population based on the principle of 'basic medical protection, wide population coverage' (*bao ji ben, guang fu gai*). The government introduced the NRCMS in 2002, the URBMI in 2007 and the CIIS in 2012. All these three medical insurance schemes are voluntary in nature. But each individual scheme has its distinct funding structure, medical coverage and reimbursement level.

The NRCMS was implemented in October 2002 when the Central Committee of the Communist Party of China and the State Council jointly issued *Decision on Further Strengthening Rural Health Work* (hereafter the 2002 State Council Decision), which announced the government's decision to gradually implement the NRCMS in order to reduce medical induced poverty (The Central Committee of the Communist Party of China and the State Council 2002). The 2002 State Council Decision stated that the NRCMS was expected to provide health care coverage for the entire rural population by 2010 and could be adjusted in accordance with the local social and economic development, the financial capacity of peasants and medical expenses. Following the 2002 State Council Decision, MOH, MOF and Ministry of Agriculture (MOA) in January 2003 jointly issued *Opinions on Establishing the New Rural Cooperative Medical System*, which contained four specific guidelines for the design and implementation of the NRCMS (Ministry of Health *et al.* 2013). First, participation in the NRCMS was voluntary but must be at the household level to avoid adverse selection. In other words, either all or none of the members in a household participate in the NRCMS. Second, the funding for the NRCMS came from three main sources, which included individual contribution, subsidies from the central government, and from local (mainly provincial) governments. Each NRCMS participant was required to contribute no less than Renminbi (RMB) 10 per year, with the local government subsidizing at least RMB 10 per year for each NRCMS participant (Ministry of Health *et al.* 2013). The central government would also match with RMB 10 per year for each NRCMS participant in the central and western provinces (Ministry of Health *et al.* 2013). Third, the NRCMS mainly focused on catastrophic illnesses. Fourth, management and operation of the NRCMS was at county level. County-level governments were given discretion to determine the deductible, reimbursement ceiling and reimbursement ratio in accordance with their own socio-economic conditions. NRCMS committees were set up by county governments to carry out insurance implementation.

The URBMI was implemented in July 2007 when the State Council issued the *Guiding Opinions on Piloting Basic Medical Insurance for Urban Residents* (The State Council 2007). It required qualified provinces to select two or three cities for implementing the URBMI. The URBMI was a subsidized voluntary scheme for non-working urban residents, including young children, primary and secondary school students, the severely disabled and the elderly. It required individual contribution, with moderate subsidies shared by the central and local governments. It focused on covering inpatient and outpatient services for catastrophic illnesses. In 2007, the minimum government subsidy was RMB 40 per enrollee per year (The State Council 2007). For the severely disabled students and children, the government would give an additional subsidy of no less than RMB 10 per enrollee per year (The State Council 2007). For the severely disabled adults and low-income seniors over 60 years of age, the government would give an additional subsidy of no less than RMB 60 per enrollee per year (The State Council 2007).

The CIIS was implemented in August 2012 when the National Development and Reform Commission (NDRC), MOH, MOF, Ministry of Human Resources and Social Security, Ministry of Civil Affairs (MCA) and the China Insurance Regulatory Commission (CIRC) jointly issued *The Guiding Opinions on the Launch of the Work on Critical Illness Insurance for Urban and Rural Residents* (hereafter the Guiding Opinions) (National Development and Reform Commission *et al.* 2012). According to the Guiding Opinions, the CIIS could be bought from a qualified commercial insurer by using the surplus of the URBMI and NRCMS funds or by increasing the funds collected from the URBMI and the NRCMS. Those insured by the URBMI or the NRCMS would be compensated for no less than 50 per cent of their out-of-pocket medical expenses incurred by treatments for critical illnesses, on top of their basic medical insurance reimbursement (National Development and Reform Commission *et al.* 2012). The main objective of the CIIS was to insure urban and rural residents against catastrophic health expenditures and prevent them from falling into poverty (*yin bing zhi pin*) or falling back into poverty (*yin bing fan pin*). The operation of the CIIS was entrusted to a qualified commercial insurer that was selected through a competitive, open bidding process. When operating the CIIS, the qualified commercial insurer needed to follow the principles of 'balancing revenue and expenditure, and capital preservation with narrow profit margin' (*shou zhi ping heng, bao ben wei li*). The insurer was responsible for its own profits and losses. The CIIS provided an extra layer of protection for people who did not have to pay extra insurance premium. In February 2014, the Health Care Reform Office of the State Council issued *The Notification of Accelerating the Implementation of the Critical Illness Insurance Scheme for Urban and Rural Residents,* which called for full implementation of the pilot CIIS scheme in the nation by June 2014 (Health Care Reform Office of the State Council 2014).

Complex interplay of forces that shape health insurance reforms over time

After almost three decades of effort, a multi-layered health insurance system has been established to provide financial protection against illnesses for different segments of the population. The reforms have been implemented in a gradual and peaceful manner. Health insurance reform in China is not a one-time event but an ongoing process responding to changing circumstances (Luk 2014: 150). Careful examination reveals that health insurance reform is shaped by a complex interplay of forces, which include (i) a top-down decision-making model and competing bureaucratic interests; (ii) the discretionary power of local governments; (iii) policy feedback effects; (iv) environmental triggers; and (v) ideational forces.

Top-down decision-making model and competing bureaucratic interests

The process of health insurance reforms involves competing bureaucratic interests because reform usually leads to the redistribution of interests among stakeholders. Strains can emerge 'between those who would not benefit or could not adjust to the new conditions and those who saw the new opportunities' (Narayanan 2006: 329). This situation is particularly true in China when 'there were about 20 ministries containing certain degrees of responsibilities for health care' (Luk 2014: 60). It was not an easy task to coordinate among ministries because there was no clear division of authority among these ministries (Luk 2014: 61). Besides, the ministries 'operated largely independently on a daily basis, [and] had different interests to defend' (Luk 2014: 61). The Chinese idiom of 'nine dragons harnessing floods' (*jiu long zhi shui*) was used by Chinese scholars and experts to describe the 'complex institutional arrangement for health care' (Luk 2014: 61). This can be substantiated by the documents or notification on health insurance schemes that are jointly issued by ministries.

The highly centralized political system and top-down decision-making model allowed top party leaders to enjoy the monopoly on setting health care goals and making decisions on major polices of a nationwide character (Wang 2002: 406). The principles of health reform were outlined jointly by the Central Committee and the State Council (Ho 2011: 2). The Central Committee was the highest authority within the Chinese Communist Party (CCP) containing top Party leaders while the State Council 'was the highest executive organ and the command headquarter exerting leadership over the ministries, bureau, commissions and committees' (Luk 2014: 59). Once the Central Committee indicated in which direction health care reform should proceed, 'the State Council would administer various ministries below it to actualize the health care reform' (Luk 2014: 59).

Under the leadership of the State Council, trans-ministry committees, leading small groups or research groups that were ad hoc in nature, were formed so that representatives of various ministries could gather together to exchange ideas and reach a consensus on the contents of health insurance reform programmes. Competing policy orientation and competing interests usually led to disagreement, heated debates and time-consuming discussion among ministries (Luk 2014: 62). For example, the MOF, which had a fiscally conservative position, favored 'reducing the government's financial burden caused by rising medical costs and shrinking the government's role in funding health care' (Luk 2014: 62). The MOH, which had the duty of overseeing hospitals, wanted to ensure that the interests of hospitals and physicians would not be affected by health insurance reform. Nevertheless, representatives from different ministries would find ways to reconcile differences and to reach agreements by consensus in the bargaining process.

The discretionary power of local governments

While the government during Deng's era continued to centralize the policy-making powers in its hands, it decentralized the administrative power to local governments to implement health insurance reforms (Luk 2014: 62). Decentralization had the advantage of increasing 'the autonomy, discretion, efficiency, enthusiasm, flexibility incentives and support of local governments' (Luk 2014: 62) when implementing health insurance reforms. During the initial stage of reform in the mid-1980s, local governments were encouraged to experiment with different solutions that could reduce health care spending. In the mid-1990s, local governments used the successful experience of Zhenjiang and Jiujiang as reference and adopted various models that could suit their needs and socioe-conomic conditions. The health insurance models in Shanghai, Hainan and Shenzhen were some well-known models that gained national recognition due to their virtues of reducing supply-side and demand-side moral hazard and reducing health care spending (Luk 2014). When the UEBMI was implemented in 1998, local governments enjoyed a high degree of autonomy in policy enforcement. They had discretion to determine the contribution rate, funding structure, payment structure, medical coverage and reimbursement ratio of health insurance schemes. But the high degree of autonomy enjoyed by local governments in implementing health insurance reform had unavoidably created some problems. The self-interests of local government led to the original purpose of health insurance reform being disregarded or being distorted. For example, some local governments used the participation rate of the NRCMS as their political achievement, thereby forcing rural peasants to join the scheme that was originally voluntary in nature (Chen and Li 2012: 96; Xia 2013).

Positive and negative policy feedback effects

Both positive and negative policy-feedback effects shaped the development of health insurance reform. In the 1980s, the free health care system established during Mao's era generated negative policy-feedback effects of supply-side and demand-side moral hazard. Overconsumption of medical services and waste of medical resources led to substantially increased health care expenditures, which in turn imposed a heavy financial burden on both work units and the government. The negative socio-economic consequences undermined the fiscal sustainability of the free health care system and resulted in the collapse of the LIS and GHS in the 1980s. In the mid-1990s, the two-*jiang* model, which combined individual MSA and the SPF, succeeded in promoting the ideas of individual responsibility and social solidarity. These two ideas generated the positive effects of increasing cost consciousness of the insured and promoting risk pooling in health care. The successful experience of implementing the two-*jiang* model created a lock-in effect, which paved the way for subsequent development of a basic medical insurance model characterized by the combination of an individual MSA and the SPF. Although the institutional design of the NRCMS and the URBMI did not contain the individual MSA, the ideas of individual responsibility and social solidarity were introduced to these health insurance programs. Participants were required to pay a lump sum and their medical expenses were covered by the SPF. The positive policy-feedback effects generated by the two-*jiang* model since the mid-1990s has created a policy continuity that the direction of health insurance reform revolved around the ideas of individual responsibility and social solidarity.

Environmental triggers

In the 1980s, the new leadership and the transformation from a centrally planned economy to a market economy were two domestic environmental triggers that opened a window of opportunity for the government to implement an initial stage of health insurance reform. Population ageing is another domestic trigger that has created a window of opportunity for different generations of leadership and the government to implement health insurance reform in the later stage. Population aging is closely related to epidemiological transition from infectious disease to chronic diseases (Lee 2015). For this reason, the government since 2002 has focused on providing rural and urban residents with financial protection against outpatient and inpatient catastrophic illnesses.

Ideational forces

The shift of old ideas to new ideas also shapes the development of the health care financing system over time. Ideological orientation affects the policy preferences of Party leaders (Narayanan 2006: 331). Ideology is 'the vehicle for communicating regime values to the Party rank and file and to the whole population' (Narayanan 2006: 331). Mao's endorsement of communist ideologies and egalitarianism led to the establishment of a free health care system so that health care became accessible and affordable to the majority of the population. When Deng Xiaoping came to power in 1978, however, he embraced the ideas of market forces and efficiency, which led to Mao's revolutionary ideologies and populist egalitarianism being abandoned and the 'iron rice bowl' policy being discarded. Marketization became trendy in health care (Ngok 2014: 98). The ideas of individual responsibility and shared responsibility were introduced to the free health care system. Those who were entitled to the LIS and GHS had to bear part of their financial costs when seeking medical care. The idea of financial contracting was also introduced to the relationship between the government and work units and the relationship between work units and public hospitals in order to derive optimal securities in the presence of incentive conflicts (Roberts and Sufi 2009: 3). Deng's successor Jiang Zemin embraced Deng's reform philosophy. He continued to advance economic reforms (Tisdell 2009) and 'managed to guide the Chinese economy on to a high growth path' (Narayanan 2006: 335). This led to the creation of a new contributory health insurance system for urban employees.

During Jiang's era, the establishment of a health insurance system combined with individual MSA and SPF reflected the ideas of individual responsibility and social solidarity (Luk 2014: 67). These two ideas 'could achieve political prominence because they fitted into the market-oriented economic context well' (Luk 2014: 67). Jiang had been resolutely pro-open-door (Nathan 1999: 5). The ideas of individual responsibility and social solidarity were borrowed from international experience and then introduced to the institutional design of the new insurance model (Luk 2014: 67). The individual MSA of the new insurance model was similar to the compulsory medical savings scheme in Singapore (Luk 2014: 67) while 'the SPF and the mandatory contribution from both work units and employees was similar to the sickness fund of the social insurance scheme in Germany' (Luk 2014: 67). The individual MSA emphasized individual responsibility and could increase the cost consciousness of the insured. The SPF could achieve social solidarity because it served the purposes of redistributive financing and providing a risk pool among the insured (Luk 2014: 68). Meanwhile, the institutional design of the new insurance model also reflected the path-dependent logic of policy makers. While the Singaporean government required the self-employed to participate into the compulsory medical insurance scheme, the Chinese government excluded the self-employed from participating in the UEBMI. The exclusion of the self-employed from joining the UEBMI reflected the path-dependent logic that health care benefit was work-unit based (Luk 2014: 66).

Economic reforms since 1978 have led to China experiencing drastic economic growth and improving citizens' economic welfare. Nevertheless, decades of economic reforms had 'produced a disturbing degree of social inequality and injustice' (Zhou 2011: 16). This led to Jiang's successor Hu Jintao embracing the idea of harmonious society, which represented 'a dramatic shift away from the growth-at-all-cost of the developing model of his predecessors' (Zhou 2011: 16). '[T]aking people as the basis' and 'comprehensive development' became two main elements of the concept of harmonious society (Zhou 2011: 16). In Hu's view, it was important to take care of the interests of the majority of the population. He emphasized the development of a more equitable and sustainable social security system (Hu 2012) and the provision of basic medical care for the Chinese people (Hu 2007). The concept of harmonious society was introduced into health insurance reform. The principle of 'basic medical protection, wide population coverage' became the direction of health insurance reform. Different types of medical insurance schemes, including the NRCMS, the URBMI and the CIIS, were implemented to provide financial protection for different segments of the population. Reimbursement levels of these health insurance schemes have continued to increase so that the level of medical protection enjoyed by the insured also increased.

Conclusion

To conclude, a multi-layered health insurance system that promotes the ideas of individual responsibility and social solidarity has been established after three decades of effort. Health insurance reform in China is an ongoing process that has undergone four different stages. It is a political process involving a range of players and stakeholders with competing values and interests. It is also a complex process in which different types of forces interact with each other and have shaped the development of health insurance reforms over time.

5 A multi-layered health insurance system

Composition, models and characteristics

Introduction

Since the mid-1980s, a series of health insurance reforms have been implemented in order to provide different segments of the population with financial protection against illnesses. After three decades of effort, a multi-layered health insurance system has been established. This health insurance system consisted of the Urban Employee Basic Medical Insurance (UEBMI), the New Rural Cooperative Medical System (NRCMS), the Urban Resident Basic Medical Insurance (URBMI) and the Critical Illness Insurance Scheme (CIIS). Meanwhile, a medical financial assistance (MFA) system has also been established to help people with limited financial means to participate in the URBMI or the NRCMS. Health insurance has expanded constantly both in coverage and scope in China.

During the health insurance reform process, local governments were encouraged to experiment with different models that could suit their local circumstances. Some of the health insurance models implemented by local governments gained national recognition because they were able to yield some useful experience. This chapter aims at introducing these health insurance models, examining their contents and highlighting their characteristics. It will examine four representative models in the experimental phase: (i) the two-*jiang* model, (ii) the Shenzhen model, (iii) the Hainan model and (iv) the Shanghai model. Besides, it will examine different types of reimbursement models in the NRCMS and different models in the CIIS. It will also examine the MFA System in urban and rural areas.

Four representative models in the experimental phase (1993–7)

In the experimental phase of health insurance reform, there were four representative models that gained national recognition because they were able to yield some useful experience. They were the two-*jiang* model, (ii) the Shenzhen model, (iii) the Hainan model and (iv) the Shanghai model. The institutional design of these models revolved around the ideas of individual responsibility and social solidarity and demonstrated the efficacy of individual medical savings accounts (MSA) and the social pooling fund (SPF) in restraining moral hazard and reducing health care spending.

The two-jiang model

In the mid-1990s, the cities of Zhenjiang in Jiangsu Province and Jiujiang in Jiangxi Province were selected by the central government to experiment with a health insurance model that combined an individual MSA with a SPF. This pilot health insurance model came to be known as the two-*jiang* model because this was where the model was implemented. It was also called the 'Pathway Model' because it had the prominent feature of paying medical expenses through three tiers (Liu *et al.* 2004: 48). According to the 1994 Opinions, government organs, institutions, public and private enterprises (except township and village enterprises) and their incumbent employees and retirees had to participate in this medical insurance scheme. Under this medical insurance system, premium contribution was jointly shared by employers and employees. The contribution rate for the employers was 10 per cent of their total annual payroll for the previous year while the contribution rate for the employees was 1 per cent of their annual salary. Retirees did not have any premium contributions. Premium contribution was respectively split into the individual MSA and the SPF. The full amount of the employees' contribution and no less than 50 per cent of the employers' contribution were allocated to the individual MSA, with the rest being allocated to the SPF.

This medical insurance system has a three-tiered payment structure. The first tier was the use of the individual MSA to pay medical expenses. The second tier was out-of-pocket expenses when the individual MSA was insufficient to pay medical expenses or when it was fully depleted. The insured was required to have self-payment if the medical expenses were below 5 per cent of his or her annual salary. The third tier was the use of the SPF and co-payment when medical expenses exceeded 5 per cent of the insured employee's annual salary. The percentage of co-payment decreased when the amount of medical expenses increased. The co-payment rate was set as follows: (i) 10 to 20 per cent if medical expenses exceeded 5 per cent of the insured employee's annual salary but was below Renminbi (RMB) 5,000; (ii) 8 to 10 per cent if medical expenses fell within the range of RMB 5,000 to RMB 10,000; and (iii) 2 per cent if medical expenses exceeded RMB 10,000 (The State Commission for Restructuring the Economic Systems *et al.* 1994). Old Red Army, disabled revolutionary soldiers and retired senior officials did not have to pay any insurance premium and an individual MSA was not set up for them (The State Commission for Restructuring the Economic Systems *et al.* 1994). Their medical expenses were fully covered by the SPF.

The Shenzhen model

In May 1996, the Shenzhen municipal government promulgated the *Shenzhen Provisional Regulations on Basic Medical Insurance* (hereafter the 1996 Provisional Regulations). According to the 1996 Provisional Regulations, the Basic Medical Insurance was applicable to all public and private enterprises, government organs, institutions, social organizations and their incumbent employees, retirees and those receiving unemployment benefits (The Shenzhen Municipal Government 1996). Under the umbrella term of Basic Medical Insurance, there were three types of medical insurance designed for different population groups: (i) combined health insurance for incumbent employees and retirees who were Shenzhen permanent residents; (ii) hospitalization insurance for employees who were Shenzhen temporary residents and those receiving unemployment benefits; and (iii) a special medical insurance plan for retired senior officials and disabled revolutionary soldiers.

Combined health insurance covered both inpatient and outpatient expenses of the insured. The contribution rate of combined health insurance was 9 per cent of monthly salary, out of which 7 per cent was borne by the employer and 2 per cent was borne by the employee. The contribution rate was 12 per cent of monthly pension for retirees, which was borne by the employer. The insurance premium was split into the individual MSA and the SPF. The entire amount of insurance premium paid by the employee was allocated to his or her individual MSA. As to the insurance premium paid by the employer, 2 per cent of it was deducted by the Shenzhen Municipal Social Insurance Management Bureau for management fees and 4 per cent of it was deducted for risks reserve funds. After deduction, 50 per cent of the insurance premium paid by the employer was allocated to the individual MSA if the employee was 44 years old and below; 60 per cent if the employee was 45 years old or above. The individual MSA covered outpatient expenses. The SPF covered 90 per cent of hospitalization expenses for incumbent employees and 95 per cent for retirees, with the rest being paid out of pocket. If no money was left in the individual MSA, the insured must first pay on his or her own, up to a level of 10 per cent of the previous year's annual salary of urban employees of Shenzhen, after which the SPF would cover 65 per cent of the excess if the insured sought medical treatment at the third-tiered or municipal hospitals, 70 per cent if the insured sought medical treatment at the second-tiered or district-level hospitals and 75 per cent if the insured sought medical treatment at the first-tiered hospitals or street-level health stations (The Shenzhen Municipal Government 1996).

Hospitalization insurance only contained the SPF. The contribution rate of hospitalization insurance was 2 per cent of the previous year's average monthly salary of urban employees in Shenzhen, which was borne by the employer. The SPF covered 90 per cent of hospitalization expenses, whereas the insured paid 10 per cent out of pocket. The insured had to bear outpatient expenses on their own. For retired senior officials and disabled revolutionary soldiers, they did not have any individual MSA. They could still enjoy free medical services and drugs under the special medical insurance plan. The Shenzhen model received national recognition 'by virtue of its broader coverage and the differentiation of members according to age, residence and status' (Rösner 2004: 73). Its heterogeneity in tailoring three different insurance plans to meet the needs of different population groups could improve the social pooling capacity (Liu *et al.* 2004: 50).

The Hainan model

In July 1995, the Standing Committee of the People's Congress of Hainan Province respectively promulgated *Medical Insurance Ordinance for Urban Employees of the Hainan Special Economic Zone* (hereafter the 1995 Hainan Medical Insurance Ordinance) and *Implementation Details of Medical Insurance Ordinance for Urban Employees of the Hainan Special Economic Zone* (hereafter the 1995 Implementation Details). According to the 1995 Hainan Medical Insurance Ordinance, the medical insurance scheme was applicable to all public and private enterprises, government organs, institutions, social organizations and their incumbent employees, retirees, retired senior officials, together with owners of individual economic entities and their employees. The contribution rate of the medical insurance scheme was 11 per cent of monthly salary, out of which 10 per cent was borne by the employer and 1 per cent was borne by the employee (The Standing Committee of the People's Congress of Hainan Province 1995). The contribution rate was 10 per cent for owners of individual economic entities and 1 per cent for their employees. Depending on the age of the insured participants, different proportions of the employer's and employee's contribution were allocated to the individual MSA, with the rest being allocated to the SPF. Four per cent of the employer's and employee's contribution were respectively allocated to the individual MSA if the employee was 40 years old and below; 5 per cent if the employee was aged between 41 and 50; 6 per cent if the employee was 51 years old or above (The Standing Committee of the People's Congress of Hainan Province 1995). Retirees did not have to pay any insurance premium, but 8 per cent of their pensions were allocated to the individual MSA.

Individual MSA mainly covered outpatient expenses. The SPF mainly covered the expenses of catastrophic illnesses listed in the Disease Catalogue, such as acute leukemia, lung cancer and kidney disease, and the medical expenses of retired Old Red Army and disabled revolutionary soldiers (The People's Government of Hainan Province 1995). Insured employees had to pay on their own if the medical expenses were lower than two months' average salary of the previous year. The SPF would cover 85 to 95 per cent of employees' medical expenses that exceeded two months' average salary of the previous year, with the rest being paid by employees on their own. Retirees had to pay on their own if the medical expenses were lower than one month's average salary of the previous year. The SPF would cover 92.5 to 97.5 per cent of retiree's medical expenses that exceeded one month's average salary of the previous year, with the rest being paid by retirees on their own. For retired senior officials, they had to pay 2 per cent of outpatient expenses and 1 per cent of inpatient expenses on their own, with the rest being covered by the SPF (The People's Government of Hainan Province 1995). The Hainan model was also called the 'Compartmental Model' (Liu *et al.* 2004: 49) because the individual MSA and the SPF were operated separately and independently. Since it required co-payment, participants were more cost-conscious and had greater incentives to make cost-effective health care choices.

The Shanghai model

The Shanghai municipal government implemented the pilot medical insurance reform in three phases. But before implementing the medical insurance reform, the government in July 1994 implemented a global budget policy in hospitals with the aims of reducing the rapid increase of medical costs and minimizing pharmaceutical waste. It set the annual allowable growth rate of hospital drug revenues every year to match the growth rate of gross domestic product (Luk 2014: 48–9). It also adjusted the charges of different medical services in order to provide stable sources of revenues for hospitals. Drug revenues that exceeded the target allowable growth rate would be taxed by the Shanghai Health Bureau. The global budget policy was an effective supply-side cost-control mechanism that subsequently facilitated the implementation of pilot medical insurance schemes in Shanghai.

In April 1996, the Shanghai municipal government promulgated the *Shanghai Provisional Regulations on Hospitalization Insurance for Urban Employees* (the 1996 Shanghai Provisional Regulations). According to the 1996 Shanghai Provisional Regulations, a hospitalization insurance scheme was introduced to cover incumbent employees and retirees. The hospitalization insurance scheme only contained the SPF and covered inpatient expenses of the insured participants. Employers were required to contribute 4.5 per cent of total annual payroll to the insurance fund. The SPF covered 85 per cent of inpatient expenses that exceeded the threshold of RMB 1,500 for first-tiered hospitals, RMB 2,000 for second-tiered hospitals and RMB 2,500 for third-tiered hospitals (The Shanghai Municipal Government 1996). The remaining medical expenses were jointly shared by employers and employees. The hospitalization insurance scheme was implemented on 1 May 1996.

In April 1997, the Shanghai municipal government promulgated the *Shanghai Provisional Regulations on Partial Outpatient and Emergency Services Medical Insurances for Urban Employees*. It introduced another medical insurance scheme that covered some of the outpatient and emergency services of incumbent employees and retirees. A SPF was established for this medical insurance scheme. The insurance scheme required the employers to contribute 1 per cent of total annual payroll to the medical insurance fund. Meanwhile, 1 per cent of total annual payroll contributed by the employers to the old-age pension fund was allocated to the medical insurance fund (The Shanghai Municipal Government 1997). The SPF covered 85 per cent of medical expenses at emergency observation rooms if the medical expenses exceeded the threshold of RMB 2,000 for second-tiered hospitals and RMB 2,500 for third-tiered hospitals (The Shanghai Municipal Government 1997). It also covered 70 per cent of medical expenses at outpatient sections of designated hospitals (The Shanghai Municipal Government 1997). The remaining medical expenses were jointly shared by employers and employees. This medical insurance scheme was implemented on 1 May 1997. In November 1998, the Shanghai municipal government extended this insurance scheme to cover all the outpatient and emergency services of retirees. Under this insurance scheme, the SPF covered 50 per cent of medical expenses of retirees, with the remaining medical expenses jointly shared by employers and retirees (The Shanghai Municipal Government 1998).

The pilot health insurance reform was implemented steadily in Shanghai. The Shanghai model received national recognition by virtue of implementing both demand-side and supply-side cost-control mechanisms. While deductibles and co-payment of medical insurance schemes made insured participants more cost conscious, the global budget policy made hospitals more cost conscious in treating patients and gave hospitals greater incentive to manage medical resources more effectively and efficiently.

Urban Employee Basic Medical Insurance (UEBMI)

In December 1998, a nationwide, compulsory scheme known as Urban Employee Basic Medical Insurance (UEBMI) was implemented nationwide. The UEBMI required the participation of all urban work units in both the public and private sectors and their employees. The UEBMI was implemented to replace the previous LIS and GHS. It was different from the previous LIS and GHS in five ways. First, the UEBMI was a compulsory scheme while the previous LIS and GHS were employment-based welfare benefits. Second, the UEBMI had more diversified sources of finance than the previous LIS and GHS. It was financed by contributions from both urban work units and employees while the previous LIS and GHS were financed by the state budget. Third, the ideas of individual responsibility and social solidarity were introduced to the institutional design of the UEBMI while these two ideas did not exist in the previous LIS and GHS. Fourth, the UEBMI covered employees and retirees from the private sector, such as foreign investment enterprises and private non-enterprise entities, while the previous LIS and GHS did not. Fifth, the UEBMI did not provide any coverage for direct dependents of employees while the previous LIS and GHS provided partial or full coverage for direct dependents of employees. Nevertheless, the implementation of the UEBMI did not mean that the provision of free health care came to an end. As stated in the 1998 Decree, free health care would still be provided to three special groups of people: retired cadres, old Red Army and disabled revolutionary soldiers whose military rank was Grade Two or above. These special groups of people could still enjoy free medical services and drugs, with their medical expenses paid by the Basic Medical Insurance (BMI) fund.

In 2009, Ministry of Human Resources and Social Security and the Ministry of Finance (MOF) jointly issued *The Guiding Opinions on Further Strengthening the Management of the Basic Medical Insurance Fund*, which stated that in principle the accumulated surplus of the UEBMI fund in any regions should be sufficient to pay six to nine months of average medical expenditures. The accumulated surplus that could pay more than 15 months of average medical expenditure was regarded as too high while the accumulated surplus that could pay less than three months of average medical expenditure was regarded as too low (Ministry of Human Resources and Social Security and Ministry of Finance 2009a). If the accumulated surplus of UEBMI fund in any regions was too high for two consecutive years, the government in that region could either reduce the fund-raising level of UEBMI in stages or appropriately increase the medical insurance coverage of insured persons.

The New Rural Cooperative Medical System (NRCMS)

There were four types of reimbursement models under the NRCMS: (i) 'inpatient expenses and household account for outpatient expenses' model, (ii) 'inpatient expenses only' model, (iii) 'inpatient expenses and catastrophic outpatient expenses' model, and (iv) 'inpatient expenses and collective funds for outpatient expenses' model (Du and Zhang 2007: 92–3). 'Inpatient expenses and household account for outpatient expenses' model was the most popular model used in about 65 per cent of rural counties. It was implemented in central and west regions, such as Anhui and Jiangxi provinces. Under this model, inpatient services were reimbursed according to certain formula while outpatient services were reimbursed by a household MSA with deductibles and cap lines. Every household had its own MSA that was jointly used by insured household members who made contributions to it (Du and Zhang 2007: 92). 'Inpatient expenses only' model was used in about 17 per cent of rural counties. It was implemented in economically developed areas, such as Tianjin, Zhejiang, Jiangsu and Fujian provinces. It mainly reimbursed inpatient services with deductibles and cap lines. The insured had to pay out-of-pocket for other expenses. 'Inpatient expenses and catastrophic outpatient expenses' model was used in about 11 per cent of rural counties, such as Beijing. It reimbursed inpatient and outpatient expenses for chronic or catastrophic diseases (e.g. diabetes and kidney diseases) with separate deductibles and cap lines. 'Inpatient expenses and collective funds for outpatient expenses' model was used in about 7 per cent of rural counties, such as Shandong. It reimbursed inpatient expenses according to certain formula with cap lines while outpatient expenses were reimbursed with collective funds without any deductibles or cap lines (Du and Zhang 2007: 93). Some counties provided free medical checkup for participants who did not use any collective funds within that year (Du and Zhang 2007: 93). All four models emphasized inpatient reimbursement. It was because inpatient expenses usually imposed a heavy financial burden on patients and hence, inpatient reimbursement was the best way of providing financial protection for participants.

Over the past decade, both individual contribution and the government's annual subsidies for each NRCMS participant have increased steadily as part of the government's effort to increase health care coverage and the participation rate of the NRCMS. In January 2006, the Ministry of Health (MOH), National Development and Reform Commission (NDRC), the Ministry of Civil Affairs (MCA), the MOF, Ministry of Agriculture (MOA), China Food and Drug Administration, and State Administration of Traditional Chinese Medicine jointly issued *Notice on Accelerating Pilot Work of the New Rural Cooperative Medical System*. Starting in 2006, the central government increased its annual subsidies for each NRCMS participant in the central and western provinces to RMB 20 while local governments were required to increase their annual subsidies for each NRCMS participant by RMB 10 as well. In March 2008, the MOH and the MOF jointly issued *Notice on Accomplishing the Task of New Rural Cooperative Medical System*. Starting in 2008, individual contribution was raised from RMB 10 to RMB 20 per year. Meanwhile, the government's annual subsidies for each

NRCMS participant were raised to RMB 80, with the central and local governments respectively contributing RMB 40. In March 2009, the Central Committee of the Communist Party of China and the State Council issued *Opinions on Deepening the Health Care System Reform*, which stated that the government's annual subsidies for *each* NRCMS participant should be gradually raised to RMB 120 by 2010. In 2010, individual contribution was raised to RMB 30 per year. From 2011 to 2014, individual contribution increased from RMB 50, RMB 60, RMB 70, to RMB 90. From 2011 to 2014, the government's annual subsidies increased by RMB 40 every year. It increased from RMB 200 in 2011 to RMB 320 in 2014. In 2015, individual contribution was raised to RMB 120 while the government's annual subsidies were raised to RMB 380 (The National Health and Family Planning Commission and Ministry of Finance 2015).

From 2009 to 2011, the reimbursement rate for inpatient expenses of the NRCMS was raised from 55 per cent, 60 per cent to 70 per cent (Ministry of Health 2010, 2012b). In 2012, the reimbursement rate for inpatient expenses of the NRCMS was raised to 75 per cent, with the payment cap no less than eight times of the average annual per capita net income of peasants and no less than RMB 60,000 (Ministry of Health 2012b). In 2015, the reimbursement rate for inpatient expenses would maintain at 75 per cent while the reimbursement rate for outpatient expenses was raised to 50 per cent (The National Health and Family Planning Commission and Ministry of Finance 2015).

Over the past decade, the participation rate of the NRCMS has continued to increase. In 2003, the NRCMS was piloted in 310 counties with about 69 million participants (Ministry of Health 2004). Until the end of 2007, the NRCMS had been piloted in 2,451 counties with a total of 730 million participants (Ministry of Health 2008). Until the end of 2013, the NRCMS had been piloted in 2,489 counties with about 800 million participants (Ministry of Health 2014). The participation rate reached 98.7 per cent (Ministry of Health 2014).

The Urban Resident Basic Medical Insurance for (URBMI)

In 2007, the Urban Resident Basic Medical Insurance (URBMI) was piloted in 79 cities (Xinhua News 2007) to provide financial protection for non-working urban residents, including young children, primary and secondary school students, the severely disabled and the elderly. It was a subsidized voluntary scheme requiring individual contribution, with moderate subsidies shared by the central and local governments. It focused on covering inpatient and outpatient services for catastrophic illnesses. Over the past few years, the URBMI has been extended to cover different segments of the population. In October 2008, the State Council issued *Guiding Opinions on Including University Students in the Pilot Basic Medical Insurance for Urban Residents* (hereafter the 2008 Guiding Opinions). The 2008 Guiding Opinions stated that full-time undergraduate and postgraduate students would be included in the URBMI. University students were encouraged to participate in the URBMI based on the principle of voluntary participation. They had to contribute to the URBMI, with local and central government subsidies. They were also encouraged to buy commercial health insurance in order to increase the level of health protection. For university students having economic difficulties to contribute to the URBMI, they could get subsidies through multiple channels, such as Medical Financial Assistance (MFA) System and charitable donations (The State Council 2008). The URBMI was implemented nationwide in the second quarter of 2009 (Ministry of Human Resources and Social Security and Ministry of Finance 2009b). In 2010, the URBMI was extended to include urban residents without formal employment, urban residents with flexible employment and migrant peasant workers in urban areas (Ministry of Human Resources and Social Security 2010). In 2011, the URBMI was further extended to include minors from low-income families. Besides, the maximum reimbursement amount of the URBMI should be no less than RMB 50,000 (Ministry of Human Resources and Social Security 2011).

From 2008 to 2010, the minimum government subsidy was raised from RMB 80 per enrollee per year to RMB 120 per enrollee per year (Ministry of Human Resources and Social Security and Ministry of Finance 2008; Ministry of Human Resources and Social Security 2010). From 2011 to 2015, the minimum government subsidy was raised from RMB 200 per enrollee per year to RMB 380 per enrollee per year (Ministry of Human Resources and Social Security 2011; Ministry of Human Resources and Social Security and Ministry of Finance 2015). In order to strike a balance between individual and government responsibility and ensure a sustainable funding mechanism, the average per capita premium was raised from RMB 50 in 2011 to RMB 90 in 2014 and RMB 120 in 2015 (Ministry of Human Resources and Social Security 2011; Ministry of Human Resources and Social Security and Ministry of Finance 2015). According to China Statistical Yearbook 2014, the URBMI covered more than 274 million people in 2013 (National Bureau of Statistics of the People's Republic of China 2014a).

Critical Illness Insurance Scheme (CIIS): four representative models

In August 2012, the Critical Illness Insurance Scheme (CIIS) was implemented to provide URBMI and NRCMS participants with financial protection against critical illnesses, on the top of their basic medical insurance reimbursement. Local governments are asked to formulate specific plans regarding the CIIS in accordance with local economic and social conditions (National Development and Reform Commission *et al.* 2012).[1] They can design local regulations on fundraising, scope of reimbursement, the minimum compensation rate, settlement management and other details (National Development and Reform Commission *et al.* 2012).[2] In 2013, the State Council called for the overall advancement of the CIIS in urban and rural areas (The State Council 2013).

The Taicang model

The Taicang model, which combines public health insurance with commercial insurance, is highly recognized by Medical Reform Office of the State Council.

It provides a blueprint for the Chinese government to design and implement the CIIS in 2012. Taicang is one of the most developed county-level cities in the southeastern part of Jiangsu province. It has been one of the top 10 counties in terms of comprehensive strength in China. Petrochemicals, electricity and energy, and light industrial papermaking are three pillar industries supporting the city's continued prosperity (Wu 2013). In 2008, the NRCMS and the URBMI merged to become the Basic Medical Insurance for Urban and Rural Residents (BMIFURR). The BMIFURR co-exists with the UEBMI and is managed by Ministry of Human Resources and Social Security of Taicang city. In 2010, the accumulated surplus of UEBMI fund in Taicang was about 465 million, which could pay 25 months of average medical expenditures (Zheng and Zhang 2013: 22). The large amount of accumulated surplus of UEBMI fund laid a good foundation for implementing the CIIS. In July 2011, the Taicang government implemented a pilot version of CIIS. It bought the CIIS from the qualified commercial insurer by using the surplus of the UEBMI funds and the BMIFURR funds. Employees contribute RMB 50 to the UEBMI fund as annual insurance premium while urban and rural residents contribute RMB 20 to the BMIFURR fund as annual insurance premium.

The operation of the CIIS fund is entrusted to Jiangsu Branch of PICC Health Insurance Company Limited after an open bidding process. The commercial insurer reimburses the insured person if the amount of his/her medical expenses exceeds the average annual per capita net income of rural residents. The average annual per capita net income of rural residents is determined by the Taicang government. Reimbursement is offered to the insured person whose out-of-pocket medical expenses exceed RMB 10,000, on the top of the basic medical insurance reimbursement. The reimbursement rate ranges from 53 per cent to 82 per cent. The reimbursement rate increases when individual medical expenses increase. The reimbursement rate is 53 per cent for individual medical expenses ranging from RMB 10,000 to RMB 20,000. For the interval between RMB 20,000 and RMB 100,000, there is a 2.5 per cent increase in the ratio of insurance compensation for every increase of RMB 10,000. The reimbursement rate is 75 per cent for individual medical expenses ranging from RMB 100,000 to RMB 150,000, 78 per cent for individual medical expenses ranging from RMB 150,000 to RMB 200,000, 81 per cent for individual medical expenses ranging from RMB 200,000 to RMB 500,000 and 82 per cent for individual medical expenses over RMB 500,000. There is no reimbursement ceiling. Both employees and residents are treated the same. What makes the Taicang model special is that reimbursement is based on out-of-pocket medical expenses rather than types of critical illnesses (Zeng 2012a). This makes the CIIS easier to operate and to get public acceptance (Zeng 2012a).

The Zhanjiang model

Zhanjiang is an underdeveloped port city in Guangdong Province because of its backward transport infrastructure. It lags behind the prosperous Pearl River Delta in economic development. In 2012, its GDP per capita only ranked sixteenth among cities in Guangdong Province and was just 69 per cent of China's average GDP (Zhao 2013). In January 2009, the NRCMS and the URBMI merged to become the BMIFURR, which has been managed by Ministry of Human Resources and Social Security of Zhanjiang city ever since. Residents who join the BMIFURR can voluntarily contribute RMB 20 or RMB 50 as an annual insurance premium, depending on their ability to pay. The cover limit per insured person is RMB 15,000. The BMIFURR is supplemented by the CIIS. The Zhanjiang government allocated 15 per cent of the BMIFURR fund to buy CIIS from Zhanjiang branch of PICC Health Insurance Company Limited. On the top of the cover limit per insured person of the BMIFURR, the cover limit per insured person of the CIIS is respectively RMB 35,000 for those who contribute RMB 20 to the BMIFURR per year and RMB 65,000 for those who contribute RMB 50 to the BMIFURR per year.

In order to facilitate the appropriate use of medical resources, the Zhanjiang government sets up different payment thresholds and reimbursement rates in different tiers of hospitals. According to the *Trial Implementation of Basic Medical Insurance for Urban and Rural Residents*, the payment threshold of the CIIS is RMB 100 in first-tiered hospitals, RMB 300 in second-tiered hospitals and RMB 500 in third-tiered hospitals (Ministry of Human Resources and Social Security of Zhanjiang City).[3] In 2008, the reimbursement rate was 70 per cent in first-tiered hospitals, 60 per cent in second-tiered hospitals and 40 per cent in third-tiered hospitals (Ministry of Human Resources and Social Security of Zhanjiang City).[4] Since 2010, the reimbursement rate has become 75 per cent in first-tiered hospitals, 65 per cent in second-tiered hospitals and 45 per cent in third-tiered hospitals (Jiang 2010). A one-stop hotline service is established to answer public enquires about the BMI, commercial health insurance, health care management and health insurance policies (Jiang 2010; Wang Y. *et al.* 2011). Besides, a one-stop payment and settlement platform is established for the designated hospitals, commercial insurance company and Ministry of Human Resources and Social Security to share information about patients' medical payment (Jiang 2010). It helps simplify both the reimbursement procedures and the reimbursement approval process (Jiang 2010) while at the same time reducing the long-existing phenomenon of default in the payment for medical services (Zheng 2011). Also, an inspection team consisting of 40 members of the commercial insurance company is authorized by Ministry of Human Resources and Social Security of Zhanjiang city to inspect medical services of third-tiered hospitals and examine the checklist of medical expenses (Wang Y. *et al.* 2011). It ensures that patients can receive appropriate treatment and pay appropriate medical fees (Wang Y. *et al.* 2011). The Zhanjiang model is able to increase the management and service efficiency of medical insurance while reducing administrative costs. Besides, it is able to restrict hospitals from selling expensive drugs and doctors from overprescribing drugs or prescribing expensive drugs.

The Jiangyin model

Jiangyin is a county-level city located in the southern part of Jiangsu province. It has been ranked No.1 among the top 100 counties in terms of basic competitiveness of county-level economy in China for 11 consecutive years (2003–13). Since 2001, the Jiangyin government has encouraged peasants who have already participated in the NRCMS to buy non-compulsory supplemental critical illness insurance provided by the commercial insurance company called China Pacific Insurance (Group) Co., Ltd. Peasants contribute RMB 50 to the supplemental critical illness insurance as an annual insurance premium. In return, their reimbursement rate can increase 10 per cent, on top of the reimbursement of the NRCMS. Besides, the supplemental critical illness insurance covers consultation charges that are given to specialists who work in third-tiered hospitals outside Jiangyin but visit patients' homes in Jiangyin (Li 2012). The insured patients can enjoy high-quality medical resources of third-tiered hospitals in Shanghai, Beijing and other big cities without leaving Jiangyin (Li 2012). Due to having rich management experience, Jiangyin branch of China Pacific Insurance (Group) Co., Ltd used RMB 3 million to set up the Rural Medical Insurance Management Centre and is responsible for managing the funds of the supplemental critical illness insurance (Gu 2002). Besides, it developed an automatic settlement and reimbursement software and established a settlement and reimbursement platform (Gu 2002). It makes the settlement and reimbursement processes easier and more efficient. In 2011, the reimbursement rate on hospitalization is near 50 per cent, which is 4 per cent higher than that of nearby regions having the same fundraising level (Li 2012). The Jiangyin model fully demonstrates the professional services provided by commercial insurance company, effectively prevents the unreasonable growth of medical costs and facilitates equity and efficiency (Yang 2012). Since 2002, the participation rate of the NRCMS has maintained 100 per cent (Yang 2012). China Pacific Insurance has applied the Jiangyin model into different places, including Sanshui and Chancheng in Foshan city in Guangdong, Chinkang city in Fujian, and Longyou county in Zhejiang (Yang 2012).

The Xunyi model

Xunyi is a county of Xianyang city in Shaanxi province. It is the apple-growing capital of China (Wang 2004). In 2010, the Xunyi government implemented the New Rural Cooperative Medical Allowance System for Critical Illnesses (hereafter the *Medical Allowance System*) in order to tackle illness-led poverty. Funds are raised from different sources, including funds from NRCMS, local government finance, medical assistance from the MCA and business donations. In 2010, the *Medical Allowance System* collected RMB 5 million. RMB 2 million came from the NRCMS fund, RMB 2 million came from local government finance, RMB 0.5 million came from medical assistance and RMB 0.5 million came from business donations (Zeng 2012b). Illnesses such as leukemia and congenital heart diseases suffered by children aged 0 to 14 years old, breast cancer, cancer of the cervix, drug-resistant tuberculosis, chronic renal disease, aplastic anemia and the single hospitalization fees over RMB 100,000 are included in the *Medical Allowance System* (Zhang Y. 2012). In 2012, 58 illnesses were included in the *Medical Allowance System* (Zeng 2012b). In 2011, the NRCMS and the URBMI merged to become the *New Rural Cooperative Medical System for Urban and Rural Residents*. Under the new system, peasants and residents in urban and rural areas have the same fund-raising standard and reimbursement ratio. Their annual insurance premium was RMB 30 in 2011 and RMB 50 in 2012 (Wang and Lu 2011). In 2015, their annual insurance premium is RMB 100 for each person while the government subsidizes RMB 400 for each person (Xunyi County Cooperative Medical Website 2014b). The insured residents are all covered by the *Medical Allowance System*. The cover limit per insured person of the *Medical Allowance System* is no more than RMB 400, 000 a year (Wang and Lu 2011). Since 2010, the *Medical Allowance System* has reimbursed about 23.74 million to 552 insured patients (Xunyi County Cooperative Medical Website 2014a).

Global budget is adopted in order to pose a fixed budget cap on hospitals in order to contain the overall medical costs and improve the quality of care for patients. Whenever the patient's self-payment medicines exceed 5 per cent, the excess part of expense will be borne by the relative hospital (Xunyi County Government 2011). The *Medical Allowance System* is managed by the New Rural Cooperative Medical Handling Center, which plays an important role in supervising the operation of the *Medical Allowance System*. The Center reports the usage, revenues and expenditures of the fund to the county government and county commission every month (Zeng 2012b). It inspects designated hospitals every season and evaluates their performance every six months (Zeng 2012b). The Xunyi model does not buy critical illness insurance from commercial insurance companies. By merging the NRCMS with URBMI, the Xunyi government is able to save medical insurance management resources.

Medical Financial Assistance (MFA) System

Medical Financial Assistance (MFA) System, which protects poor households against illness-led poverty, is implemented in both rural and urban areas. Rural MFA System piloted in Shanghai in early 2001. But the decision to implement rural MFA System nationwide was announced in the 2002 State Council Decision. In November 2003, the MCA, together with the MOH and the MOF, issued *Opinions on the Implementation of Rural Medical Financial Assistance*. This document stated that rural MFA System was established to provide financial assistance mainly for rural five-guaranteed households[5] and rural poor households to join the NRCMS in localities or cover part of their catastrophic medical expenses (The Central People's Government of the People's Republic of China 2003). Rural MFA System was financed by multiple channels, which included transfer payments from the central government, revenues of local governments and donations from societies. It was implemented and managed by the MCA. Provincial governments were required to select two or three counties or cities as demonstration cases to experiment MFA System. County authorities were given discretion to design and implement rural MFA System in accordance with local socio-economic conditions.

In February 2005, the MCA, together with the MOH, Ministry of Labor and Social Security, and the MOF, issued *Opinions on Establishing Pilot Urban*

Medical Financial Assistance System. The document stated that the primary aim of the establishment of the pilot urban MFA System was to help urban residents in receipt of the Minimum Livelihood Guarantee Scheme, whether they were covered by the UEBMI or not, get access to basic health care through the provision of subsidies (The Central People's Government of the People's Republic of China 2005). Urban MFA System was financed by multiple channels, which included financial and budgetary provisions, dedicated lottery funds and donations from societies. Governments in provinces, autonomous regions and municipalities could select two or three counties or cities as demonstration cases to experiment urban MFA System. The level of medical assistance should match socio-economic development at the local level. The pilot urban MFA System would run for two years. It would take another two or three years to establish an institutionalized and standardized urban MFA System nationally after the two-year pilot scheme.

In June 2009, the MCA, together with the MOF, the MOH and the Ministry of Human Resources and Social Security, issued *Opinions on Further Improving Urban and Rural Medical Financial Assistance Systems* (hereafter the 2009 Opinions). According to the 2009 Opinions, the MFA System would be extended to include those facing economic hardship, such as low-income patients with catastrophic illnesses. Besides, the MFA System should take into account medical assistance for both inpatient and outpatient medical services, but more attention should be given to medical assistance for inpatient medical services. The surplus of the medical assistance fund should not exceed 15 per cent of the medical assistance fund collected within that year (Ministry of Civil Affairs 2009).

In January 2012, the MCA, together with the MOF, the Ministry of Human Resources and Social Security and the MOH, issued *Opinions on Implementing Pilot Medical Financial Assistance System for Catastrophic Illnesses* (hereafter the 2012 Opinions). According to the 2012 Opinions, the introduction of pilot medical financial assistance system for catastrophic illnesses aimed at reducing patients' financial burden caused by catastrophic health expenditures. The target groups for medical financial assistance for catastrophic illnesses included recipients of the Minimum Livelihood Guarantee Scheme, five-guaranteed households, low-income seniors, the severely disabled and those who could not pay catastrophic health expenditures from their own pockets (Ministry of Civil Affairs 2012). Priority for medical financial assistance for catastrophic illnesses would be given to children who suffered from acute leukemia or congenital heart diseases, women who suffered from cervical cancer or breast cancer, and those who suffered from severe mental illnesses (Ministry of Civil Affairs 2012). Those who were eligible for medical financial assistance for catastrophic illnesses should seek medical treatment at designated medical institutions where the URBMI or the NRCMS participants sought medical treatment. The scope and level of medical financial assistance for catastrophic diseases should be extended and raised in accordance with the scale of medical assistance fund and the socio-economic development at the local level.

In April 2015, the MCA, together with the MOF, Ministry of Human Resources and Social Security, National Health and Family Planning Commission, China

Insurance Regulatory Commission, issued *Opinions on Further Improving Medical Financial Assistance System and Implementing Medical Financial Assistance System for Catastrophic Illnesses in Full Swing* (hereafter the 2015 Opinions). The 2015 Opinions highlighted the importance of integrating urban and rural medical financial assistance system by the end of 2015 in order to reduce urban–rural disparities in health care and ensure urban and rural residents' equal access to basic health care (Ministry of Civil Affairs 2015). Besides, much greater magnitude of medical financial assistance should be given to children that were critically ill or severely disabled. Those who experienced special hardship due to having no physical work capacity, financial resources or family resources would be given a full subsidy to participate in the URBMI or the NRCMS. Those who were in receipt of the Minimum Living Standard Scheme would be given a fixed amount of subsidy to participate in the URBMI or the NRCMS (Ministry of Civil Affairs 2015). Also, the maximum amount and percentage of medical financial assistance for catastrophic illnesses should take into account individual affordability, family affordability and sources of funding at the local level.

Conclusion

To conclude, many efforts have been made to implement health insurance reforms over the past 30 years. A multi-layered medical insurance system has been established to provide different segments of the population with comprehensive or partial medical coverage. Some of the health insurance models developed by local governments gained national recognition because they were able to address the problems of moral hazard and high health care costs. They could yield useful experience for the central government and other local governments as reference.

Notes

1 Please refer to Section Two No.4 of *The Guiding Opinions on the Launch of the Work on Critical Illness Insurance of Urban and Rural Residents.*
2 Please refer to Section Five No.1 of *The Guiding Opinions on the Launch of the Work on Critical Illness Insurance of Urban and Rural Residents.*
3 Please refer to Section 20 of The Trial Implementation of Basic Medical Insurance for Urban and Rural Residents.
4 Please refer to Section 20 of The Trial Implementation of Basic Medical Insurance for Urban and Rural Residents.
5 'Five-guaranteed households' refer to those without sufficient family resources to provide food, clothing, housing, medical care and burial expenses.

6 Problems in the current multi-layered social health insurance system

Introduction

After three decades of effort, the government has transformed the free health care system into a contributory social health insurance system. It has established a multi-layered health insurance system, which includes the Urban Employee Basic Medical Insurance (UEBMI), the New Rural Cooperative Medical System (NRCMS), the Urban Resident Basic Medical Insurance (URBMI) and the Critical Illness Insurance Scheme (CIIS). And the reform process is still going on. The government under the leadership of Xi Jinping has the goal of providing accessible and affordable health care for all the Chinese people. However, this is not an easy task because many problems have to be solved before the government can carry out further reform and move forward to achieve universal health care (UHC).

This chapter examines problems in the current multi-layered social health insurance system and explains why these problems act as impediments to achieving UHC. It argues that although the social medical insurance system upholds the principle of 'basic healthcare protection and wide population coverage', it contains lots of problems. These problems include deep inequality and wide disparity in treatment between different population groups, floating population and rural migrant workers being uninsured, poor portability and transferability of health insurance schemes, health insurance fraud, deficit of health insurance fund, non-compliance, adverse selection, peasants being forced to join the health insurance scheme, and people's lack of understanding about health insurance schemes. Together, these problems limit the efficacy and sustainability of the basic social medical insurance system.

Deep inequality and wide disparity in treatment between different population groups

The multi-layered medical insurance system is established to provide different levels of financial protection against the cost of illness, depending on which scheme a person opts for. However, the institutional design of this medical insurance system has unavoidably created deep inequality and wide disparity in treatment between different population groups. The current medical insurance system is similar to a feudal hierarchy in ancient China, which divides people into different classes and ranks (Luk 2014: 74). It privileges retired cadres, old Red Army and disabled revolutionary soldiers who can enjoy free health care with their medical expenses paid by the Basic Medical Insurance (BMI) fund. The privilege of enjoying free health care is a way for the Chinese government to express gratitude to these special groups of people who 'fought for their country when they were young and showed deep and continuing loyalty to the [Chinese Communist Party] CCP' (Luk 2014: 74). But the use of the BMI fund to pay for the medical expenses of this privileged group has put incumbent employees in a very unequal and disadvantageous position because the medical expenses of this privileged group have drained the fund that is supposed to cover incumbent employees' medical expenses (Luk 2014: 74–5).

Due to its compulsory nature, the UEBMI is the most dominant medical insurance scheme with the largest number of participants in China. Nevertheless, it is an inherently discriminatory scheme because retirees can enjoy more favorable treatment than incumbent employees. Retirees who are not required to pay any premium can enjoy higher reimbursement ratios and lower self-payment rates than incumbent employees. For example, the social pooling fund (SPF) of the UEBMI in Shanghai covers 92 per cent of inpatient expenses of retirees but 85 per cent of inpatient expenses of incumbent employees (Luk 2014: 51–2). Compared with other medical insurance schemes, the UEBMI is more favorable than the NRCMS and URBMI in terms of medical coverage. It provides more comprehensive coverage to cover both inpatient and outpatient medical expenses. Due to low premium contribution, the NRCMS mainly covers inpatient illnesses while the URBMI is limited to covering inpatient and outpatient expenses for catastrophic illnesses. Hence, the amount of self-payment for the NRCMS and URBMI participants remain high.

In rural China, NRCMS participants do not seem to benefit from joining the health insurance scheme because their out-of-pocket expenses for inpatient and outpatient services have continued to increase. In the southwest part of China, there was an increase in both outpatient and inpatient expenses and out-of-pocket costs for NRCMS participants in Yunnan Province from 2004 to 2008. During this period, the average inpatient cost increased by about 43 per cent while the average out-of-pocket cost for NRCMS inpatients increased by 23 per cent (Du *et al.* 2009: 696). In 2008, the growth rate of average inpatient cost in Yunnan Province was about 8.6 per cent higher than that of average inpatient cost in the nation and 2.1 per cent higher than that of average inpatient cost in the western part of China (Du *et al.* 2009: 696). Meanwhile, the average outpatient cost increased by 23.5 per cent from 2004 to 2008 and the average out-of-pocket cost of outpatient expenses increased by 10.4 per cent during the same period (Du *et al.* 2009: 696). It showed that the implementation of the NRCMS did not reduce the financial burden of rural participants (Jin *et al.* 2012: 58).

Meanwhile, the URBMI participants have similar thoughts that the scheme is not useful for providing medical protection. In Hunan Province, about 58 per cent of the 290 urban residents surveyed thought that the URBMI could only reduce part of their financial burden while almost 20 per cent of the urban residents surveyed thought that the URBMI did not reduce their financial burden at all (Song *et al.* 2012: 73). In Guangxi, about 79 per cent of 439 university students surveyed thought that the URBMI they joined had a rather low reimbursement ratio (Xu and Zhang 2012: 696).

Since the current basic medical insurance schemes are only able to alleviate part of the financial burden caused by illnesses, the problem of falling into poverty due to illness is still very serious and the risk of falling back to poverty due to illness remains very high in China. The NRCMS participants, especially those who are seriously ill, suffer from heavy financial burdens caused by expensive medical bills and expenses for transportation, accommodation and meals incurred by seeking medical care in urban hospitals (Interview 16KM1). A nurse who worked in a municipal hospital said in the interview that most of the NRCMS patients she came across encountered lots of difficulties in coping with expenses for meals and accommodation:

> I feel very sorry for these NRCMS patients and my heart aches when I know that many of them can only afford to eat one meal a day in the hospital canteen. I mean one meal that is shared by the patient and his wife or her husband, can you imagine that? . . . These patients are seriously ill and they must be accompanied by family members in order to seek medical care in urban area. They borrow lots of money from their sons and daughters, relatives and friends in the village. They treat every penny seriously. Some of the family members of NRCMS patients told me that they have to sleep on the bench of the railway station at night because they cannot afford the accommodation costs. One time, I saw the family members carry large sheets of cardboard in hand. They told me that they were going to sleep on the floor of the ward. I feel sad when I hear it. It is late at night and the floor is cold. So I let the family members sleep on the hospital beds in an empty ward. I know that it is not right to let them sleep on the beds because they do not pay for it. If my boss finds out, she will chase them away. Last time, my boss was angry when she found out that I let a patient's family members sleep in an empty ward. And I was scolded by her. The patients and their family members have gone through so much pain but there is nothing much I can do. All I can do is to be a good listener and say some comforting words to them.
>
> (Interview 16KM1)

The nurse interviewed also said that many NRCMS patients she met were either broke or seriously in debt due to seeking medical treatment in an urban area (Interview 16KM1). As she said during the interview:

> The hospital I work for receives lots of NRCMS patients who come from mountainous areas of Guizhou, Sichuan and Yunnan Provinces to seek medical treatment or get medical surgery. Many of them live a miserable life. Some of them told me that they have to sell their farmlands, water buffalo

and pigs to other peasants or neigbours in the village in order to pay for some procedures and services that are not covered by the NRCMS. These non-covered procedures and services have to pay in full prior to services rendered. Some of them have already delayed in getting needed medical care, partly due to poor health care facilities in their home provinces and partly due to spending time to borrow money from different people. Some of them are so unfortunate that their health has significantly deteriorated by the time they arrived hospitals. Then, they are told that they need to get a more complicated surgery because of worsened health condition. So, extra money is needed to cover the surgical charges. And they have to call home immediately to borrow money. In fact, the medical expenses incurred by a single hospitalization is already enough to drive many NRCMS patients into debt. Some of the patients told me that they have to find some low-paid jobs when they discharge from hospital or recover from their illness. It is because they have to pay off debt.

(Interview 16KM1)

Although the CIIS was established in 2012 as a top-up scheme to provide the NRCMS and URBMI participants with financial protection against critical illnesses, it is still a voluntary scheme and is only implemented in some pilot cities and provinces. It is undeniable that the implementation of the CIIS is a historic step taken by the Chinese government to achieve better medical protection and increase the risk-pooling capacity by breaking the rural–urban dichotomy that has traditionally characterized China's health care financing system (General Office of the State Council 2015a). But more time is needed to see if the CIIS can effectively alleviate the financial burden of patients.

Floating population and rural migrant workers remain uninsured

Since 1998, the Chinese government has implemented different types of medical insurance schemes that target different segments of the population. Unfortunately, floating population and rural migrant workers are still excluded from the basic medical insurance (BMI) system due to the household registration (*hukou*) system. Introduced in the 1950s, the household registration system 'functions as a domestic passport system to regulate the migration of people, especially from rural to urban areas, and from small cities to large cities' (Luo 2012: 121–2). Its classification is dual in nature, which contains the place of *hukou* registration and type of *hukou* registration (Chan and Zhang 1999: 821–2). The former requires a person to 'register in one and only one place of regular residence' (Chan and Zhang 1999: 821). The latter, which essentially refers to urban and rural *hukou*, determines a person's entitlement and access to social services (Luo 2012: 129–30). Specifically, urban *hukou* can be subdivided into permanent urban *hukou* and valid local urban *hukou* (Luo 2012: 129), 'the former of which grants [a person] full rights and access to the urban social welfare system, with the latter giving only partial access' (Luo 2012: 129–30). Rural *hukou* status 'grants more limited rights in every regard' (Luo 2012: 130). Since the household registration system ties one's access to social services to his/her original registration location, floating population and rural migrant workers that leave their hometowns for work are subject to institutionalized discrimination. They are treated as second-class citizens and lack equal access to social services like their urban counterparts. They cannot enjoy medical, educational and housing benefits.

Floating population and rural migrant workers work for low pay. The wages of rural migrant workers 'have been consistently lower than the national average' (China Labour Bulletin 2015). When floating population or rural migrant workers are sick, most of them cannot afford medical treatment. A rural migrant worker who got injured while working in a construction site told the news reporter that he could not afford to see a doctor that could cost him RMB 100 to 200 because he only received a daily salary of RMB 30 (Wuxi Daily 2006). Not seeking medical attention, buying and using over-the-counter (OTC) drugs on their own and delays in seeking medical care are common practices among floating population and rural migrant workers when they are sick (Wuxi Daily 2006). For those who see a doctor, most of them have to pay their medical expenses out of pocket (Wuxi Daily 2006). Some migrant workers who want to save medical expenses choose to seek medical care at 'black clinics'. 'Black clinics' are unlicensed clinics that have poor hygiene and are run by untrained and unlicensed medical practitioners who prescribe medicines from unknown sources (Beijing Youth Daily 2016). Practice at 'black clinics' puts patients' health and lives at risk because incorrect diagnosis and treatment worsen patients' health conditions and even cause the patients' deaths. In 2014, the Chinese government shut down a total number of 5,088 'black clinics' in the nation (Beijing Youth Daily 2016). But 'black clinics' can still survive and flourish again because they are still the main recourse for floating population and rural migrant workers to seek medical treatment and the current penalty for unlicensed clinics is too mild to have any deterrent effect (Beijing Youth Daily 2016).

Poor portability of medical insurance schemes

At present, the portability of medical insurance schemes remains poor in China. People can only enjoy basic medical coverage and get reimbursed in the place where they register to participate into the scheme (Luo and Guo 2014: 86). Due to uneven health care capacities across provinces, public hospitals in affluent provinces usually excel in treating exceedingly difficult and complicated cases and have better health care facilities to diagnose and treat patients. More often than not, patients have to seek medical treatment across provinces when medical services required are not available at their home provinces. If they want to get reimbursement after seeking medical treatment outside their home province, they have to fulfill two requirements. First, they must obtain a medical referral letter that is vetted and approved by the health insurance office of the public hospital at their home province. Second, they must notify and obtain approval from the Health Insurance Bureau in advance concerning seeking medical treatment outside their home province. These two requirements are so rigid, inflexible and impersonal that many people who are originally insured end up paying medical expenses on their own, especially those who suddenly fall ill or get injured while travelling outside their home provinces.

When people seek medical treatment outside their home province, they must first pay out of pocket for the medical expenses. Poor people who have to seek necessary medical care outside their home province usually borrow money from their friends, relatives and neighbors before leaving their home so as to pay their medical bills. However, having fulfilled the requirements of obtaining the medical referral letter and obtaining approval from the Health Insurance Bureau in advance does not guarantee that people can get reimbursed or get full reimbursement eventually. Problems arise when people fail to provide all necessary supporting documentation within a specific period of time (Interview 15KM3) or the time for people to get reimbursement takes months or more (Mo 2014: 701). Problems also arise when the Health Insurance Bureau at the home province only reimburses medical costs that fall within the category defined in its medical insurance policy (Interview 15KM3). Besides, the Health Insurance Bureau reserves the right to refuse any reimbursement claims that it considers excessive, inappropriate or unreasonable – notwithstanding any supporting documentations or appropriate receipts submitted (Interview 15KM6). It can entirely decline a reimbursement claim that it suspects is fraudulent (Interview 15KM3).

In December 2009, the Ministry of Human Resources and Social Security and Ministry of Finance (MOF) jointly issued *Opinions on Basic Medical Insurance Settlement Service for Medical Expenses Incurred outside Home Territory*, which proposed implementing a uniform policy, standard, management approach and settlement service for medical insurance policy in order to reduce self-payment of patients who seek medical treatment outside their home territory (Ministry of Human Resources and Social Security and Ministry of Finance 2009c). In November 2014, the Ministry of Human Resources and Social Security, MOF and the National Health and Family Planning Commission jointly issued *Guiding Opinions on Further Improving Basic Medical Insurance Settlement Service for Medical Expenses Incurred outside Home Territory*, which proposed the establishment of a national platform for settling medical expenses incurred outside home territory in 2015 and the full implementation of settlement service for retired persons' inpatient medical expenses incurred outside home territory in 2016 (Ministry of Human Resources and Social Security *et al.* 2014). However, lukewarm support and resistance from local governments, poor coordination among health insurance authorities at the provincial level and tremendous variation in the level of information technology capacity across provinces are major impediments to implementing settling service for medical expenses incurred outside home territory. For example, the development of health insurance software varies in different places in China (Zhong and Tao 2015: 36). Many public hospitals lack a unified information system for registering patients' personal and insurance information or platform for settling medical expenses (Interview 15KM5). They also lack a uniform coding system to identify medical items, services and procedures for which they bill medical insurance schemes (Interview 15KM5). Several items or services that exist in the coding system of one hospital may not exist in the coding system of another hospital (Interview 15KM5). Disease code also varies among public hospitals (Zhong and Tao 2015: 36).

In recent years, some provinces such as Sichuan and Chongqing have established a unified platform that interconnects the information system of some public hospitals through the Internet to facilitate basic medical insurance settlement service (Yong 2015). Reciprocal service and billing agreements are signed among local governments for the provision of settling service for medical expenses incurred outside home territory. By interconnecting the information systems of public hospitals among provinces, public hospitals in one province can provide medical insurance settlement service for patients who come from another province. The advantage is that patients can get reimbursed instantly by presenting a valid medical insurance card to public hospitals where the medical treatment takes place (Yong 2015). Patients no longer have to pay first and seek reimbursement later (Yong 2015). Nevertheless, the current basic medical insurance settlement service is only available in some designated public hospitals and is used for settling inpatient medical expenses only (Yong 2015). Hence, it is inconvenient and time-consuming for those who still have to get reimbursed from health insurance centers after going back to their home province.

The sustainability of health insurance funds becomes questionable

Over the past few years, the financial sustainability of medical insurance funds has become a major concern for both the central and local governments. Like many other developed countries, China faces the problems of ageing population and heightened demands for health care, both of which lead to higher users of health services and rising medical costs. But in China the situation is more complex. On one hand, the basic medical insurance schemes have been extended to cover more people and have increased reimbursement rates (Diao 2014: 60). On the other hand, the deeply flawed health care system, poor hospital management, an immature legal system and the lack of supervision provide health care providers, medical professions, drug manufacturers and patients with lots of opportunities to cheat and abuse the medical insurance system for personal gain. All these result in draining a substantial amount of medical insurance funds. In recent years, the BMI funds have experienced deficits in some provinces. It inevitably raises concern over the financial sustainability of the BMI fund in the long run and the erosion of coverage in the BMI system.

The problems of ageing population and early retirement

The problems of ageing population and early retirement present challenges to the financial sustainability of the BMI fund, which are especially serious in the UEBMI.

The annual average growth rate of the number of retirees participating in the UEBMI is higher than that of the number of incumbent employees participating in the UEBMI. From 2009 to 2014, the annual average growth rate of the number of retirees participating in the UEBMI was 5.6 per cent while the annual average growth rate of the number of incumbent employees participating in the UEBMI was 5.1 per cent (Economic Information Daily 2015a). If this trend continues, there will be structural imbalance in the UEBMI. Medical costs in retirement are one of the biggest financial concerns for retirees. It is because their health conditions usually get worse with age and they need to spend more money on health care (Ni and Yu 2012: 47). At present, retirees' average medical expenses that are paid by BMI fund are three times higher than that of incumbent employees (Economic Information Daily 2015a). Retirees who do not have to pay any insurance premiums will substantially deplete the SPF of health insurance (Diao 2014: 60). Besides, the problem of early retirement has become a hidden danger to the BMI fund (Economic Information Daily 2015a). For those who opted for early retirement, the average retirement age was below 55 years old for men and below 46 years old for women (Economic Information Daily 2015a). They stop the premium contribution, which will reduce the revenue of the UEBMI fund.

Continuous rise in medical expenses and the problem of Supplier-Induced Demand (SID)

The continuous rise in medical expenses due to supply-side moral hazard has led to an unnecessary waste of health care resources and the unnecessary drain of BMI funds. The SID phenomenon has been very pervasive in China for decades. In order to earn more revenues, doctors falsify patients' diagnosis or their medical conditions to justify the use of expensive or overseas medicines and the conduction of medical tests and surgeries that are medically unnecessary. It is also common for hospitals to overcharge patients through 'unbundling', which splits one service item into several sub-items (Liu *et al.* 2000: 159). Overcharging can bring substantial amount of revenues to hospitals. For example, some of the county hospitals in Shandong overcharged 'by a margin of 86 to 90 per cent of the regulated fees' (Liu *et al.* 2000: 159). The actual charges for 85 per cent of their surgical operation services were priced high above the costs, with the cost recovery rate amounting to 124 per cent (Liu *et al.* 2000: 159). The profit-seeking behavior of health care providers and doctors not only jeopardizes patients' health, but also imposes heavy financial burdens on patients and their families, who usually have to pay out-of-pocket expenses. For example, in Hunan Province, 74 per cent of urban residents surveyed thought that 'seeing doctors was expensive' because of high drug fees (36.2 per cent), high medical examination fees (35.1 per cent), and high inpatient expenses (33.1 per cent) but low reimbursement rates (21.3 per cent) (Song *et al.* 2012: 73). In Hunan Province, the problem of SID led to an increase in the hospitalization rate from 4.6 per cent in 2003 to about 8.3 per cent in 2009, leading to an unnecessary waste of the NRCMS fund (Xu *et al.* 2012: 150).

In fact, 'feeding hospitals by selling drugs' (*yi yao yang yi*) has become the most common method and the quickest way adopted by hospitals and doctors to earn substantial revenues. A study that examined the medical expenses of 16,137 inpatients in Tianjin in 2007 showed that about 89 per cent of the medical expenses of the UEBMI inpatients were constituted by drug fees (44 per cent), medical material fees (15.72 per cent), medical examination fees (14.97 per cent) and treatment fees (14.3 per cent) (Zhang and Wu 2011: 28–9). In the northwest part of China, drug revenue is the major source of income for health care providers and there was an abusive use of antibiotics. For example, a survey based on 320 NRCMS inpatients in 10 township health centers in Qingshui County, which was a poor mountainous region in Gansu Province, showed that average drug costs in 2009 accounted for about 64 per cent of total inpatient expenses and the average cost of antibiotics took up about 39 per cent of total drug costs, which was the largest component of total drug costs (Wang C. F. *et al.* 2011: 1449–50). Besides, the average use of antibiotics in 10 township health centers reached about 94 per cent in 2009, which was 14 to 24 per cent higher than the national level (Wang C. F. *et al.* 2011: 1450). In China, drug expenses in 2013 still accounted for 49.3 per cent of the total outpatient medical expenses and 39.5 per cent of the total inpatient medical expenses (National Health and Family Planning Commission of the People's Republic of China 2014).

In recent years, the doctor–patient relationship has become very fragile and tense. Rising medical costs and the problem of SID have become major causes for growing violence against doctors in public hospitals. The doctor–patient relationship is unequal in China. Doctors are in an advantageous position due to information asymmetry. Patients 'frequently cannot discern what treatment options are necessary or desirable for his or her specific medical condition' (Eggleston and Yip 2004: 345). Many patients are passive recipients and let the doctors make all decisions for them. And for patients who really ask doctors about their treatment options, they may get an embarrassingly rude response from doctors (Interview 16KM2). As the nurse said during the interview,

> Patients getting intimidated by the treating doctors happen all the time. There were several occasions that I saw the doctors threaten to force the NRCMS inpatients to stay in hospitals and not to arrange their discharge simply because the patients asked the doctors if it was possible to prescribe essential medicines for their illnesses. The patients can only get reimbursement if the doctors prescribe essential drugs from the Drug Catalogue. But the doctors have to earn more money by prescribing imported drugs. They feel very agitated when patients ask about drug prescription.
>
> (Interview 16KM2)

In fact, old people, rural residents and the NRCMS patients are very passive due to language barrier and lack of knowledge (Interview 15KM7). They fear that the doctors will not treat them if they ask questions that the doctors do not want to answer (Interview 15KM7). Hence, they choose to be silent even though they know that the doctors prescribe unnecessary medicines or ask them to do some unnecessary medical tests (Interview 15KM7).

Health insurance fraud committed by health care providers and physicians

Ever since the implementation of basic medical insurance schemes, China has experienced an enormous increase in health insurance fraud committed by health care providers and physicians, leading to substantial loss of health insurance funds. Fraudulent activities committed by health care providers and physicians include compromising or falsifying medical records, billings for medical services that are never rendered or procedures that are never performed, using genuine patient information to submit falsified claims, unnecessarily extending inpatient lengths of stay and fake hospitalization (*gua chuang zhu yuan*) (Diao 2014; Luo and Guo 2014; Zhong and Tao 2015). Over the past years, the practice of '*gua chuang zhu yuan*' has been commonly used by hospitals to earn more revenues and by physicians to earn more bonuses. '*Gua chuang zhu yuan*' refers to a practice in which physicians convince patients who do not need a hospital stay to get admitted to the hospital. This usually happens when physicians know that the patients are BMI participants. As the nurse said in the interview, many physicians have an increased incentive to encourage patients who only need outpatient visits to get admitted to the hospital:

> The logic is very simple. If this is an outpatient visit for minor illness, patients who are NRCMS or UEBMI participants have to pay out of pocket. Patients who are UEBMI participants have their medical expenses covered by their individual MSAs. The doctors usually tell the patients that getting admitted to hospital can help save money because inpatient expenses can be covered by social pooling fund and patient can enjoy higher reimbursement rate. Many patients think that the doctors are kind because doctors help them save money or reduce out-of-pocket payment. As long as the patients are willing to be admitted to the hospital, the doctors will refer the patients for admission to the hospital.
>
> (Interview 15KM5)

In order to encourage the patients to get admitted to the hospitals, some physicians guarantee patients free medication or promise them monetary rewards (Fu 2014). Once the patients register at the hospital's admission office, the hospital will assign a hospital bed and open a medical file for them (Li F. 2014). However, these hospital beds are empty most of the time because patients do not have to physically stay in hospital overnight (Interview 16KM2). They can leave the ward anytime by orally notifying the attending nurse (Interview 16KM3). Some patients go back home while some patients go to work (Interview 16KM3). They only need to go back to the hospitals to take medication or get an injection (Fu 2014). That is why the medication and treatment records of these patients are almost empty (Li and Shi 2014). But health care providers and doctors can usually find ways to fabricate a patient's medical records and pad claims (Interview 16KM4). Physicians usually avoid arranging quick discharge (Interview 16KM4). The length of this kind of inpatient hospital stay can last for few days, a week or even a month (Interview 16KM4). Longer length of inpatient stay can get higher reimbursement. The practice of *'gua chuang zhu yuan'* not only leads to inappropriate use of hospital beds, but also leads to the depletion of the medical insurance fund.

Health insurance fraud has become a very pervasive problem in both urban and rural China. For example, physicians in Wangchengpo Hospital in Changsha city of Hunan Province gave patients RMB 200 as a reward if patients could provide doctors with their medical insurance cards and had four days of inpatient hospital stay (Fu 2014). In Hainan Province, Anning Hospital, which falsified medical records of 1,812 BMI patients from 2009 and 2012, was prosecuted for committing a RMB 24.14 million medical insurance fraud (Jiang and Guo 2014). Money that was unlawfully obtained from health insurance fraud was used for hospital infrastructure, office innovation, building medical wards, buying medical devices and distributing staff bonuses (Jiang and Guo 2014). In 2013, 15 designated medical institutions in Wuhan city received the poorest credit rating due to their practice of *'gua chuang zhu yuan'* and became the targets of inspection by Wuhan Municipal Health Insurance Center (Wuhan Evening Post 2014).

In recent years, health insurance fraud has attracted much attention in news media. The news media uncovered that some hospitals in Anshun, a prefecture-level city of Guizhou Province, offered free food and pickup for NRCMS participants in exchange for the use of their medical insurance information to defraud medical insurance funds (Xinhua News 2015d). In 2015, 42 hospital staff were criminally detained by Public Security Bureau in Anshun city for defrauding NRCMS funds of more than RMB 34 million (Xinhua News 2015d). In particular, Anshu Rehabilitation Hospital was suspected of defrauding NRCMS fund of more than RMB 2.5 million due to the collusion of management staff, doctors, nurses, accountants and back office staff (Xinhua News 2015d). In June 2015, three health care centers in Xia County, Shansi Province, were uncovered by the media that they used *'gua chuang zhu yuan'* to defraud NRCMS funds (Zhang and Yan 2015). When health insurance authority carried out routine inspection, these health care centers either forced patients to physically stay in the center for 24 hours or changed a patient status from inpatient to outpatient (Zhang and Yan 2015). In sum, the fraudulent activities committed by health care providers and physicians have posed a threat to the healthy operation of the health insurance fund.

Health insurance fraud committed by patients

Patients also commit health insurance fraud due to greed and need. It is common for the uninsured patients to borrow other people's medical insurance certificate to enjoy medical insurance coverage when seeking medical treatment (Interview

15KM6). For example, the Health Insurance Bureau in Shangrao city, Jiangxi Province, opened an investigation on Shangrao Xiehe Hospital, which was suspected of letting an uninsured patient use another person's medical insurance certificate to get medical coverage (Zhu and Han 2014). Some insured BMI participants, especially young ones, borrowed their parents' or grandparents' medical insurance certificates to enjoy a higher reimbursement ratio when seeking medical treatment (Luk 2014: 70). In fact, many parents and grandparents are more than willing to lend their medical insurance certificates to their children or grandchildren. As a Shanghai lady said in an interview,

> We are family. It is normal that we share our medical insurance certificate with our children. It does not matter whether this is my medical insurance certificate or my husband's medical insurance certificate. Money stored in the medical insurance certificate is used for seeing the doctor anyway. You do not use it today. You will use it tomorrow. This is my medical insurance certificate. This is my money. I can decide how to use it. I think that my children can enjoy higher reimbursement rate if they can use my medical insurance certificate. Using my medical insurance certificate can also help my children save more money in their own MSAs. I don't think there's anything wrong with it.
>
> (Interview 10SH4)

In some regions, patients use '*gua chuang zhu yuan*' as a means to obtain higher financial compensation in lawsuits. For example, the People's Court in Nanzhao County, Hunan Province, found that the practice of '*gua chuang zhu yuan*' was commonly used by persons injured in car accidents to negotiate a higher financial compensation (Li and Shi 2014). When giving judicial advice, the People's Court criticized the practice of '*gua chuang zhu yuan*' for jeopardizing hospitals' working order and their images, increasing the compensation liability of insurance companies and leading to a serious waste of medical resources and judicial resources (Li and Shi 2014). It suggested that the Health Bureau of Nanzhao County should formulate regulatory details and carry out spot checks at hospitals in order to eradicate the practice of '*gua chuang zhu yuan*' (Li and Shi 2014).

Another fraudulent activity committed by patients is the inappropriate use of medical insurance cards to buy daily necessities at designated pharmacies. Insured people, especially the young or healthy, seldom seek medical treatment. Without seeking medical treatment, money keeps accumulating in their MSAs. According to Statistical Communiqué on Human Resources and Social Security Development, the total amount of the accumulated fund in the individual MSAs reached RMB 269.7 billion in 2012, RMB 332.3 billion in 2013 and RMB 391.3 billion in 2014 (Ministry of Human Resources and Social Security 2013, 2014, 2015). The average amount of accumulated fund in the individual MSAs per person was about RMB 1,018 in 2012, RMB 1,210 in 2013 and RMB 1,382 in 2014. As people accumulate money in their MSAs, they wish to turn it into cash (Interview

15KM8). They think that the money accumulated in the individual MSAs could have been used for other purposes as they see fit (Interview 15KM8). However, turning the money in the individual MSAs directly into cash is impossible (Interview 15KM8).

Nevertheless, designated pharmacies emerge to be a good venue for them to use their medical insurance cards as 'shopping cards' to buy daily necessities and food (Guo and Han 2012: 17), which has completely distorted the original purpose of the medical insurance card. Pharmacies provide convenience to the insured BMI participants by letting them use their medical insurance cards to buy shampoo, laundry detergent, bathroom tissue, cosmetics, peanut oil, eggs, soft drinks and instant noodles (Interview 15KM6; Interview 15KM8; Interview 16KM4). This can help pharmacies do more businesses and earn more money. Staff would usually print a fake receipt that only showed the total amount of money the customer needed to pay or used different drug names from Drug Catalogue to replace the daily necessities or food bought by the customers (Interview 15KM8; Interview 16KM4). For example, a study found that BMI participants in Guangzhou used their medical insurance card to buy daily necessities and five out of 10 pharmacies surveyed let BMI participants use their individual MSAs to buy daily necessities (Jiang *et al.* 2012: 673). In fact, the inappropriate use of medical insurance cards to buy daily necessities shows that many Chinese citizens have a poor understanding about the function of health insurance. Some of them told the news reporter that 'using individual MSAs to buy non-drug items was fair and reasonable' (Xinjiang Daily News 2014). They thought that they had the discretion to 'freely allocate the money in individual MSAs to buy cosmetics if the money is not used for buying drugs' (Xinjiang Daily News 2014).

Patients also engage in fraud by using their medical insurance certificates to buy prescription drugs from designated pharmacies and then resell the drugs to other pharmacies or other patients. Alternatively, some insured patients sell their redundant medicines to drug dealers directly or based on the demand of drug dealers (Procuratorial Daily 2008). Drug dealers usually wander around the entrance of hospitals and take the initiative in approaching patients to see if patients can sell drugs to them. In general, drug dealers would first purchase drugs from patients using a discount of 30 or 40 per cent off the market prices of drugs and then resell the drugs to other people or places using a discount of 10 or 20 per cent off the market prices of drugs (Anhui Commercial News 2015).

Since 2008, some people have been arrested and sentenced to imprisonment due to involving in illegal purchase and resale of drugs. In 2008, 11 people were arrested for collectively involving in the illegal purchase of drugs from insured patients and reselling them in Zhejiang Province from 2005 to 2007, with the money involved amounting to more than RMB 52 million (Procuratorial Daily 2008). According to Mr. Tao Tian, the People's Procuratorate of Shangcheng District, Hangzhou city, a fixed chain of interests had been formed from the processes of dispensing, purchasing, reselling and selling medicines (Procuratorial Daily 2008). In 2013, the Beijing police arrested five people who were collectively involved in illegal purchase and resale of drugs (The Beijing News

2013). These five people first purchased drugs from insured patients in hospitals and pharmacies and then resold them to rural hospitals, clinics and pharmacies through an underground drug market (The Beijing News 2013). The amount of money involved in this illegal purchase and resale of drugs amounted to about RMB 3 million (The Beijing News 2013). In the same year, the Health Insurance Centre of Chaoyang District in Beijing temporarily banned 201 citizens from using their medical insurance certificates due to involving in the illegal purchase and resale of drugs and having unlawful gains from lending their medical insurance certificates to other people (Beijing Youth Daily 2013). These citizens had to pay out of pocket when seeking medical treatment (Beijing Youth Daily 2013).

In July 2014, two men were sentenced to prison by the Intermediate People's Court of Hefei Municipality in Anhui Province due to their unlawful gains of more than RBM 1 million through the purchase and resale of drugs outside large hospitals (Jianghuai Moring Post 2014). In 2015, a patient with uremia was sentenced to 10 years in prison and penalized RMB 2 million for illegally reselling drugs that were used to treat high blood pressure (Anhui Commercial News 2015). He was prosecuted for substantially purchasing drugs from places such as Shanghai, Nanjing and Ningbo at discounted prices and reselling them to Sichuan, Henan and Zhengzhou from 2011 to 2013 (Anhui Commercial News 2015). The drugs were sold for more than RMB 30.3 million, which was the largest amount of money involved in the illegal sale of drugs so far in Hefei city (Anhui Commercial News 2015). In fact, the illegal purchase and resale of drugs constitutes an unfair form of competition. Besides, it does not guarantee any drug quality and safety (Anhui Commercial News 2015). People illegally purchase and resell drugs because of greed. But the practice of illegal purchase and resale of drugs reflects that there are serious loopholes in both health insurance management and hospital management.

Concern over the deficit and accumulated deficit in health insurance fund

According to the 2014 *China Statistical Yearbook*, the BMI fund in the nation in 2013 had about RMB 144.7 billion surplus (National Bureau of Statistics of the People's Republic of China 2014a). The revenue of the BMI fund was about RMB 824.8 billion while the expense of the BMI fund was about RMB 680.1 billion (National Bureau of Statistics of the People's Republic of China 2014a). However, official figures in *China Statistical Yearbook* might not be able to accurately reflect reality because of two main reasons. First, the revenue of the BMI fund is overstated when money borrowed from the MOF is used to cover the deficit of the BMI fund (Luk 2014: 158). Second, individual cities and provinces experience a deficit in the BMI fund due to differences in economic development, the number of incumbent employees participating in the BMI and the level of medical consumption. For example, Jixi city and Mudanjiang city in Heilongjiang Province respectively reported a deficit of RMB 70 million and RMB 20 million in the UEBMI fund in 2013 due to rising medical costs, an increase in reimbursement ratio and an increase in the number of UEBMI participants who were patients with chronic diseases (Wang 2014). In fact, data reported by Ministry of Human Resources and Social Security indicated that the rate of expenditure growth of the BMI fund since 2013 has been more than 5 per cent higher than the rate of revenue growth (Economic Information Daily 2015a).

As regards the *Green Book of Health Reform and Development 2014*, it predicted that the expenditure of the UEBMI fund would exceed revenue in 2017 and the UEBMI fund would have an accumulated deficit of RMB 735.3 billion in 2024 (Economic Information Daily 2015b). In fact, Mr. Wei-gang Jin, Director-general of the Research Institute for Social Security, Ministry of Human Resources and Social Security, said that in 2013, the problem of expenditures exceeding revenues in the UEBMI fund was founded in 225 regions, which accounted for 32 per cent of regions where the UEBMI was implemented (Economic Information Daily 2015b). In the same year, 22 out of these 225 regions spent all the accumulated revenues in the UEBMI fund (Economic Information Daily 2015b). In 2013, the problem of expenditures exceeding revenues in the URBMI fund was also found in 108 regions in China (Economic Information Daily 2015b). And for regions that reported a surplus in the UEBMI fund, the surplus of fund was unevenly distributed within the region. For example, in 2013, 87 per cent of the surplus in the UEBMI fund in Guangdong Province concentrated in seven cities in the Pearl River Delta (Economic Information Daily 2014). As regards the NRCMS fund, it experienced a deficit of RMB 384,100 in 2009 due to an increase in the reimbursement ratio in medical institutions at county and township levels (Chen *et al.* 2012: 105). The problem of ageing population in Jiangsu Province, together with an increase in the hospitalization rate of people aged 60 and above, may affect the sustainability of the NRCMS fund in the long run (Chen *et al.* 2012: 105). In sum, the shortage of the medical insurance fund may lead to inadequate medical protection for legitimate participants or the collapse of health insurance system.

Other problems in the basic medical insurance system

Non-compliance at the enterprise level and fraud committed by employers

At present, some UEBMI-eligible employees remain uninsured due to non-compliance of their work units or employers. This is a common practice for work units or employers to reduce their operation costs. Some employers use 'a lump sum cash payment as a substitute for premium contribution' (Luk 2014: 69), the amount of which is usually less than the premium contribution an employer needs to pay (Interview 10SH1). Some employees favor receiving cash payment because they think that 'the lump sum cash payment was like increasing their salary and could be used in a more flexible way' (Luk 2014: 69). It is also common for some employers to reduce premium contribution by willfully falsifying the number of employees they hire, altering employees' time sheets and pay records

(Luk 2014: 69; Interview 15KM9). But employees who encounter this situation usually choose to remain silent in order to keep their jobs (Interview 10SH1).

Poor transferability of individual medical savings accounts

At present, the poor transferability of individual MSAs across different regions not only discourages workforce mobility, but also puts those with high geographical mobility in a disadvantageous position to enjoy medical insurance coverage. Many employees fail to transfer their individual MSAs from one city or province to another when they change their place of work (Guo 2014) because local governments or new work units do not allow them to do so (Interview 15KM8). In theory, the premium contribution years in different locations can be calculated cumulatively (Interview 15KM5). As stated in *Framework Plan for Social Security Development under the 12th Five Year Plan*, the transferability of medical insurance should be implemented and the premium contribution years in different locations should be calculated cumulatively (The Ministry of Human Resources and Social Security *et al.* 2012). In practice, however, the premium contribution years in one place are not recognized by the local government in another place due to local variations in medical insurance policy (Interview 15KM5).

Local governments can decide upon the implementation details of medical insurance policy in accordance with their own economic and social conditions. Different premium contribution rates and different minimum premium-paying periods are two main reasons the local government chooses to reject the transferability of individual MSAs (Interview 15KM5). In China, the minimum premium-payment period is the least number of years in which a UEBMI participant has to pay the premium before he/she can continue to enjoy medical insurance benefit upon retirement without paying premiums. For example, the minimum premium-paying period in Yunnan Province is 30 years for male employees and 25 years for female employees (Human Resources and Social Security Bureau of Yunnan Province 2009) while the minimum premium-paying period in Shanghai is 15 years for both male and female employees (Shanghai Municipal Government 2013). More often than not, employees try in vain to transfer their individual MSAs because they are told to follow the rules of the health insurance policy of the new place where they work (Interview 15KM8). Some of them feel very frustrated because the simple response of 'different locations' or the vague responses of 'encountering a technical difficulty' or 'causing an administrative mess' is already a sufficient reason for the local government to immediately reject the transferability of their individual MSAs to the new place (Interview 15KM6; Interview 15KM10). They usually have no choice but to give up their old individual MSAs and then set up a new one. Giving up the old individual MSAs means that employees have to give up all the money they have contributed for all those years because 'complicated procedures and costs of travel to obtain documentary proof are causing too much trouble to get back the money in the individual MSAs' (Interview 15KM10). They feel terrible because money in the old individual MSAs belongs to them and is their private property (Interview

15KM8). Giving up the old individual MSAs 'is like throwing money into the sea' (Interview 15KM8).

Meanwhile, setting up new individual MSAs means that employees have to start paying premium and satisfying the minimum premium-paying period over again in the new location, irrespective of the amount of premium they have already paid and the number of years they have contributed premium in the old location (Interview 16KM4). Employees who change their place of work said that giving up an old individual MSAs and setting up a new one is a precondition for starting their new job (Interview 15KM8). The new employer or work unit most likely does not want the employees to sign an employment contract or allow them to go to work unless such employees promise to set up new individual MSAs (Interview 15KM8). Hence, some employees with high geographical mobility ask the new employer not to let them join the UEBMI because the procedures of transferring the individual MSAs are too annoying (Guo 2014). They would rather pay out of pocket for medical care to save all the trouble. But their financial protection against unexpected or critical illnesses is greatly reduced when they have no medical insurance coverage.

The problem of adverse selection

Being a voluntary scheme, the URBMI faces the problem of adverse selection. Older people are more willing to join the scheme than younger people. People who have poorer health and suffer from chronic illnesses join the scheme while healthy people choose not to join the scheme (Xue and Liu 2009: 65). For example, in Ningxia, older people and urban residents aged 60 and above had higher URBMI participation rates (93 per cent) than those aged between 18 and 45 (79 per cent) (Liang *et al.* 2012: 200). Besides, those who had poorer health status had higher URBMI participation rates (97 per cent) than healthy people (83 per cent) (Liang *et al.* 2012: 200). The URBMI highly relies on government subsidies, which increases the financial burden of local government in the long run (Meng 2014: 87).

Rural population was forced by the local government to join the NRCMS

The participation rate of the NRCMS was very high, reaching almost 99 per cent in the nation in 2014. However, high participation rate does not truly reflect the willingness of rural residents to join the scheme. Being a voluntary scheme, the NRCMS is treated as a compulsory scheme by the local governments. The reason is that the participation rate of the NRCMS is used by the local governments as one of their political achievements and one of the indicators to measure the performance of rural cadres (Chen and Li 2012: 96). Rural cadres who failed to meet the participation rate of the NRCMS would face penalty, such as salary deduction (Chen and Li 2012: 96) or being disqualified from excellence awards that year (Xia 2013). When meeting the participation rate of the NRCMS became a top-down mission, rural cadres had to force rural residents to join the scheme (Chen and Li 2012: 96). For example, rural cadres in regions such as Dingnan County in Jiangxi Province, Yizhou city in Guangxi Province and some rural villages in Anhui, Hebei and Jiangsu Provinces, forced the peasants to join the scheme and required them to make compulsory contribution (Chen and Li 2012: 96; Xia 2013).

Rural cadres used whatever means that were necessary to mobilize or force rural residents to join the scheme (Chen and Li 2012: 96). Some rural cadres used the money that was originally intended for ecological forestry to pay for peasants' mandatory contribution to the NRCMS (Xia 2013). Other rural cadres paid out of pocket for peasants who could not afford to make the contribution and let the peasants return the money to them later (Chen and Li 2012: 96; Xia 2013). Due to economic difficulty, some of the peasants failed to return the money to rural cadres. Rural cadres ended up involving in health insurance fraud in order to get back the money. For example, in May 2013, four rural cadres and a village doctor in Yizhou city, Guangxi Province, were arrested for collectively involving in health insurance fraud by using peasant's medical insurance cards and then falsifying peasants' outpatient reimbursement records to get money from the NRCMS fund (Xia 2013). They claimed that their involvement in health insurance fraud was a way to compensate for the money that 57 peasants were unable to return to them when they paid out of pocket for these peasants to join the NRCMS (Xia 2013). Meanwhile, in places such as Meili Village in Jiangsu Province, land-lost peasants had to think of their own way to pay the mandatory contribution to the NRCMS (Tao 2009: 14). In sum, the original purpose of the NRCMS to protect the rural population against critical illness has been totally distorted by local governments and rural cadres. It is unfortunate that the NRCMS has been manipulated by the local governments to achieve personal gain.

People's lack of understanding about health insurance scheme

At present, those who are eligible for joining the URBMI do not have strong desire to join the scheme because of two main reasons. First, they do not understand the scheme well due to the lack of government promotion and education (Ouyang *et al.* 2012: 960). They do not know about the existence of the scheme or how to join the scheme (Yang *et al.* 2009: 260). They do not know about designated hospitals where they can seek medical treatment, the reimbursement procedures or reimbursement ratio (Yuan *et al.* 2012: 61). For example, in Ningxia, about 14 per cent of 2,024 urban residents surveyed did not join the URBMI because they did not understand the scheme (62.3 per cent) (Liang *et al.* 2012: 199). Similarly, in Hebei Province, about 17.3 per cent of 588 university students surveyed did not join the URBMI because they did not understand the URBMI system (59 per cent) (Yuan *et al.* 2012: 62). In Taiyuan city, Shanxi, about 29 per cent of 2,653 university students surveyed did not join the URBMI (Yang *et al.* 2009: 260). And among those who did not join the scheme, 40.5 per cent of them never thought of issues related to health insurance while about 21 per cent of them did not know how to join the scheme (Yang *et al.* 2009: 260).

Second, there is a perception that it is unnecessary for healthy people to join the scheme. This thought is quite common among university students because university students are young and in general have better health (Ouyang *et al.* 2012: 960). For example, among 102 Hebei university students who did not join the URBMI, 20 per cent of them thought that they were healthy and had little risk of having critical illnesses (20 per cent) (Yuan *et al.* 2012: 62). In Enshi city, Hubei, 17 per cent of 800 university students surveyed did not join the URBMI (Xu 2010: 76). And among those who did not join the scheme, 65 per cent of them were due to rarely getting sick (Xu 2010: 76).

But those who join the URBMI also do not understand the scheme well because they lack adequate channels from which to receive information and there is the lack of government promotion (Chou *et al.* 2009: 13–4). A study that examined university students in Enshi city, Hubei, found that most of the university students did not know about the real purpose for joining the URBMI (Xu 2010: 76). Among 608 university students who joined the URBMI, 51 per cent of them were due to knowing that most of their classmates had joined the scheme while 35 per cent of them were due to their response to the university's call for joining the scheme (Xu 2010: 76). Only 14 per cent of the university students surveyed joined the URBMI because they thought that the scheme could be protection against medical risks (Xu 2010: 76).

As regards the NRCMS, people also do not understand the scheme and its reimbursement policy well. This may due to the lack of government education and promotion. For example, in central and Western China, about 42 per cent of 1,040 rural households surveyed had little understanding about the NRCMS while 10 per cent of them had no understanding about the NRCMS at all (Li *et al.* 2012: 48). Besides, 31 per cent of rural households surveyed said that they did not have a clear understanding about reimbursement ratio for hospital inpatient services while 21 per cent of them gave incorrect answers about reimbursement ratio for hospital inpatient services (Li *et al.* 2012: 48). In eastern and northern China, many people also did not understand the NRCMS well. A survey conducted in Shandong, Jiangsu and Hebei Provinces showed that about 63 per cent of 245 rural households surveyed had little understanding about the NRCMS while about 2 per cent of them had no understanding about the NRCMS (Fan *et al.* 2009: 54). The lack of understanding about the NRCMS affects people's desire to join the scheme. And for those who joined the NRCMS, their lack of understanding about the scheme may act as an impediment for them to get reimbursement.

Conclusion

To conclude, there are many problems plaguing the multi-layered social health insurance system. They severely limit the effectiveness and sustainability of the health insurance system and impede further health insurance reform. They must be addressed without hesitation by the government in order to hold up the promise of providing accessible and affordable health care for all Chinese people.

7 Ways to ensure the financial sustainability of health insurance systems

Introduction

At present, there are many problems plaguing the social health insurance system. These problems cannot be solved overnight. But they must be addressed by the government carefully so that the government can carry out further reform and achieve universal health coverage (UHC) in the future. This chapter borrows some international experience that can be constructive and pragmatic for maintaining financial sustainability of the social health insurance system. It also examines the current policies adopted by the government to deal with high drug costs. This chapter argues that there is a pressing need for the Chinese government to strengthen its anti-fraud capacity, utilize data mining technology, improve health insurance management and perfect the centralized drug procurement system in order to ensure the financial sustainability of health insurance system and achieve UHC in the long run.

Anti-fraud measures

Health insurance fraud is a pervasive problem and truly undesirable conduct. It is an unethical and illegal act that increases the strain on health insurance funds and may put the health of patients at risk. The defects of the current health care system and the loopholes in the legal system have created a breeding ground for health insurance fraud in China. Over the past few years, China has witnessed an increased participation by public hospitals and doctors in an ongoing and large-scale health insurance fraud to obtain business or individual advantage. Dishonest patients also involve in small or large-scale health insurance fraud that drains the fund away from legitimate applicants. Money that could have been used to provide medicine and medical services ends up being wasted on greed. Under these unhealthy circumstances, the Chinese government needs to develop and strengthen its anti-fraud capacity.

Strengthen law enforcement/legislative efforts

One way to combat health insurance fraud is to promulgate state laws that address health insurance fraud. In the United States (US), there are bodies of law imposing civil or criminal liability on individuals or health care entities that engage in health insurance fraud, including the Medicare and Medicaid Anti-Kickback Statute (Rogers 1993), Medicaid False Claims Act or Health Care Fraud Statute (Centers for Medicare & Medicaid Services 2015a). However, China has yet to form state law that specifically targets health care fraud and abuse. At present, Social Insurance Law of the People's Republic of China (SILPRC) and Criminal Law of the People's Republic of China (CLPRC) are the only existing laws applicable to health insurance fraud, but nevertheless are too vague to adequately address such conduct. Effective on 1 July 2011, SILPRC is the first ever national legislation on social insurance with the aim of protecting the lawful rights and interests of citizens participating in social insurance. It broadly covers medical, pension, maternity, unemployment and occupational injury insurances. Under Article 79 (3) of SILPRC, the Social Insurance Administrative Department shall be entitled to deter any acts to conceal, transfer, misappropriate or encroach upon the social insurance fund and require those who exhibit such behavior to make corrections (The Central People's Government of the People's Republic of China 2010). But how to make corrections is not mentioned in SILPRC and the idea of 'making corrections' is subject to broad interpretation. Under Article 88 of SILPRC, any individuals committing insurance fraud shall return the money fraudulently obtained to Social Insurance Fund and face a fine of two to five times the amount of money fraudulently obtained (The Central People's Government of the People's Republic of China 2010). Under Article 87 of SILPRC, any health care entities committing insurance fraud shall return the money fraudulently obtained to Social Insurance Fund; face a fine of two to five times the amount of money fraudulently obtained; face termination of its service agreement if it provides social insurance service; or revoke practice qualifications of its staff who commit insurance fraud (The Central People's Government of the People's Republic of China 2010). Nevertheless, penalties for those in violation of SILPRC seem to be too mild and do not produce a strong deterrent effect, letting fraudsters continue to take advantage of the inadequacy of the existing legal system.

Effective on 1 January 1980, CLPRC was promulgated to 'use criminal punishments to fight against all criminal acts [in law]' (National People's Congress 1997). Article 266 of CLPRC addresses crime of fraud, which broadly refers to the use of false facts to swindle either public or private property in a relatively large amount. Depending on the value of the property that is allegedly swindled and the seriousness of the crime, the punishment varies. If the circumstances are especially serious, a guilty person shall be sentenced to fixed-term imprisonment of not less than 10 years or life imprisonment, pay fines and face confiscation of property; in less serious cases, a guilty person shall pay fines and shall be sentenced to fixed-term imprisonment of not less than 3 years, but not more than 10 years, or shall be sentenced to fixed-term imprisonment of not more than 3 years, subject to criminal detention or put under public surveillance (National People's Congress 1997). Article 266 of CLPRC is applicable to health insurance fraud because health insurance fraud is the use of false facts to swindle public property for the purpose of illegal possession. However, health insurance fraud is a specific crime that can be ongoing and large-scale and committed by individuals, organized groups, medical profession and health care entities. For this reason, the limited language and terminology of Article 266 of CLPRC hinder both investigative and prosecutorial efforts.

At present, both SILPRC and CLPRC are too broad and too vague to pursue health insurance fraud properly and effectively. Besides, the state authority provides little guidance for SILPRC and CLPRC compliance. In response to the pervasive problem of health insurance fraud, the state authority should consider amending SILPRC and CLPRC. Penalties for those in violation of SILPRC should be elevated in order to make it harder, more risky, or less rewarding for individuals to commit the crime or re-offend. Article 266 of CLPRC can be expanded to specify the crime of health insurance fraud and clearly state the criminal liability of such conduct committed by individuals, medical professionals or health care entities. Alternatively, China should consider promulgating specific state laws that authorize law enforcement agencies and their personnel at central and local levels to detect, investigate and prosecute cases of alleged health insurance fraud more easily. The state authority should prepare tougher laws against health insurance fraud offenders, especially health care providers and physicians because they violate patients' trust for the sake of increasing revenue and profit margin and take advantage of their professional environment and knowledge to cheat. They let greed or financial incentive override their medical judgment and sacrifice the integrity of the medical insurance system. The state authority should propose laws that clearly state the civil or criminal penalties for health insurance fraud offenders to reflect the serious harms they cause to the economy and society. Penalties should be significant enough to produce a deterrent effect, including fines, restitution, confiscation of property and imprisonment. Otherwise, offenders might simply regard the penalties as part of the cost of committing health insurance fraud and think that they have little to lose. Heavier penalties should be imposed on those who have had previous convictions for fraud. If the harms associated with health insurance fraud involve serious bodily injury or death of patients, offenders should face stiff penalties such as life sentence, the suspension or loss of professional licenses if they are physicians or debarments from participating in health insurance schemes if they are health care providers.

Setting up insurance fraud bureaus/fraud control units

Another way to combat health insurance fraud is to establish an Insurance Fraud Bureau (IFB) or set up fraud control units at the local level to conduct and coordinate investigation systematically; collect, share and analyze information or data related to health insurance fraud; and facilitate civil and criminal enforcement actions. At present, the anti-fraud capacity of the Chinese government is limited by the lack of personnel to monitor and supervise the operation of the health insurance fund and provide audit and reimbursement service. For example, Xixiu District of Guizhou Province, which had about 500 designated medical institutions for the New Rural Cooperative Medical System (NRCMS), only had four to five staff to monitor and supervise the operation of the NRCMS (Xinhua News 2015d). The number of NRCMS outpatient and inpatient visits of Xixiu District was respectively 800,000 and 50,000 per year (Xinhua News 2015d). The substantial amount of caseloads makes it very hard for the staff to perform a detailed and comprehensive check on every case or insurance claim.

Besides, China lacks a law enforcement agency dedicated exclusively to combating all forms of insurance fraud through interagency or cross-provincial collaboration and the coordination of information exchange. The Chinese government never officially discloses the way in which cases of suspected health insurance fraud are detected, investigated and prosecuted to the public. But information from state-run media indicates that cases of alleged health insurance fraud, from investigation to conviction, have to go through different procedures that involve different government agencies. If the Commission for Discipline Inspection or Audit Bureau identifies a potentially fraudulent claim or suspicious claim made by public hospitals, such claim would be referred to the Public Security Bureau for further investigation (Xinhua News 2015d). The Public Security Bureau, once receiving the case referral, opens an investigative file. After thorough investigation and gathering enough evidence, the Public Security Bureau places suspects under criminal detention (Xinhua News 2015d), which leads to formal arrest. In China, criminal detention precedes formal arrest. Formal arrest is usually followed by indictment by the People's Procuratorate and then trial in court (Jiang and Guo 2014).

In China, official statistics on cases of health insurance fraud or health insurance fraud prosecutions are not publicly available. One possible explanation is that the Chinese government has not specifically established health insurance fraud as a separate offence, thereby being impossible to provide precise statistics that have an accurate representation of the level of health insurance fraud. Another possible explanation is that much health insurance fraud remains undetected, unreported and unproven. Even if there are statistics on health insurance fraud prosecutions, such statistics reveal merely a partial picture. Having said that, however, there is reason to believe that health insurance fraud is a pervasive and growing problem that must be addressed by the Chinese government actively and aggressively. It is because many health insurance fraud prosecutions that have been reported by mass media over the past few years collectively involve hundreds or thousands of victims, most of whom are patients, and involve hundreds of millions or millions of dollars in losses. There is a pressing need for the government to establish anti-fraud institutions, agencies or network in order to coordinate fraud detection, investigation and prosecution in a timely and more effective manner. In this aspect, China can turn to the US experience for reference.

In the US, IFBs have been established in 41 states as law enforcement agencies to 'detect and apprehend those who commit insurance fraud and to change the public perception of insurance fraud as a victimless crime' (New York State Division of Criminal Justice Services 2009: 9). For example, the IFB established within the New York State Insurance Department has a specialized unit that investigates health insurance fraud committed by doctors, health care providers and policyholders (Department of Financial Services 2016). Other examples include Medicare Fraud Strike Force (MFSF) Teams and Medicaid Fraud Control Units (MFCUs) in the US. MFSF Teams 'are teams comprising staff from federal, state, and local investigation agencies, designed to combat Medicare fraud by using data-analysis techniques' (Stallone 2013: 9). Through interagency collaboration, MFSF Teams have conducted multi-district national takedowns, 'charged over 2,100 individuals involved in more than [US] $6.5 billion in fraud' (Centers for Medicare & Medicaid Services 2015b) and 'recovered millions of taxpayer dollars' (Office of Inspector General's 2016a). As regards MFCU, they are single, identifiable entities of state government that employ teams of auditors, investigators, prosecutors and attorneys to investigate and prosecute civil and criminal Medicaid fraud (Stallone 2013: 11; Office of Inspector General's 2016b). Establishing an IFB or fraud control unit(s) requires a substantial amount of money and effort and its effective operation depends upon a pool of highly trained, skilled and experienced personnel in the areas of fraud detection, investigation and prosecution. But considering all of the positive impacts that IFB or fraud control unit(s) can bring to the economy and society, such as recovering a substantial amount of money and improving public awareness of insurance fraud, the establishment of IFB or fraud control unit(s) is worthy of government and community support.

Public fraud reporting system and the incentive reward scheme

Combating health insurance fraud cannot be achieve by the government alone, but, instead, must involve the public at large. International experience shows that the use of public fraud reporting systems is an effective approach to assist the state authority in detecting and combating all forms of fraud. A public fraud reporting system is one of the proactive detection methods around the globe. In order to stem the rising tide of health insurance fraud and assist law enforcement, the Chinese government should let the health insurance system become subject to greater scrutiny by society through the establishment of a health insurance fraud reporting system. The system can allow the general public, employees or informants to promptly make a good-faith report of known or suspected incidence of health insurance fraud by providing tips and evidence (e.g. documentation or data) through a 24-hour telephone hotline, email or fraud reporting website. For the fraud hotline, callers can identify themselves and leave contact information for trained hotline staff or representative to reach them for future follow-up. They can also choose to speak to hotline staff anonymously if they wish. Alternatively, to ensure anonymity and confidentiality, a reference number can be assigned to callers for calling back any time to check on the status of their report or update information. Information provided by callers will be kept on a secure electronic database to prevent unauthorized access, disclosure, misuse or distribution of such information. To encourage the public at large to come forward, the government can introduce an incentive reward scheme that offers incentive payments to those who are able to provide relevant information, tips and evidence that subsequently lead to an arrest, successful prosecution and conviction, or fraud monetary recoveries.

The use of data mining technology to detect health insurance fraud

The traditional method of detecting health care fraud and abuse that relies on manual, paper-based auditing procedures is often time-consuming and practically ineffective (Joudaki *et al.* 2015b). In recent years, data mining technology has emerged as a more systematic and precise tool in developed countries for identifying trends or patterns of unusual billing, inconsistent billing, duplicate claims, reimbursement irregularities, and predicting future fraud and abuse in large set of insurance claim data (Kirlidog and Asuk 2012; Rawte and Anuradha 2015; Joudaki *et al.* 2015a; Joudaki *et al.* 2015b). Data mining is the mathematical core of Knowledge Discovery in Databases (KDD), which is 'an automatic, exploratory analysis and modeling of large data repositories' (Maimon and Rokach 2010: 1). It 'involves statistical, mathematical, artificial intelligence and machine learning techniques to extract and identify useful information and subsequent knowledge from large databases' (Kirlidog and Asuk 2012: 990). It has been 'proved to successfully detect fraudulent activities such as money laundering, e-commerce credit card fraud, telecommunications fraud, insurance fraud, and computer intrusion' (Muhammad 2014: 62). There are three types of data mining approaches that can be adopted to detect health care fraud: supervised data mining, unsupervised data mining and hybrid data mining (Joudaki *et al.* 2015b). Supervised data mining, such as neutral networks, decision tree or genetic algorithms (Joudaki *et al.* 2015a: 196), uses samples of previously known fraudulent and non-fraudulent records to 'construct models which allow assigning a new observation into one of the [two] groups of records' (Joudaki *et al.* 2015b: 2). Unsupervised data mining, such as outliner detection, clustering or association rules (Joudaki *et al.* 2015a 197), is 'used when there is no labeled historical fraud data' (Liu and Vasarhelyi 2013: 1), involving the comparison of 'individual claims with the norms observed in the sample of claims under analysis' (Joudaki *et al.* 2015b: 2). It 'can be applied to identify new types of fraud or abuse' (Joudaki *et al.* 2015b: 3). Hybrid data mining, which combines both supervised and unsupervised approaches, usually uses 'unsupervised approaches to improve the performance of supervised approach' (Liu and Vasarhelyi 2013: 1).

Facing serious challenges caused by continuous expansion of the medical insurance system, the rapid increase in the number of designated health care institutions and the number of the insured (21st Century Business Herald 2015) and the increase in the reimbursement levels, Health Insurance Bureaus in China are strained with acute shortages of trained and qualified personnel to perform audits and reviews of health insurance claims data. For example, the average number of inpatient claims reviewed by each auditor in Health Insurance Bureau of Chengdu, Sichuan Province, increased from 6,708 in 2011 to 8,654 in 2013 (21st Century Business Herald 2015). The development of an intelligent system in auditing is expected to relieve workload pressure and combat health insurance fraud. In its initial stage of exploration, the Chinese government has launched a pilot intelligent system in auditing in Health Insurance Bureaux of Hangzhou in Zhejiang Province, Chengdu in Sichuan Province and Zhanjiang in Guangdong Province to identify suspicious claims and correct the problem of over-prescription (21st Century Business Herald 2015). It can quickly and accurately perform audits at an average speed of 0.37 seconds (21st Century Business Herald 2015). When the intelligent system in auditing can be launched nationwide remains unknown and requires further study. However, the use of the intelligent system in auditing is definitely headed in the right direction and will achieve promising results in preventing health insurance fraud and abuse.

Health insurance management as one of the core contents for performance appraisal of public hospitals

In recent years, some local governments have carried out performance appraisal for designated hospitals of basic medical insurance, with health insurance management becoming one of the core contents for performance appraisal. For example, in Guangdong Province, the Dongguan Social Security Department and the Health Bureau of Dongguan City in February 2014 jointly issued the *Management of Designated Medical Institutions of Social Medical Insurance*, which clearly provided a list of fraudulent activities committed by physicians, staff or public hospitals that would lead to the punishments of temporary suspension from or termination of being an approved supplier for medical insurance services (Dongguan Social Security Department 2014). In Shandong Province, the Qingdao Municipal Bureau of Human Resources and Social Security in July 2015 issued *Methods of Assessing Designated Medical Institutions of Social Medical Insurance in Qingdao City* (hereafter the *2015 Assessment Method*), which highlighted the evaluation criteria of performance appraisal for designated hospitals of basic medical insurance. According to the *2015 Assessment Method*, performance appraisal for designated hospitals of basic medical insurance consisted of two components: 'medical insurance management assessment' and 'performance target assessment'. Full mark of the performance appraisal was 100. Fifty per cent of the total marks were allocated for 'medical insurance management assessment' and the rest was allocated for 'performance target assessment'. 'Medical insurance management assessment' was related to the quality of medical care provided to the insured, uploading medical insurance data in a timely and accurate manner and reimbursement of medical insurance. Marks would be deducted if hospitals engaged in any fraudulent behaviors, such as over-prescription or falsifying inpatient records, to obtain medical insurance funds. Hospitals that scored 80 marks or above would receive Grade A in recognition of their demonstration of a high level of integrity and reliability (Qingdao Municipal Bureau of Human Resources and Social Security 2015). If hospitals scored 60 marks or below or did not pass the performance appraisal, they would be ordered by the Municipal Human Resources and Social Security Bureau to make corrections within a certain period of time (usually one to two months) and their basic medical insurance settlement would be temporarily suspended (Qingdao Municipal Bureau of Human Resources and Social Security 2015). If their corrections failed to meet the expectation of the Qingdao Municipal Human Resources and Social Security Bureau, their designated qualifications of the basic medical insurance would be temporarily suspended or terminated.

In Gansu Province, the Health Bureau of Huining County in 2011 issued *Trial Implementation of Methods of Assessing Designated Medical Institutions of New Rural Cooperative Medical System*, which paid attention to assess the inpatient and outpatient expenses of the NRCMS participants and the prescription of generic medicine in the Drug Formulary for National Basic Medical Insurance. Depending on the seriousness of the fraudulent activity, the Health Bureau of Huining County shall be entitled to order designated medical institutions and their staff that engage in fraudulent activities to make corrections within a certain period of time, circulate a notice of criticism, retrieve the related medical expenses already disbursed by the medical insurance fund, impose disciplinary action against members convicted of health insurance fraud, or refer the case that constitutes a crime to the judiciary (Health Bureau of Huining County 2011). By using health insurance management as one of the core elements of performance appraisal, local governments can make designated medical institutions of basic medical insurance more accountable to patients, reduce the likelihood of fraudulent activity occurring, minimize fraud-related losses and the consequences associated with them, and maintain a quality workforce by properly awarding and penalizing their performance. The central government can consider adding health insurance management as an essential component required for performance appraisal of designated hospitals of basic medical institutions nationwide.

The suspension of the use of medical insurance cards of BMI participants who committed health insurance fraud

In some places, the local government penalizes the insured Basic Medical Insurance (BMI) participants who commit health insurance fraud through suspension of their use of health insurance cards and requiring them to pay medical expense out of pocket. For example, the Shanghai Municipal Human Resources and Social Security Bureau shall be entitled to ask the insured BMI participants who committed health insurance fraud to return the related medical expenses already disbursed by the medical insurance fund; issue a warning and impose a fine ranging from RMB 100 to 10,000; or suspend the use of medical insurance cards for one to six months (Shanghai Municipal Government 2011). By the end of September 2013, the Beijing Municipal Human Resources and Social Security Bureau had suspended the use of health insurance cards of 201 BMI participants who committed health insurance fraud, which included lending their health insurance cards to their family members and repeatedly visiting different designated medical institutions to get certain types of prescription drugs that are then sold on the street (Beijing Youth Daily 2013). In Kunshan city, Jiangsu

Province, the Social Insurance Fund Management Center in March 2015 issued *Notice Concerning the Temporary Suspension of the Use of Health Insurance Card of Health Insurance Participants*, which publicly announced the name and social security number of 72 health insurance participants that were blacklisted by the Centre due to abnormal medical expenses associated with the violation of health insurance regulation (Social Insurance Fund Management Center 2015). But it is believed that much health insurance fraud committed by the insured has gone unchecked due to the lack of personnel in Health Insurance Bureau to go through all the reimbursement claims.

Strengthen the usage of individual Medical Savings Accounts (MSAs)

In recent years, some of the mainland scholars and experts on health care have proposed the cancellation of MSAs so that all the premiums contributed by employers and employees can go to the social polling fund (SPF) to increase reimbursement level, achieve greater risk-pooling, maximize financial protection and promote mutual assistance efforts to a greater extent (Li T. N. 2014). At present, some of the local governments alter the original function of MSAs so that money in MSAs can be utilized in a better way. For example, local governments in Guangdong and Jiangsu make MSAs become household accounts that allow the direct dependents and spouses of BMI participants to use the money in MSAs of such participants to pay for the outpatient expenses and drug fees at pharmacies (Li T. N. 2014). Local government in Zhejiang Province allows the direct dependents of UEBMI participants to use the money in MSAs of such participants for paying charges for preventive vaccinations, including rabies vaccination and influenza and pneumonia vaccines (Li 2013). This enables MSAs to achieve risk-pooling among family members to some extent. Meanwhile, local governments in Changzhou and Suzhou of Jiangsu Province allow BMI participants to use their money in MSAs to buy supplementary commercial health insurance. It is believed that by increasing the scope of MSAs money usage, the incentives of BMI participants to use their health insurance card to buy daily necessities will decrease.

Lifting government controls on drug prices

The Chinese government's drug price control policy has long been blamed for creating a vicious circle of high drug prices. The government directly intervened in drug prices through imposing price caps on different types of drugs, which placed a ceiling on the amount pharmaceutical companies could charge for their drugs. It aimed at keeping medicines accessible and affordable to patients, especially to those of limited financial means. Since May 1998, price caps have been imposed on different types of drugs 31 times (Xia and Wang 2013). Unfortunately, the public's mounting dissatisfaction with high drug prices continued and the new problem of price-cut drugs disappearing from the market was created.

The use of price caps is regarded as a misguided effort to control spiraling drug prices because it would trigger a chain reaction in the drug distribution system. Once drug manufacturers find that they cannot reap the same profits they used to make from the price-cut drugs, they switch to producing the substitute drugs that are not affected by the drug price control policy (Luk 2014: 72, 2015: 51). Drug distributors who find the price-cut drugs unprofitable to sell would discourage health care providers from purchasing such drugs and physicians from prescribing such drugs (Interview 10SH1; Interview 16KM1). They would instead lure health care providers to purchase and physicians to prescribe expensive drugs or so-called new drugs that can guarantee lucrative profits and substantial kickbacks to them (Interview 10SH1; Interview 16KM1). Expensive drugs are usually imported drugs or substitute drugs that are not affected by the drug price control policy. They replace price-cut drugs that will quickly disappear from the market. For example, Human Tetanus Immunoglobulin (HIG), which is a sterile solution for treatment of tetanus infection, had gradually disappeared from the market after becoming a price-cut drug and 10 hospitals in Jinan, Shandong Province, ran out of HIG supply (Jinan Times 2015). Tapazole (Methimazole), a drug for treatment of hyperthyroidism that only cost Renminbi (RMB) 4.9 per bottle (100 tablets), was replaced by Thiamazole, an imported drug that cost RMB 33 (50 tablets) (Zhang and Zhang 2014). As regards the so-called new drugs, most of them are actually the same old drugs being given a new name, new packaging or new dosage before they can be sold in the market (Luk 2014: 72–3). For example, Roxithromycin, which is an antibiotic used to treat respiratory tract infections, has 40 names in China while Rocephin, which is an antibiotic used to treat bacterial infections, has 30 names in China (China Economic Net 2011). Changing the names of these two antibiotics is a trick played by drug manufacturers to make these inexpensive but efficacious essential medicines repeatedly become 'new drugs' so that the price of these 'new drugs' can be set higher (China Economic Net 2011). Drug manufacturers are always quick to respond the government's drug price control policy in order to protect their interests. Drug distributors, health care providers and physicians have also learnt to accommodate each other under the drug price control policy so as to protect their same interest of earning lucrative profits. As a result, most of the patients cannot benefit from the drug price control policy. Some of them even face a critical shortage of life saving essential medicines (Zhang and Zhang 2014).

High drug prices have seriously impeded the provision of accessible and affordable health care in China. The government's drug price control policy has proved to be far less effective than originally expected. Besides, the role of government as a price-setter on drugs is not appreciated by the public, drug manufacturers, drug distributors or medical professionals. For this reason, the government made a new move by allowing market forces to play a bigger role in setting drug prices. On April 24, 2015, the Standing Committee of the National People's Congress released amendments to the Drug Administration Law of the People's Republic of China (hereafter the Drug Administration Law). One of the amendments was deleting Article 55 of the previous Drug Administration Law, which granted the government the power to fix and guide drug prices and required drug manufacturers, drug distributors and medical institutions to implement drug prices that were fixed or guided by the government (China Food and Drug Administration 2001; The State Council Information Office of the People's Republic of China 2015). This amendment paved the way for the subsequent implementation of drug price reform.

On May 4 2015, the National Development and Reform Commission (NDRC), together with the National Health and Family Planning Commission, Ministry of Human Resources and Social Security, Ministry of Industry and Information Technology, the Ministry of Finance (MOF), Ministry of Commerce, and China Food and Drug Administration, issued *Opinions on Implementing Drug Price Reform* (hereafter the 2015 Opinions). The 2015 Opinions stated that starting from 1 June 2015, the government would lift the decade-long practice of price controls for most drugs, except for narcotic anesthetic products and Class I psychoactive drugs, and let market competition determine drug retail price. While the government continues to be the price-setter on narcotic anesthetic products and Class I psychoactive drugs, it also keeps an eye on drug prices and punishes any unlawful behaviors such as price cheating, price collusion and monopolistic pricing practices. Mr. Ming-de Yu, President of the Chinese Pharmaceutical Enterprises Association, expected that lifting the official price cap could lead to more open and transparent drug price information and drug price would not increase drastically (*Guang Ming Ri Bao* 2015). It is too early to tell whether pharmaceutical pricing liberalization can lead to reasonable pricing and the steady supply of essential medicines. But the move to a more market-oriented price setting system underlines the government's determination to solve the problem of high drug prices and achieve the goal of providing affordable health care in China.

Perfecting the centralized bidding and procurement system for essential medicines

In an effort to ensure a steady supply of essential medicines at reasonable prices, the government in 2000 piloted a centralized drug procurement system at Henan Province, Hainan Province, Liaoning Province and Xiamen City. In November 2001, the centralized drug procurement system was implemented nationwide after *Notice on Regulating the Task of the Centralized Drug Procurement System for Medical Institutions* was jointly issued by the Ministry of Health (MOH), State Planning Commission, State Economic and Trade Commission, the China Food and Drug Administration, State Administration of Traditional Chinese Medicine, and State Council's Office for Correcting Industrial Illegitimate Practice (Ministry of Health *et al.* 2001). Public hospitals were required to procure at least 80 percent of the actual quantity of essential drugs that they used in the previous year (Interview 15KM4), except for psychotropic, narcotic and radioactive drugs, through competitive bidding at the provincial level. Certified by both the MOH and the State Food and Drug Administration, a third-party drug procurement agent was responsible for running the bidding process. A bidding evaluation committee that consisted of pharmaceutical and clinical medicine experts evaluated bids submitted by drug manufacturers according to drug quality, the bid price and business reputation. The bid-winning price of drugs should not exceed the maximum retail prices or the so-called 'ceiling price' set by the government. Drug manufacturers that won the bids were required to sign a drug purchase contract with hospitals within 30 days after the notice of winning bids was issued. Drugs were then delivered by drug manufacturers directly to hospitals or through drug distributors. Hospitals were required to pay drug manufacturers according to the date and the amount of drugs specified in the contract.

In theory, the implementation of the government-led drug procurement system was able to let public hospitals obtain essential medicines at the lowest possible price because bulk purchasing of essential medicines could generate cost savings. The idea was that public hospitals joined forces to purchase essential medicines in higher volumes in pursuit of the reduction of per unit costs of drugs through economies of scale. Hence, they could secure lower drug prices from drug manufacturers. In reality, however, the bid-winning price of drugs was higher than the wholesale price of drugs in the market because of two main reasons. First, drug manufacturers collectively jacked up the tender price of drugs in order to generate a sizeable profit margin (Interview 14KM1). Hence, the bid-winning price of drugs usually deviated from the market level. For example, the bid-winning price of Sodium Bicarbonate Injection, which was used for correcting metabolic acidosis, was about 48.5 per cent higher than the market price in Zhejiang (Chen 2015). Second, bid-rigging was adopted collectively by drug manufacturers in various forms that resulted in raising the bid-winning price of drugs. For example, price fixing was a common bid-rigging practice for drug manufacturers to fix the tender price of drugs higher than the market price (Interview 14KM1). Bid rotation was another method for drug manufacturers to allocate markets or products among themselves and take turns to win an equal number of contracts or an equal dollar volume over time (Interview 14KM1). Cover bidding where drug manufacturers submitted a losing bid or bids with unacceptable terms in order to let the designated drug manufacturer win the bid was also adopted in the centralized drug procurement (Interview 14KM1). Compensation in the form of cash, goods or subcontracts would be given by a winning bidder to losing bidders (Interview 14KM1). Hence, those who won the bid through bid-rigging were not necessarily the ones who could provide drugs at the lowest possible price because the genuine competitive bidding process did not exist (Interview 14KM1).

Besides, the implementation of the centralized drug procurement system led to the shortage or disappearance of low-cost generic drugs that were therapeutically effective. It was because the profit margin of these generic drugs was too low that drug manufacturers did not have enough incentive to produce them (Zeng 2015: 38). For this reason, some winning bidders did not supply the drugs by refusing to get the bid-winning notice or they stopped supplying the drugs by using the rising prices of raw materials as an excuse (Ningxia Hui Autonomous

Region Public Resources Transaction and Management Bureau 2015). As a result, some essential drugs were out of stock in hospitals. For example, 13 drug manufacturers in Ningxia did not supply drugs after winning the bids and hence, their bid winning qualification was cancelled and their performance bonds were deducted by the Drug Procurement Office (Ningxia Hui Autonomous Region Public Resources Transaction and Management Bureau 2015). The implementation of the centralized drug procurement system also reduced patients' access to essential medicines because it changed the prescribing patterns of doctors. In order to earn more money, doctors shifted toward the use of new or more expensive drugs as substitutes. They intentionally reduced the number of drug options available for patients or increased the volumes of drugs used per patient. Hence, patients may not take the right drugs or the right dosage of drugs that could be of benefit to their health.

In February 2015, the State Council released *Guiding Opinions on Perfecting the Centralized Drug Procurement System of Public Hospitals* (hereafter the 2015 Guiding Opinions), which emphasized the importance of eradicating the practice of 'feeding hospitals by selling drugs', reducing the public's financial burden of drug costs and preventing commercial bribery in the pharmaceutical industry (The State Council 2015). The 2015 Guiding Opinions suggested that different procurement methods should be adopted for different types of medicines in order to motivate drug manufacturers and engage public hospitals in a better way. As the spokesperson for the Health Reform Office of the State Council said in the press conference, a 'double-envelope' tendering system should be adopted for essential drugs with broad clinical use and non-patented drugs (Chinanews. com 2015). The 'double-envelope' tendering system was 'designed to allocate weight to competing tenders based on a technical quality evaluation (the first envelope), as well as price (the second envelope)'(Sellers 2015). Bidding was evaluated on the basis of both quality and price. But as indicated by the 2015 Guiding Opinions, emphasis was put on quality (The State Council 2015). On the other hand, a price negotiation system was adopted for some patented drugs (The State Council 2015) because such drugs faced less competition in the market and their prices were usually more expensive (Xiang 2015). They were not suitable for being included in the centralized drug procurement system (Xiang 2015). As regards first-aid medicine and non-patented drugs for gynecology and pediatrics, they could be procured directly by public hospitals (The State Council 2015) to ensure their stable and adequate supplies. Enhancing the flexibility of drug procurement helps ensure the stable supply of essential medicines and achieve reasonable pricing. The 2015 Guiding Opinions also suggested the standardization of the drug procurement code and the realization of information sharing of drug procurement data among all the provinces through the Internet. The transparency of drug procurement would be enhanced by the government's regular announcement of drug procurement prices of hospitals, the amount of drugs procured or any misconduct of drug manufacturers and hospitals to the public (The State Council 2015). This can significantly reduce perverse incentives for unlawful tendering practices and illegal charging practices.

Zero-markup policy for essential drugs

The implementation of zero-markup drug policy is part of the government effort to eradicate the practice of 'feeding hospitals by selling drugs' and ensure affordability of essential medicines. In April 2009, the *Opinions on Deepening the Health Care System Reform*, which was jointly issued by the Central Committee of the Communist Party of China and the State Council, stated that the policy of drug sale with additional markup in public hospitals should be gradually eliminated and the zero-markup drug policy should be implemented (The Central Committee of the Communist Party of China and the State Council 2009). The zero-markup drug policy prohibits public hospitals from selling essential drugs at a 15 per cent markup. However, to compensate their loss of drug revenues, public hospitals will receive subsidies from the local government's budget and can raise other fees or introduce new fees (Luk 2015: 53). For example, public hospitals are allowed to increase registration fees, consultation fees, observation fees, hospital bed fees, surgeon fees or anesthesiologist fees to make up any shortfall in revenue (Interview 15KM3). In village clinics, the general fee for medical service was introduced by merging 'registration fee, checkup fee, injection fee (including intravenous infusion fees, excluding drug costs) and dispensing fee' (Zhang *et al.* 2015: 26). The zero-markup drug policy was initially implemented in primary medical institutions in China (Zhou *et al.* 2013), including village clinics and township health centers. By June 2011, all the government-owned primary medical institutions have adopted the zero-markup drug policy (Modern Express 2012). Since 2012, the pilot program of zero-markup drug policy has been implemented in public hospitals in 300 counties or county-level cities (General Office of the State Council 2012). In May 2015, all the public hospitals at county level were required to implement the zero-markup drug policy (General Office of the State Council 2015b).

So far, there is not much empirical research done on the effectiveness of zero-markup drug policy on reducing drug prices or medical expenses. But the results yielded from some Chinese studies and information from reports in Chinese media show that the zero-markup drug policy has brought more negative impacts than positive ones. First, the problem of high drug prices still exists. In China, the drug distribution system consists of several layers: drug manufacturer, the first-tiered drug distributor, the second-tier drug distributor, the third-tier drug distributor and hospitals (Luk 2014: 71). The zero-markup drug policy only prohibits public hospitals from adding mark-ups on drug sales. But drug manufacturers and drug distributors are still allowed to mark up a drug. 'Drug manufacturer price was the [production] cost of drug plus a 5 per cent profit' (Luk 2015: 46). Drug production costs, such as the cost of raw materials, machinery, labor and management, are usually exaggerated by drug manufacturers in order to gain more profits (Luk 2014: 71). The first-tiered drug distributors are allowed to add a 5 per cent markup over the drug manufacturer price. The second-tiered and third-tiered drug distributors are also allowed to respectively add a 5 per cent markup over the first-tiered and second-tiered drug wholesale price. Hence, although the zero-markup drug policy eliminates the additional markup on drug sales in public hospitals, drugs have already been marked up several times in the drug distribution system. Drug prices are still high.

Second, the overall medical expenditure does not decrease substantially. It is because public hospitals have to find ways to generate revenues in order to compensate for their loss of drug revenues. Public hospitals can only generate revenues by seeing more patients and doing more medical tests and treatments (Ye *et al.* 2015: 117). Hence, the zero-markup drug policy might not be able to alleviate the financial burden of patients in reality. For example, under the zero-markup drug policy, a county hospital in Jingjiang City, Jiangsu Province, respectively increased treatment fees by 10 per cent, charges for anesthesiology services by 20 per cent and surgical charges by 40 per cent (Ye *et al.* 2015: 116). Although its average inpatient drug fee per capita decreased by 11.45 per cent in 2013, its overall average inpatient expenses only decreased by 1.34 per cent in the same year (Ye *et al.* 2015: 116). As regards the average outpatient expenses, it increased by 12.04 per cent in 2013 due to an increase in observation charges and treatment fees (Ye *et al.* 2015: 116). Obviously, outpatients could hardly benefit from the zero-markup drug policy because of paying higher medical expenses.

Third, some public hospitals face deficit or are heavily indebted due to the loss of drug sales revenue and inadequate government subsidies. Before the implementation of the zero-markup drug policy, drug sales was a primary source of hospital revenue, accounting for 40–50 per cent of the total revenue of public hospitals in China (Brombal 2014: 107). Adjusting medical service charges and receiving government subsidies were the two main sources to make up for the loss of drug sales revenues. However, subsidies provided by the local government are usually unstable and far from adequate, which can be devastating to a public hospital's ability to survive. The fiscal capacity of local governments varies across regions due to different economic and social conditions. In more developed and richer regions, local governments 'are generally able to enjoy higher tax revenues coming from the development of non-agricultural sectors' (Liu and Tao 2007: 169) and 'draw on additional high income from the sale of rights to develop local land' (Liu and Tao 2007: 169). In less developed and poorer regions, however, local governments in general lack 'sufficient and dependable equalizing [fiscal] transfers from higher levels of government' (Liu and Tao 2007: 169) that can 'commensurate with ever-increasing local expenditure needs' (Liu and Tao 2007: 166). They have to draw on 'extra-budgetary revenue sources obtained through fees levied on farmers and profits generated through the expropriation of farmers' land' (Liu and Tao 2007: 167). Local government finance that heavily relies on land and real estate becomes 'subject to influence from the real estate market, causing financial instability' (Naito 2015: 71).

Many local governments have been seriously indebted due to their ongoing investment in real estate projects. 'As China's economy slides, and demand for real estate shrinks, many local governments might have trouble repaying their debt in the near future' (Xie 2016). According to the data of the National Audit Office, total debt of local governments increased from RMB 15.9 trillion at the end of 2012 to RMB 17.9 trillion at the end of 2013 (Naito 2015: 74). Over the past few years, many local governments have not been in good financial condition. Hence, it is unrealistic to expect that government subsidies can make up budget shortfall in public hospitals. For example, under the zero-markup drug policy, the People's Hospital of Pinyin County, Shandong Province, had a loss of more than RMB 30 million in drug sales revenue (Public Network 2014 March 31). But in 2013 it was RMB 222 million in debt and faced RMB 16.12 million budget shortfall because raising medical service charges generated only RMB 5 million in revenue and subsidies from county government were only RMB 8.88 million (Public Network 2014). In Anhui Province, six out of nine county-level public hospitals examined faced a budget shortfall that exceeded RMB 6 million in 2013 because the amount of government subsidies they received was 3.4 to 7.3 times less than the amount of their drug sales revenue (Li *et al.* 2015: 74). In face of budget deficit, health care providers might find alternative ways to generate revenues, which may subsequently encourage physician-induced demand. The practice of 'feeding hospitals by doing unnecessary medical tests or surgery' might emerge in future. Health care providers might also sacrifice quality of care in order to save money, which can be detrimental to patients' health and may worsen the doctor–patient relationship. Morale among physicians might become lower because they are under pressure to meet the financial targets set by the public hospitals they work for (Interview 16KM1). In sum, the zero-markup drug policy might have some unintended consequences in the long run. It should be reviewed regularly to assess overall effectiveness.

Establishing the 12358 Price Reporting System

Combating high drug prices cannot solely rely on the state authority. It also needs close community scrutiny. To seek input from the community, the NDRC in December 2014 established the 12358 Price Reporting System to handle price-related complaints in retail prices, transportation, real estate and property management, and medicine. The 12358 Price Reporting System was a unified and synchronized platform that integrated the national, provincial, municipal and county-level pricing authorities into the same one. It consisted of 'a price report call center system, online price reporting system, mobile terminal price reporting system and online price report processing platform' (Inspur 2014). It allowed the general public to provide information on known or suspected cases of illegal charging practices through various channels, including the 12358 Hotline, the Internet (http://12358.ndrc.gov.cn/) and a mobile app. The reported information would be distributed to and processed by authorities concerned. Upon completion of a price report, the general public would receive a 11-digit tracking code for a status check (China National Radio 2014). The light would flash red in the backstage management system if the price reporting complaint was not handled in due time (China National Radio 2014). In order to encourage the public to report illegal charging practices and provide important evidence, the NDRC would award RMB 10,000 to those who provided information leading to the prosecution of serious offences while raising the cash award from RMB 2,000 to RMB 5,000 for those who provided information leading to the prosecution of other offences (The Central People's Government of the People's Republic of China 2014). It was expected that the 12358 Price Reporting System could increase the transparency and efficiency of pricing authorities in handling price-related complaints.

In January 2016, the NDRC issued a report that analyzed cases of price-related complaints in the nation in 2015. The report showed that medicine ranked No.4 in terms of the number of price reports and complaints (The National Development and Reform Commission 2016). There were a total number of 7,252 cases of price reports and complaints against medicine, which amount to 6.93 per cent of the total number of price reports and complaints in 2015 (The National Development and Reform Commission 2016). Price reports and complaints against medicine included public hospitals setting their own standard charges and charging standards, drug fraud charges and price collusion (The National Development and Reform Commission 2016). It was expected that the 12358 Price Reporting System could be fully utilized in the nation, increase public awareness of fair and reasonable prices, and maintain an orderly market (The National Development and Reform Commission 2016).

Conclusion

To conclude, the Chinese government has made unremitting efforts to provide basic medical coverage for its population through the establishment of a multi-layered social health insurance system. It is moving toward UHC and is moving toward the right direction. To hold up the promise of providing accessible and affordable health care for all the Chinese people, the government should strengthen its anti-fraud capacity and improve health insurance management. Health insurance reform should be accompanied by reforms in the hospital system and strategies that can reduce drug prices or break the chain of interests in the drug distribution system. Health insurance reform is an ongoing process. With strong political will and long-term commitment, the Party leader and his government can definitely maintain a sustainable health insurance system and achieve UHC in the end.

Bibliography

ABC News (2015) 'World Health Organisation Says Cancer Rates in China Rising, Many Cases Can Be Prevented', *ABC News*, 4 February. Online. Available HTTP: http://www.abc.net.au/news/2015–02–04/cancer-rates-in-china-rising/6068954 (accessed 22 August 2015).

Alaszewski, A. and Brown, P. (2012) *Making Health Policy: A Critical Introduction*, Cambridge, UK: Polity.

Aldrich, H. E. (1979) *Organizations and Environments*, Englewood Cliffs, NJ: Prentice Hall.

Amenta, E. and Ramsey, K. M. (2010) 'Institutional Theory' in K. T. Leicht and J. C. Jenkins (eds.) *Handbook of Politics: State and Society in Global Perspective*, New York; London: Springer, pp. 15–39.

Anderson, I. (2012) *The Economic Costs of Non-Communicable Diseases in the Pacific Islands*. Online. Available HTTP: http://www.worldbank.org/content/dam/Worldbank/document/the-economic-costs-of-noncommunicable-diseases-in-the-pacific-islands.pdf (accessed 6 February 2016).

Anhui Ageing Commission Office (2008) *An Analysis of the Current Situation of Population Ageing*, Chinese Version. Online. Available HTTP: http://www.ahllb.cn/DocHtml/2/2008/8/8/11765725135.html (accessed 16 August 2015).

Anhui Commercial News (2015) 'A Patient with Uremia Is Sentenced to 10 Years in Prison for an Unlawful Gain of RMB 2 Million through Reselling Drugs', Chinese Version, *Anhui Commercial News*, 5 January. Online. Available HTTP: http://news.sina.com.cn/s/2015–01–05/164531362580.shtml (accessed 3 October 2015).

Arnold, J. and Wiener, R. (eds.) (2012) *Cold War: The Essential Reference Guide*, Santa Barbara, CA: ABC-CLIO.

Bangdiwala, S., Tucker, J., Zodpey, S., Griffiths, S., Li, L., Reddy, K., Cohen, M., Gross, M., Sharma, K. and Tang, J. (2011) Public Health Education in India and China: History, Opportunities, and Challenges, *Public Health Reviews*, 33 (1): 204–24.

Banister, J. (1987) *China's Changing Population*, Stanford, CA: Stanford University Press.

—— (1992) 'China's Changing Mortality' in D. Poston and D. Yaukey (eds.) *The Population of Modern China*, New York: Plenum Press, pp. 163–223.

Becker, J. (2000) *The Chinese*, London: John Murray.

Beijing Evening News (2015) 'Increasing the Speed of Aging: China Has the Largest Number of Elderly Population in the World', Chinese Version, *Beijing Evening*

News, 28 July. Online. Available HTTP: http://bhrb.beihai.gov.cn:8080/epaper/bhwb/html/2015/07/28/14/14_27.htm (accessed 7 August 2015).

The Beijing News (2013) 'A Group of People Purchased and Resold Drugs to Rural Clinics in Different Provinces', Chinese Version, *The Beijing News*, 17 October. Online. Available HTTP: http://www.bjnews.com.cn/news/2013/10/17/287845.html (accessed 3 October 2015).

Beijing Youth Daily (2013) '201 Citizens Were Temporarily Banned from Using Their Medical Insurance Certificates Due to Their Illegal Purchase and Resale of Drugs', Chinese Version, *Beijing Youth Daily*, 29 September. Online. Available HTTP: http://finance.chinanews.com/jk/2013/09–29/5334008.shtml (accessed 3 October 2015).

—— (2016) 'Peasants Find It Difficult to See the Doctors, "Black Clinics" Reappear Again', Chinese Version, *Beijing Youth Daily*. Online. Available HTTP: http://news.ubetween.com/2016/hotnews_0115/186959.html (accessed 5 February 2016).

Béland, D. and Wadden, A. (2012) *The Politics of Policy Change: Welfare, Medicare, and Social Security Reform in the United States*, Washington, DC: Georgetown University Press.

Berman, S. (2001) Ideas, Norms, and Culture in Political Analysis, *Comparative Politics*, 33 (2): 231–50.

Birn, A., Pillay, Y. and Holtz, T. (2009) *Textbook of International Health: Global Health in a Dynamic World*, 3rd edn, Oxford; New York: Oxford University Press.

Bloom, G. (2005) 'China' in R. Gauld (ed.) *Comparative Health Policy in the Asia-Pacific*, Maidenhead: Open University Press, pp. 23–47.

Brombal, D. (2014) 'Health Sector Reforms in Contemporary China: A Political Perspective' in K. E. Brodsgaard (ed.) *Globalization and Public Sector Reform in China*, Abingdon, Oxon: Routledge, pp. 100–24.

Bu, L. (2014) *Anti-Malaria Campaigns and the Socialist Reconstruction of China, 1950–80*. Online. Available HTTP: http://www.eastasianhistory.org/sites/default/files/article-content/39/pdfs/EAH39-BuLiping.pdf (accessed 25 August 2015).

Bu, Z. and Ji, J. (2013) A Current View of Gastric Cancer in China, *Translational Gastrointestinal Cancer*, 2 (S1): 1–4.

Cai, F., Giles, J., O'Keefe, P. and Wang, D. (2012) *The Elderly and Old Age Support in Rural China: Challenges and Prospects*. Online. Available HTTP: https://openknowledge.worldbank.org/handle/10986/2249 (accessed 12 August 2015).

Campbell, J. L. (1998) Institutional Analysis and the Role of Ideas in Political Economy, *Theory and Society*, 27 (3): 377–409.

—— (2002) Ideas, Politics, and Public Policy, *Annual Review of Sociology*, 28: 21–38.

Cao, P. (2006) The Rural Cooperative Medical System before Reform and the Opening-Up of China, Chinese Version, *Zhonggong Dangshi Ziliao*, 3: 134–44.

Centers for Medicare & Medicaid Services (2015a) *Laws Against Health Care Fraud Resource Guide*. Online. Available HTTP: https://www.cms.gov/Medicare-Medicaid-Coordination/Fraud-Prevention/Medicaid-Integrity-Education/Downloads/fwa-laws-resourceguide.pdf (accessed 1 February 2016).

—— (2015b) *The Health Care Fraud and Abuse Control Program Protects Consumers and Taxpayers by Combating Health Care Fraud*. Online. Available HTTP: https://www.cms.gov/Newsroom/MediaReleaseDatabase/Fact-sheets/2015-Fact-sheets-items/2015–03–19.html (accessed 1 February 2016).

The Central Committee of the Communist Party of China and the State Council (1997). *The Decision Concerning Health Reform and Development*, Chinese Version, Online. Available HTTP: http://www.law-lib.com/law/law_view.asp?id=64056 (accessed 17 February 2016).

────── (2002) *The Decision Concerning Further Strengthening Rural Health Work*, Chinese Version, Online. Available HTTP: http://www.people.com.cn/GB/shizheng/19/20021029/853905.html (accessed 17 February 2016).

────── (2009) *The Opinions on Deepening the Health Care System Reform*, Chinese Version, Online. Available HTTP: http://www.gov.cn/test/2009–04/08/content_1280069.htm (accessed 29 May 2015).

The Central People's Government of the People's Republic of China (2003) *Opinions on the Implementation of Rural Medical Financial Assistance*, Chinese Version, Online. Available HTTP: http://www.gov.cn/gongbao/content/2004/content_62870.htm (accessed 15 July 2015).

────── (2005) *Opinions on Establishing Pilot Urban Medical Financial Assistance System*, Chinese Version, Online. Available HTTP: http://www.gov.cn/gongbao/content/2005/content_63211.htm (accessed 15 July 2015).

────── (2010) *Social Insurance Law of the People's Republic of China*, Chinese Version. Online. Available HTTP: http://www.gov.cn/zxft/ft209/content_1748773.htm (accessed 29 December 2015).

────── (2014) *Reporting Unlawful Price Conducts Has Entered into the Information Era*, Chinese Version, Online. Available HTTP: http://www.gov.cn/jrzg/2014–02/19/content_2615054.htm (accessed 3 June 2015).

Chan, G., Lee, P. K. and Chan, L. (2012) *China Engages Global Governance: A New World Order in the Making?* Abingdon, Oxon; New York: Routledge.

Chan, K. W. and Zhang, L. (1999) The Hukou System and Rural-Urban Migration in China: Processes and Changes, *The China Quarterly*, 160: 818–55.

Chen, C. and Bunge, F. (1989) *Medicine in Rural China: A Personal Account*, Berkeley: University of California Press.

Chen, J. (1994) *China's Road to the Korean War: The Making of the Sino-American Confrontation*, New York: Columbia University Press.

Chen, K. and Chan, A. (2011) The Ageing Population of China and A Review of Gerontechnology, *Gerontechnology*, 10 (2): 63–71.

Chen, M. (2001) 'The Great Reversal: Transformation of Health Care in the People's Republic of China' in W. C. Cockerham (ed.) *The Blackwell Companion to Medical Sociology*, Malden, MA: Blackwell, pp. 456–82.

Chen, W., Zheng, R., Baade, P. D., Zhang, S., Zeng, H., Bray, F., Jemal, A., Yu, X. Q. and He, J. (2016). Cancer Statistics in China, 2015, *CA: A Cancer Journal for Clinicians* (Early view): 1–18. Online. Available HTTP: http://onlinelibrary.wiley.com/doi/10.3322/caac.21338/pdf (accessed 14 February 2016).

Chen, W., Zheng, R., Zeng, H., Zhang, S. and He, J. (2015) Annual Report on Status of Cancer in China, 2011, *Chinese Journal of Cancer Research*, 27 (1): 2–12.

Chen, W., Zheng, R., Zhang, S., Zhao, P., Li, G., Wu, L. and He, J. (2013) Report of Incidence and Mortality in China Cancer Registries, 2009, *Chinese Journal of Cancer Research*, 25 (1): 10–21.

Chen, X. J. and Li, F. F. (2012) The Thoughts about Establishing a United Health Insurance System in Urban and Rural China, Chinese Version, *Agricultural Economy*, 10: 95–7.

Chen, X. J., Wang, Z. and Chen, J. Y. (2012) Investigation of the Fund Operation and the Cost of Hospitalization of New Rural Cooperative Medical Scheme of a City in Jiangsu Province, 2008–2010, Chinese Version. *Acta Universitatis Medicinalis Nanjing (Social Sciences)*, 2: 102–6.

Chen, Z. (2015) 'The Bid-Winning Price Was 48.5% Higher Than the Market Price', Chinese Version, *Zhejiang News Site*, 10 April. Online. Available HTTP: http://news.zj.com/detail/2015/04/10/1573296.html (accessed 17 June 2015).

Cheng, C. (1991) A Speculative Analysis of Socio-economic Influences on the Fertility Transition in China, *Asia-Pacific Population Journal*, 6 (3): 3–79.

Cheng, F. (2009) 'The Nutrition Transition and Obesity in China' in P. Pinstrup-Andersen and F. Cheng (eds.) *Case Studies in Food Policy for Developing Countries, Volume 1: Policies for Health, Nutrition, Food Consumption, and Poverty*, Ithaca, NY: Cornell University Press, pp. 103–15.

Cheung, A. and Gu, X. (2004) 'Health Finance' in L. Wong, L. White and S. Gui (eds.) *Social Policy Reform in Hong Kong and Shanghai: A Tale of Two Cities*, Armonk, NY: M.E. Sharpe, pp. 23–52.

China Development Research Foundation (2013) *China's New Urbanization Strategy*, New York: Routledge.

China Economic Herald (2012) *China's Total Fertility Rate Was Only 1.18 in 2010*, Chinese Version, 10 July. Online. Available HTTP: http://www.ceh.com.cn/ceh/jryw/2012/7/10/121921.shtml (accessed 14 August 2015).

China Economic Net (2011) *If Drug Prices Have to Be Cut Again, the Phenomenon of Price-Cut Drugs Disappearing from the Market Must Be Prevented*, Chinese Version. Online. Available HTTP: http://news.cntv.cn/20110807/102966.shtml (accessed 5 February 2016).

China Food and Drug Administration (2001) *Drug Administration Law of the People's Republic of China*, Chinese Version. Online. Available HTTP: http://www.sda.gov.cn/WS01/CL0064/23396.html (accessed 5 February 2016).

The China Health Care Study Group (1974) *Health Care in China, an Introduction: The Report of a Study Group in Hong Kong*, Geneva: Christian Medical Commission.

China Health Study Group (1974) *Health Care in China: An Introduction*, Geneva: Christian Medical Commission.

China Labour Bulletin (2015) *Wages and Employment*, Online. Available HTTP: http://www.clb.org.hk/en/content/wages-china (accessed 5 February 2016).

China National Radio (2014) *The Pilot 12358 Price Reporting System Will Be Operated on January 1 Next Year*, Chinese Version, 3 December. Online. Available HTTP: http://china.cnr.cn/news/201412/t20141203_516957588.shtml (accessed 2 June 2015).

China National Working Commission on Ageing (2011) *China's Aging Statistics Compendium, 1953–2009*, Chinese Version, Beijing: Hua Ling Press.

China News of Medicine (2015) 'Correct Poor Dietary Habit in Order to Stay Away from Colorectal Cancer', Chinese Version, *China News of Medicine*, 27 March. Online. Available HTTP: http://www.cnpharm.cn/kepu/kxyy/yszd/2015/0327/89467.html (accessed 22 August 2015).

Chinanews.com (2015) *The Health Reform Office of the State Council: Perfecting the Centralized Drug Procurement System Is Conducive to Eradicate the Practice of Feeding Hospitals by Selling Drugs*, Chinese Version, 28 February. Online. Available HTTP: http://www.chinanews.com/gn/2015/02-28/7088562.shtml (accessed 13 June 2015).

Chinese Academy of Social Sciences, Indian National Science Academy, Indonesian Academy of Sciences, National Research Council of the U.S. National Academies and Science Council of Japan (2011) *Preparing for the Challenges of Population Aging in Asia: Strengthening the Scientific Basis of Policy Development.* Online. Available HTTP: http://www.ncbi.nlm.nih.gov/books/NBK53399/pdf/Book shelf_NBK53399.pdf (accessed 6 February 2016).

Chou, Y. L., Zhang, J. Y., Xu, C., Xu, X. L. and Huang, H. Y. (2009) The Study on Satisfaction Level of the Basic Medical Insurance for Urban Residents in Tiantai County, Chinese Version, *Chinese Journal of Health Policy*, 2 (2): 11–17.

Chow, G. (2004) Economic Reform and Growth in China, *Annals of Economics and Finance*, 5: 127–52.

Cohen, M., Henderson, G., Aiello, P. and Zheng, H. (1996) Successful Eradication of Sexually Transmitted Diseases in the People's Republic of China: Implications for the 21st Century, *The Journal of Infectious Diseases*, 174 (Suppl 2): S223–29.

Cortell, A. P. and Peterson, S. (1999) Altered States: Explaining Domestic Institutional Change, *British Journal of Political Science*, 29 (1): 177–203.

Daemmrich, A. (2013) The Political Economy of Healthcare Reform in China: Negotiating Public and Private, *SpringerPlus*, 2: 448.

Department of Comprehensive Statistics of National Bureau of Statistics (2005) *China Compendium of Statistics 1949–2004*, Beijing: China Statistics Press.

Department of Financial Services (2016) *More About the Insurance Frauds Bureau.* Online. Available HTTP: http://www.dfs.ny.gov/insurance/frauds/fd1abouc. htm (accessed 1 February 2016).

Diao, H. H. (2014) Some Thoughts about Monitoring Health Insurance Fund, Chinese version, *Manager's Journal*, 7: 60.

Dong, W. (2003) Healthcare-Financing Reforms in Transitional Society: A Shanghai Experience, *Journal of Health Population and Nutrition*, 21 (3): 223–34.

Dongguan Social Security Department (2014) *The Management of Designated Medical Institutions of Social Medical Insurance*, Chinese Version. Online. Available HTTP: http://dgsi.dg.gov.cn (accessed 5 February 2016).

Du, L. and Zhang, W. (eds.) (2007) *The Development Report on China's Health No.3*, Chinese version, Beijing: Social Sciences Academic Press (China).

Du, S., Lu, B., Zhai, F. and Popkin, B. (2007a) 'A New Stage of the Nutrition Transition in China' in F. Di (ed.) *Essay Collections for China Health and Nutrition Survey*, Beijing: China Science Publishing & Media Ltd., pp. 431–7.

Du, S., Mroz, T., Zhai, F. and Popkin, B. (2007b) 'Rapid Income Growth Adversely Affects Diet Quality in China Particularly for the Poor' in F. Di (ed.) *Essay Collections for China Health and Nutrition Survey*, Beijing: China Science Publishing & Media Ltd., pp. 263–74.

Du, Y. J., Yang, T. Y., Chen, P., Jiang, M. and Li, H. W. (2009) Analysis on the Financial Burden of Peasants Who Joined the New Rural Cooperative Medical System in Yunnan Province During the Period of 2004 and 2008, Chinese Version, *Chinese Health Service Management*, 10: 695–7.

Duckett, J. (2011) *The Chinese State's Retreat from Health: Policy and the Politics of Retrenchment*, Abingdon, Oxon; New York: Routledge.

Ebrahim, S., Pearce, N., Smeeth, L., Casas, J. P., Jaffar, S. and Piot, P. (2013) Tackling Non-Communicable Diseases in Low- and Middle-Income Countries: Is the Evidence from High Income Countries All We Need? *PLOS Medicine*, 10 (1): e1001377.

Economic Information Daily (2014) 'Ministry of Human Resources and Social Security Said That the Problem of Expenditures Exceeding Revenues in the Basic Medical Insurance Fund Was Found in Many Provinces', Chinese Version, *Economic Information Daily*, 27 January. Online. Available HTTP: http://www.js.xinhuanet.com/2014–01/27/c_119147179.htm (accessed 22 September 2015).

—— (2015a) 'The Ratio of Retiree in the Basic Medical Insurance for Urban Employees Continues to Increase: Expert Suggests Extending the Retirement Age', Chinese Version, *Economic Information Daily*, 21 July. Online. Available HTTP: http://news.xinhuanet.com/finance/2015–07/21/c_128040159.htm (accessed 22 September 2015).

—— (2015b) 'The Rate of Expenditure Growth of the Basic Medical Insurance Fund Is Higher Than the Rate of Revenue Growth: A Funding Gap Will Occur in Year 2020', Chinese Version, *Economic Information Daily*, 5 June. Online. Available HTTP: http://news.xinhuanet.com/politics/2015–06/05/c_127880367.htm (accessed 22 September 2015).

Eggleston, K. and Yip, W. (2004) Hospital Competition under Regulated Prices: Application to Urban Health Sector Reforms in China, *International Journal of Health Care Finance and Economics*, 4: 343–68.

Fan, J., Wang, J., Jiang, Y., Xiang, W., Liang, H., Wei, W., Qiao, Y. and Boffetta, P. (2013) Attributable Causes of Liver Cancer Mortality and Incidence in China, *Asian Pacific Journal of Cancer Prevention*, 14: 7251–6.

Fan, L. M., Jie, E. and Yin, L. (2009) Analysis on Peasants' Satisfaction with the New Rural Cooperative Medical System: Using the Survey on 245 Rural Households in Three Provinces, Chinese Version. *Journal of Shandong University (Philosophy and Social Sciences)*, 1: 52–7.

Fierlbeck, K. (2011) *Health Care in Canada: A Citizen's Guide to Policy and Politics*, Toronto: University of Toronto Press.

Fischer, J. (2012) 'Health: A Development Perspective' in J. Spear and P. D. Williams (eds.) *Security and Development in Global Politics: A Critical Comparison*, Washington, DC: Georgetown University Press, pp. 171–88.

Fu, Y. T. (2014) *How Can the Practice of Invalid Inpatient Stays (gua chuang zhu yuan) Be Used to Commit Health Insurance Fraud of RMB 20 Million?*, Chinese Version. Online. Available HTTP: http://www.banyuetan.org/chcontent/jrt/2014113/116169.html (accessed 23 September 2015).

Galperin, H. (2004) Beyond Interests, Ideas, and Technology: An Institutional Approach to Communication and Information Policy, *The Information Society*, 20 (3): 159–68.

Gelman, H. (1980) 'Outlook for Sino-Soviet Relations' in E. P. Hoffmann and F. J. Fleron, Jr. (eds.) *The Conduct of Soviet Foreign Policy*, 2nd edn, New York: Aldine Pub. Co., pp. 608–32.

General Office of the State Council (2012) *The Opinions on Comprehensive Pilot Reform in Public Hospitals at the County Level*, Chinese Version. Online. Available HTTP: http://www.gov.cn/gongbao/content/2012/content_2169155.htm (accessed 5 February 2016).

—— (2015a) *Opinions on the Full Implementation of Critical Illness Insurance for Urban and Rural Residents*, Chinese Version. Online. Available HTTP: http://www.gov.cn/zhengce/content/2015–08/02/content_10041.htm (accessed 5 February 2016).

—— (2015b) *Opinion on the Full Implementation of the Comprehensive Reform in Public Hospitals at the County Level,* Chinese Version. Online. Available HTTP: http://www.gov.cn/zhengce/content/2015–05/08/content_9710.htm (accessed 5 February 2016).

Government Administration Council (1951) *Regulations Regarding Labour Insurance in the People's Republic of China,* Chinese Version. Online. Available HTTP: http://www.law-lib.com/law/law_view.asp?id=686 (accessed 22 December 2015).

—— (1952) *The Directive Regarding the Precaution to Implement the Government Insurance Scheme for Personnel of the People's Governments, Parties, Organizations and Institutions at Various Levels in the Nation,* Chinese Version. Online. Available HTTP: http://www.china.com.cn/guoqing/2012–09/05/content_26746358.htm (accessed 24 December 2015).

Gu, H. (2002) 'China Pacific Insurance (Group) Co., Ltd Implements Commercial Health Insurance in Jiangyin', Chinese Version, *Xinhua News,* 16 September. Online. Available HTTP: http://finance.sina.com.cn/roll/20020916/1425255297.html (accessed 10 October 2014).

Guang Ming Ri Bao (2015) 'Three Questions about Lifting Official Price Caps on Drugs', Chinese Version, *Guang Ming Ri Bao,* 7 May. Online. Available HTTP: http://news.gmw.cn/2015–05/07/content_15586031.htm (accessed 2 June 2015).

Guo, J. P. (2014) *Why Does Health Insurance Fund Report A Surplus of RMB 764.4 Billion?* Chinese Version. Online. Available HTTP: http://finance.eastmoney.com/news/1365,20140410375502071.html (accessed 21 September 2015).

Guo, S. (2013) *Chinese Politics and Government: Power, Ideology, and Organization,* Abingdon, Oxon; New York: Routledge.

Guo, S. S. and Han, J. J. (2012) Examining and Analyzing the Solutions to the Existing Problems of the Basic Medical Insurance for Urban Employees in China, Chinese Version, *Labor Security World,* 7: 16–8.

Gu, X. (2000) 'State Corporatism and Civil Society' in G. Wang and Y. Zheng (eds.) *Reform, Legitimacy and Dilemmas: China's Politics and Society,* Singapore: Singapore University Press; Singapore; Hong Kong: World Scientific, pp. 71–102.

—— (2001) Market Transition and the Transformation of the Health Care System in Urban China, *Policy Studies,* 22 (3/4): 197–215.

Hall, P. A. and Taylor, R. C. R. (1996) Political Science and the Three New Institutionalisms, *Political Studies,* 44 (5): 936–57.

Hanson, M. (2008) The Art of Medicine: Maoist Public-Health Campaigns, Chinese Medicine, and SARS, *The Lancet,* 372 (9648): 1457–8.

Health Bureau of Huining County (2011) *Trial Implementation of Methods of Assessing Designated Medical Institutions of New Rural Cooperative Medical System,* Chinese Version. Online. Available HTTP: http://www.doc88.com/p-911954557945.html (accessed 5 February 2016).

Health Care Reform Office of the State Council (2014) *The Notification of Accelerating the Implementation of the Critical Illness Insurance Scheme for Urban and Rural Residents,* Chinese Version. Online. Available HTTP: http://www.nhfpc.gov.cn/tigs/s7846/201402/3e605fe2f3e64c46be3e516fc1fb8f62.shtml (accessed 17 February 2016).

Henderson, G. (1989) 'Issues in the Modernization of Medicine in China' in D. F. Simon and M. Goldman (eds.) *Science and Technology in Post-Mao China,* Cambridge, MA: Council on East Asian Studies, Harvard University, pp. 199–222.

Higo, M. and Williamson, J. B. (2011) 'Global Aging' in R. A. Settersten, Jr. and J. L. Angel (eds.) *Handbook of Sociology of Aging*, New York: Springer, pp. 117–30.

Hillier, S. M. (1983) 'The Cultural Revolution and After: Health Care, 1965–82' in S. M. Hillier and J. A. Jewell (eds.) *Health Care and Traditional Medicine in China, 1800–1982*, London: Routledge & K. Paul, pp. 103–46.

Hillier, S. M. and Zheng, X. (1994) 'Rural Health Care in China: Past, Present and Future' in D. Dwyer (ed.) *China: The Next Decades*, Essex: Longman Scientific & Technical Harlow, pp. 95–115.

Hipgrave, D. (2011) Communicable Disease Control in China: From Mao to Now, *Journal of Global Health*, 1 (2): 224–38.

Ho, C. S. (2011) 'China's Healthcare Reform: Background and Policies' in C. W. Freeman III and X. Lu (eds.) *Implementing Health Care Reform Policies in China: Challenges and Opportunities*. Online. Available HTTP: http://csis.org/files/publication/111202_Freeman_ImplementingChinaHealthReform_Web.pdf (accessed 17 February 2016).

Hong, F. and Lu, Z. (2013) *The Politicisation of Sport in Modern China: Communists and Champions*, Oxen: Routledge.

Hsü, I. C. Y. (2000) *The Rise of Modern China*, 6th edn, New York: Oxford University Press.

Hsu, J. C. (1989) 'The Role of Foreign Trade in China's Economic Reforms, 1978–85' in Y. C. Jao, V. Mok and L. Ho (eds.) *Economic Development in Chinese Societies : Models and Experiences*, Hong Kong: Hong Kong University Press, pp. 129–42.

Hu, J. (2007) *Report to the Seventeenth National Congress of the Communist Party of China*. Online. Available HTTP: http://www.china.org.cn/english/congress/229611.htm (accessed 17 February 2016).

—— (2012) *Full Texts of Hu Jintao's Report at the 18th Party Congress*. Online. Available HTTP: http://english.cntv.cn/20121118/100129.shtml (accessed 17 February 2016).

Hu, Y. (2013) *Rural Health Care Delivery: Modern China from the Perspective of Disease Politics*, Berlin, Heidelberg: Springer.

Huang, Y. (2013) *Governing Health in Contemporary China*, Milton Park, Abingdon, Oxon; New York: Routledge.

Human Resources and Social Security Bureau of Yunnan Province (2009) *Notification of the Minimum Years of Premium Payment for Basic Medical Insurance for Urban Employees*, Chinese Version, Online. Available HTTP: http://yn.cnpension.net/sbylj/2009–07–15/924563.html (accessed 21 September 2015).

Immergut, E. M. (1998) The Theoretical Core of the New Institutionalism, *Politics & Society*, 26 (1): 5–34.

Inspur (2014) *Tiansuo K1 System Won the Bid for 12358 System: Sharing of Price Information Nationwide*. Online. Available HTTP: http://www.inspur.com/inspur/495255/494903/2069113/index.html (accessed 3 June 2015).

International Institute of Social History (2008) *Chinese Propaganda Posters*. Online. Available HTTP: http://www.iisg.nl/publications/chineseposters.pdf (accessed 25 August 2015).

Islam, S. M. S., Purnat, T. D., Phuong, N. T. A., Mwingira, U., Schacht, K. and Fröschl, G. (2014) Non-Communicable Diseases (NCDs) in Developing Countries: A Symposium Report, *Globalization and Health*, 10: 81.

Jiang, D. and Guo, Y. H. (2014) ' "*Gua chuang zhu yuan*": The New Method of Health Insurance Fraud', Chinese Version, *Procuratorial Daily*, 18 September. Online. Available HTTP: http://newspaper.jcrb.com/html/2014-09/18/content_168658. htm (accessed 22 September 2015).

Jiang, R. (2010) 'The Government Buys Insurance Service: Upgrading the Basic Medical Insurance for Urban and Rural Residents in Zhanjiang', Chinese Version, *Xinhua News*, 27 April. Online. Available HTTP: http://news.xinhuanet.com/fortune/2010-04/27/c_1259391.htm (accessed 10 October 2014).

Jiang, R. R., Bai, L. P. and Liang, P. P. (2012) The Survey Analysis on the Individual Medical Savings Account of the Basic Medical Insurance for Urban Employees in Guangdong City, Chinese Version, *Chinese Health Service Management*, 9: 672–4.

Jianghuai Moring Post (2014) 'Two Men Was Sentenced to Prison Due to Reselling Drugs Near Hospitals', Chinese Version, *Jianghuai Moring Post*, 8 July. Online. Available HTTP: http://news.hf365.com/system/2014/07/08/014081007. shtml (accessed 3 October 2015).

Jin, H. (2014) *China National Working Commission on Ageing: About 90 Per Cent of the Elderly Population Relied on Pensions as Their Main Source of Income*. Online. Available HTTP: http://jjckb.xinhuanet.com/2014-03/01/content_493748. htm (accessed 6 February 2016).

Jin, L. Q., Wang, J. K., Hu, F. and Li, Y. C. (2012) Survey Analysis on Peasants' Satisfaction with the New Rural Cooperative Medical System in Ouhai District, Wenzhou City, Chinese Version, *Chinese Journal of Disease Control & Prevention*, 16 (1): 57–9.

Jinan Times (2015) Essential Medicine in Jinan Disappeared from the Market After Becoming Price-Cut Drug, Chinese Version, *Jinan Times*, 18 October. Online. Available HTTP: http://help.3g.163.com/0402/15/1018/08/ B66QL5E70402008V.html# (accessed 5 February 2016).

Johnston, L. (2012) *Getting Old After Getting Rich: Comparing China with Japan*. Online. Available HTTP: http://www.eastasiaforum.org/2012/12/22/getting-old-after-getting-rich-comparing-china-with-japan/ (accessed 12 August 2015).

Joudaki, H., Rashidian, A., Minaei-Bidgoli, B., Mahmoodi, M., Geraili, B., Nasiri, M. and Arab, M. (2015a) Using Data Mining to Detect Health Care Fraud and Abuse: A Review of Literature, *Global Journal of Health Science*, 7 (1): 194–202.

——— (2015b) Improving Fraud and Abuse Detection in General Physician Claims: A Data Mining Study, *International Journal of Health Policy and Management*, 4 (x): 1–8.

Kirlidog, M. and Asuk, C. (2012) A Fraud Detection Approach with Data Mining in Health Insurance, *Procedia – Social and Behavioral Sciences*, 62: 989–94.

Krasner, S. D. (1984) Approaches to the State: Alternative Conceptions and Historical Dynamics, *Comparative Politics*, 16 (2): 223–46.

Kraus, W. (1982) *Economic Development and Social Change in the People's Republic of China*, New York: Springer-Verlag.

Lampton, D. M. (1974) *Health, Conflict and the Chinese Political System*, Ann Arbor: Center for Chinese Studies, University of Michigan.

——— (1977) *The Politics of Medicine in China: the Policy Process, 1949–1977*, Boulder, CO: Westview Press.

Larus, E. F. (2012) *Politics and Society in Contemporary China*, Boulder, CO: Lynne Rienner Publishers.

Lee, A. (2015) *Population Aging in the Asia-Pacific Region*. Online. Available HTTP: https://oia.stanford.edu/news/population-aging-asia-pacific-region (accessed 17 February 2016).

Lee, L. (2004) The Current State of Public Health in China, *Annual Review of Public Health*, 25: 327–39.

Li, F. (2014) 'The Practice of Invalid Inpatient Stays Has Become an Open Secret: Two Hospitals in Wangcheng District Are Heavily Penalized for Health Insurance Fraud', Chinese Version, *Xinhua News*, 29 April. Online. Available HTTP: http://www. hn.xinhuanet.com/2014–04/29/c_1110469032.htm (accessed 23 September 2015).

Li, H. (2012) 'The Pilot Critical Illness Insurance Scheme Prevents Citizens from Falling into Poverty', Chinese Version, *People's Daily*, 2 September. Online. Available HTTP: http://politics.people.com.cn/n/2012/0902/c1026–18895548. html (accessed 10 October 2014).

Li, J. (1991) *Taxation in the People's Republic of China*, New York: Praeger.

—— (2014) 'China the Hardest Hit by Global Surge in Cancer, Says WHO Report', *South China Morning Post*, 7 February. Online. Available HTTP: http://www.scmp.com/news/china/article/1422475/china-hardest-hit-global-surge-cancer-says-who-report (accessed 16 February 2016).

Li, J., Tian, G. and Zhou, D. (2015) Analysis on Drug Income and Expenditure of Nine County-Level Public Hospitals in Anhui Province Before and After the Reform, *Chinese Health Economics*, 34 (1): 73–5.

Li, M. and Gu, J. (2005) Changing Patterns of Colorectal Cancer in China over a Period of 20 Years, *World Journal of Gastroenterology*, 11 (30): 4685–4688.

Li, Q. (2009) *The Study on Realizing the Path to Universal Health Insurance in China*, Chines Version, Beijing: People's Publishing House.

Li, R. F., Hu, L. J. and Gao, Li. M. (2012) Study on the Sustainable Development of New Rural Cooperative Medical System from the Perspective of Peasants: Using the Rural Household Survey in 10 Counties of 7 Provinces in Central and Western China, Chinese Version, *Chinese Journal of Health Policy*, 5 (7): 45–51.

Li, T. N. (2013) 'Low Usage Rate of Individual Medical Savings Account (MSA), Experts Said that the Cancellation of MSA Will Become the Trend', *Economic Information Daily*, 12 July. Online. Available HTTP: http://finance.people.com. cn/n/2013/0712/c1004–22173277.html (accessed 5 February 2016).

—— (2014) 'Medical Insurance Fund Has Surplus of 900 Billion', Chinese Version, *Economic Information*, 28 April. Online. Available HTTP: http://jjckb. xinhuanet.com/2014–04/28/content_502253.htm (accessed 5 February 2016).

Li, Y. Y. and Shi, H. J. (2014) 'Handling the Practice of Invalid Inpatient Stays: Regulate the Working Order of Hospitals', Chinese Version, *People's Court Daily*, 11 September. Online. Available HTTP: http://rmfyb.chinacourt.org/paper/ html/2014–09/11/content_87355.htm?div=-1 (accessed 23 September 2015).

Liang, P. F., Ma, J. and Guo, Z. Q. (2012) Factor Analysis on the Impacts and Current Status of Basic Medical Insurance for Urban Residents in Yinchuan City, Chinese Version, *Chinese Journal of Health Statistics*, 29 (2): 199–201.

Lin, Y., Ueda, J., Kikuchi, S., Totsuka, Y., Wei, W., Qiao, Y. and Inoue, M. (2011) Comparative Epidemiology of Gastric Cancer between Japan and China, *World Journal of Gastroenterology*, 17 (39): 4421–4428.

Liu, B. (2015) *The Working-Age Population Has Decreased for Three Consecutive Years in China and Demographic Dividend Is Declining*, Chinese Version. Online.

Available HTTP: http://news.qq.com/a/20150122/001709.htm (accessed 12 August 2015).

Liu, D. (2013) *China's New Rural Cooperative Medical Scheme: Evolution, Design and Impacts*, Frankfurt am Main: PL Academic Research.

Liu, G., Yuen, P., Hu, T., Li, L. and Liu, X. (2004) 'Urban Health Insurance Reform: What Can We Learn from the Pilot Experiments?' in A. Chen, G. G. Liu and K. H. Zhang (eds.) *Urbanization and Social Welfare in China*, Aldershot, Hants; England; Burlington, VT: Ashgate, pp. 38–62.

Liu, H. Q. (2013) *Government-Funded Health Care Scheme: The Memory That Is Fading Away*, Chinese Version. Online. Available HTTP: http://news.ifeng. com/history/zhongguoxiandaishi/special/maozedongshidaiyiliao/detail_2013_ 11/20/31420417_1.shtml (accessed 26 December 2015).

Liu, J. (2014) Ageing, Migration and Familial Support in Rural China, *Geoforum*, 51: 305–12.

Liu, M. and Tao, R. (2007) 'Local Governance, Policy Mandates and Fiscal Reform in China' in V. Shue and C. Wong (eds.) *Paying for Progress in China: Public Finance, Human Welfare and Changing Patterns of Inequality*, London; New York: Routledge, pp. 166–89.

Liu, Q. and Vasarhelyi, M. (2013) *Healthcare Fraud Detection: A Survey and a Clustering Model Incorporating Geo-Location Information*. Online. Available HTTP: http://raw.rutgers.edu/ (accessed 5 February 2015).

Liu, S. (1997) Some Thoughts about Population Ageing in Different Regions of China, Chinese Version, *Population Journal*, 3: 33–40.

Liu, X. (2015) 'China Home to 25% of Cancer Deaths: WHO', *Global Times*, 4 February. Online. Available HTTP: http://www.globaltimes.cn/content/905992. shtml (accessed 22 August 2015).

Liu, X., Liu, Y. and Chen, N. (2000) The Chinese Experience of Hospital Price Regulation, *Health Policy and Planning*, 15 (2): 157–63.

Liu, X. and Mills, A. (2005) *The Effect of Performance-Related Pay of Hospital Doctors on Hospital Behaviour: A Case Study From Shandong, China*. Online. Available HTTP: http://www.human-resources-health.com/content/3/1/11 (accessed 4 October 2015).

Liu, Y. (2009) 'The Anatomy of China's Public Health System' in X. Lu (ed.) *China's Capacity to Manage Infectious Diseases: Global Implications*. Online. Available HTTP: http://csis.org/files/media/csis/pubs/090325_freeman_chinacapacity_ web.pdf (accessed 25 August 2015).

——— (2010) The National Immunization Plan: China, *Australasian Medical Journal*, 3 (7): 375–79.

Liu, Z. (2014) 'Cancer Rates on the Rise', *China Daily USA*, 9 April. Online. Available HTTP: http://usa.chinadaily.com.cn/epaper/2014–04/09/content_17419605. htm (accessed 16 February 2016).

Lo, C. (2015) *HIV/AIDS in China and India: Governing Health Security*, New York: Palgrave Macmillan.

Loh, C. and Yip, Y. Y. (2004) 'SARS and China: Old vs New Politics' in C. Loh and Civic Exchange (eds.) *At the Epicentre: Hong Kong and the SARS Outbreak*, Hong Kong: Hong Kong University Press, pp. 163–78.

Luk, S. (2014) *Health Insurance Reforms in Asia*, Abingdon, Oxon; New York, NY: Routledge.

—— (2015) The Politics of Drug Price Control Policy in China: Regulation, Deregulation and Re-Regulation, *The Journal of Contemporary China Studies*, 4 (1): 41–54.

Luo, J. and Guo, W. (2014) The Problems of and Solutions to Health Insurance Fund in China, Chinese Version, *Journal of Social Science of Hunan Normal University*, 4: 84–88.

Luo, R. (2012) Across the Institutional Passage of Migration: The Hukou System in China, *InterDisciplines*, 1: 120–47.

Ma, S. and Sood, N. (2008) *A Comparison of the Health Systems in China and India*. Online. Available HTTP: http://www.rand.org/content/dam/rand/pubs/occasional_papers/2008/RAND_OP212.pdf (accessed 30 November 2015).

Maimon, O. and Rokach, L. (2010) 'Introduction to Knowledge Discovery and Data Mining' in O. Maimon and L. Rokach (eds.) *Data Mining and Knowledge Discovery Handbook*, 2nd edn, Boston, MA : Springer Science+Business Media, LLC, pp. 1–15.

Marsh, C. (2005) *Unparalleled Reforms: China's Rise, Russia's Fall, and the Interdependence of Transition*, Lanham, MD: Lexington Books.

Meng, X. (2014) The Analysis on Basic Medical Insurance for Urban Residents: Using City A in Guangdong Province as an Example, Chinese Version, *South China Finance*, 8: 86–7.

Ministry of Civil Affairs (2009) *Opinions on Further Improving Urban and Rural Medical Financial Assistance Systems*, Chinese Version, Online. Available HTTP: http://www.mca.gov.cn/article/zwgk/fvfg/zdshbz/200906/20090600031974.shtml (accessed 19 July 2015).

—— (2012) *Opinions on Implementing Pilot Medical Financial Assistance System for Catastrophic Illnesses*, Chinese Version, Online. Available HTTP: http://dbs.mca.gov.cn/article/csyljz/zcfg/201203/20120300283129.shtml (accessed 19 July 2015).

—— (2015) *Opinions on Further Improving Medical Financial Assistance System and Implementing Medical Financial Assistance System for Catastrophic Illnesses in Full Swing*, Chinese Version, Online. Available HTTP: http://www.mca.gov.cn/article/zwgk/fvfg/zdshbz/201504/20150400809653.shtml (accessed 19 July 2015).

Ministry of Health (1985) *Report Concerning a Number of Policy Issues Connected with the Health Service Reforms*, Chinese Version, Online. Available HTTP: http://www.china.com.cn/law/flfg/txt/2006–08/08/content_7060220.htm (accessed 17 February 2016).

—— (2004) *Conference on the Pilot Work of the New Rural Cooperative Medical System in 2004 Was Held in Beijing*, Chinese Version, Online. Available HTTP: http://www.moh.gov.cn/wsb/pM30109/200804/18576.shtml (accessed 29 May 2015).

—— (2008) *Statistical Bulletin of China's Health Development in 2007*, Chinese Version, Online. Available HTTP: http://www.moh.gov.cn/mohbgt/s6689/200804/33525.shtml (accessed 29 May 2015).

—— (2010) *Advancing the Rural Health Work and Actively Implementing Payment Reform*, Chinese Version, Online. Available HTTP: http://www.moh.gov.cn/jws/s6477/201002/71ea088d2abf48038f999c87c06f01a5.shtml (accessed 29 May 2015).

—— (2012a) *China Health Statistics Yearbook 2012*, Beijing: China Union Medical College Publishing.

—— (2012b) *The Work Progress of the New Rural Cooperative Medical System in 2011 and Key Points of the New Rural Cooperative Medical System in 2012*, Chinese Version, Online. Available HTTP: http://www.moh.gov.cn/mohbgt/s3582/201202/54209.shtml (accessed 29 May 2015).

—— (2014) *Statistical Bulletin of China's Health Development and Family Planning in 2013*, Chinese Version, Online. Available HTTP: http://www.moh.gov.cn/guihuaxxs/s10742/201405/886f82dafa344c3097f1d16581a1bea2.shtml (accessed 29 May 2015).

Ministry of Health, Ministry of Finance, and Ministry of Agriculture (2013) *Opinions on Establishing the New Rural Cooperative Medical System*, Chinese Version, Online. Available HTTP: http://www.law-lib.com/law/law_view.asp?id=43058 (accessed 17 February 2016).

Ministry of Health, State Planning Commission, State Economic and Trade Commission, the China Food and Drug Administration, State Administration of Traditional Chinese Medicine, and State Council's Office for Correcting Industrial Illegitimate Practice (2001) *Notice on Regulating the Task of the Centralized Drug Procurement System for Medical Institutions*, Chinese Version. Online. Available HTTP: http://www.gov.cn/gongbao/content/2002/content_61499.htm (accessed 5 February 2016).

Ministry of Human Resources and Social Security (2010) *Notice on Accomplishing the Task of the Basic Medical Insurance for Urban Residents in 2010*, Chinese Version, Online. Available HTTP: http://www.law-lib.com/law/law_view.asp?id=317105 (accessed 21 July 2015).

—— (2011) *Notice on Accomplishing the Task of the Basic Medical Insurance for Urban Residents in 2011*, Chinese Version, Online. Available HTTP: http://www.hyl2333.gov.cn/News_1957.html (accessed 21 July 2015).

—— (2013) *Statistical Communiqué on Human Resources and Social Security Development in 2012*, Chinese Version, Online. Available HTTP: http://education.news.cn/2013–05/28/c_124776442.htm (accessed 3 October 2015).

—— (2014) *Statistical Communiqué on Human Resources and Social Security Development in 2013*, Chinese Version, Online. Available HTTP: http://www.chinanews.com/gn/2014/05–28/6223421.shtml (accessed 3 October 2015).

—— (2015) *Statistical Communiqué on Human Resources and Social Security Development in 2014*, Chinese Version, Online. Available HTTP: http://www.mohrss.gov.cn/SYrlzyhshbzb/dongtaixinwen/buneiyaowen/201505/t20150528_162040.htm (accessed 3 October 2015).

Ministry of Human Resources and Social Security and Ministry of Finance (2008) *Notice on Accomplishing the Task of the Pilot Basic Medical Insurance for Urban Residents in 2008*, Chinese Version, Online. Available HTTP: http://www.lawtime.cn/info/shengchan/aqscfg/201107046495.html (accessed 29 May 2015).

—— (2009a) *The Guiding Opinions on Further Strengthening the Management of the Basic Medical Insurance Fund*, Chinese Version, Online. Available HTTP: http://www.chinajob.gov.cn/gb/insurance/2009–08/10/content_318435.htm (accessed 16 October 2014).

—— (2009b) *Notice on Implementing the Basic Medical Insurance for Urban Residents Nationwide*, Chinese Version, Online. Available HTTP: http://www.gov.cn/zwgk/2009–08/05/content_1383950.htm (accessed 21 July 2015).

—— (2009c) *Opinions on Basic Medical Insurance Settlement Service for Medical Expenses Incurred Outside Home Territory*, Chinese Version, Online. Available HTTP: http://www.gov.cn/ztzl/ygzt/content_1661142.htm (accessed 5 February 2016).

———— (2015) *Notice on Accomplishing the Task of the Basic Medical Insurance for Urban Residents in 2015*, Chinese Version, Online. Available HTTP: http://www.mohrss.gov.cn/SYrlzyhshbzb/ldbk/shehuibaozhang/yiliao/201502/t20150209_151708.htm (accessed 29 May 2015).

Ministry of Human Resources and Social Security, Ministry of Finance and National Health and Family Planning Commission (2014) *Guiding Opinions on Further Improving Basic Medical Insurance Settlement Service for Medical Expenses Incurred Outside Home Territory*, Chinese Version, Online. Available HTTP: http://www.mohrss.gov.cn/SYrlzyhshbzb/ldbk/shehuibaozhang/yiliao/201412/t20141224_147142.htm (accessed 5 February 2016).

The Ministry of Human Resources and Social Security, National Development and Reform Commission, Ministry of Civil Affairs, Ministry of Finance, Ministry of Health, and National Council for Social Security Fund (2012) *Framework Plan for Social Security Development under the 12th Five Year Plan*, Chinese Version, Online. Available HTTP: http://www.gov.cn/zwgk/2012–06/27/content_2171218.htm (accessed February 5 2016).

Ministry of Human Resources and Social Security of Zhanjiang City (2008) *The Trial Implementation of Basic Medical Insurance for Urban and Rural Residents*, Chinese Version, Online. Available HTTP: http://www.zhanjiang.gov.cn/fileserver/newshtml/d2f07510–2f74–468d-96bb-d7038b3a1354.htm (accessed 10 October 2014).

The Ministry of Labour and the All-China Federation of Trade Unions (1966) *The Circular on Several Questions Concerning the Improvement of the Labour Health Insurance System*. Online. Available HTTP: http://laws.66law.cn/law-17700.aspx (accessed 22 December 2015).

Mo, J. Y. (2014) Increasing the Operation Efficiency of Basic Medical Insurance Fund in Urban China: Based on the Experience in Reforming the Basic Medical Insurance Policy in Guangdong Province, Chinese Version, *Soft Science of Health*, 28 (11): 701–3.

Modern Express (2012) 'Primary Medical Institutions Adopted the Zero-Markup Drug Policy', Chinese Version, *Modern Express*, 3 August. Online. Available HTTP: http://kb.dsqq.cn/html/2012–08/03/content_199155.htm (accessed 5 February 2016).

Morrison, W. (2015) *China's Economic Rise: History, Trends, Challenges, and Implications for the United States*. Online. Available HTTP: https://www.fas.org/sgp/crs/row/RL33534.pdf (accessed 1 December 2015).

Muhammad, S. A. (2014) *Fraud: The Affinity of Classification Techniques to Insurance Fraud Detection*. Online. Available HTTP: http://www.ijitee.org/ (accessed 5 February 2016).

Naito, J. (2015) China's Fiscal Position and Policy: Current Status of Local Government Debt Problems and Challenges, *Public Policy Review*, 11 (1): 67–91.

Narayanan, R. (2006) The Politics of Reform in China: Deng, Jiang and Hu, *Strategic Analysis*, 30 (2): 329–53.

Nathan, A. J. (1999) 'Introduction: Dilemmas of Development' in A. J. Nathan, Z. Wong and S. R. Smith (eds.) *Dilemmas of Reform in Jiang Zemin's China*, Boulder, CO: Lynne Rienner Publishers, pp. 1–12.

National Bureau of Statistics of the People's Republic of China (1986) *Statistical Yearbook of China 1986*, Beijing: China Statistics Press.

———— (1990) *Statistical Yearbook of China 1990*, Beijing: China Statistics Press.

—— (2012) *Statistical Reports on 2011 National Economic and Social Development*, Chinese Version, Online. Available HTTP: http://www.stats.gov.cn/tjsj/tjgb/ndtjgb/qgndtjgb/201202/t20120222_30026.html (accessed 10 August 2015).

—— (2013a) *China Statistical Yearbook 2013*, Beijing: China Statistics Press.

—— (2013b) *Statistical Reports on 2012 National Economic and Social Development*, Chinese Version, Online. Available HTTP: http://www.stats.gov.cn/tjsj/tjgb/ndtjgb/qgndtjgb/201302/t20130221_30027.html (accessed 10 August 2015).

—— (2014a) *China Statistical Yearbook 2014*, Chinese Version, Online. Available HTTP: http://www.stats.gov.cn/tjsj/ndsj/2014/indexeh.htm (accessed 10 August 2015).

—— (2014b) *Statistical Reports on 2013 National Economic and Social Development*, Chinese Version, Online. Available HTTP: http://www.stats.gov.cn/tjsj/zxfb/201402/t20140224_514970.html (accessed 10 August 2015).

—— (2015) *Statistical Communiqué of the People's Republic of China on the 2014 National Economic and Social Development*, Chinese Version, Online. Available HTTP: http://www.stats.gov.cn/tjsj/zxfb/201502/t20150226_685799.html (accessed 10 August 2015).

The National Development and Reform Commission (2016) *Analysis on Price Reporting in China in 2015*, Chinese Version. Online. Available HTTP: http://12358.ndrc.gov.cn/EC0F227DDDC5E2B6D6F8943EA8FE957C/2016–01–18/35290B922C99A6C9FD6D4C4D256A307B.htm (accessed 5 February 2016).

National Development and Reform Commission, Ministry of Health, Ministry of Finance, Ministry of Human Resources and Social Security, Ministry of Civil Affairs, and China Insurance Regulatory Commission (2012) *The Guiding Opinions on the Launch of the Work on Critical Illness Insurance for Urban and Rural Residents*, Chinese Version, Online. Available HTTP: http://www.gov.cn/gzdt/2012–08/31/content_2214223.htm (accessed 17 February 2016).

National Health and Family Planning Commission of the People's Republic of China (2013) *China Health and Family Planning Yearbook 2013*, Chinese Version, Online. Available HTTP: http://www.nhfpc.gov.cn/htmlfiles/zwgkzt/ptjnj/year2013/index2013.html (accessed 7 February 2016).

—— (2014) *Statistical Communiqué of the People's Republic of China on the 2013 National Health Care and Family Planning Development*, Chinese Version, Online. Available HTTP: http://www.moh.gov.cn/guihuaxxs/s10742/201405/886f82dafa344c3097f1d16581a1bea2.shtml (accessed 17 August 2015).

National Health and Family Planning Commission and Ministry of Finance (2015) *Notice on Accomplishing the Task of New Rural Cooperative Medical System in 2015*, Chinese Version, Online. Available HTTP: http://www.moh.gov.cn/jws/s3581sg/201501/98d95186d494472e8d4ae8fa60e9efc5.shtml (accessed 29 May 2015).

National People's Congress (1997) *Criminal Law of the People's Republic of China*, Online. Available HTTP: http://www.npc.gov.cn/englishnpc/Law/2007–12/13/content_1384075.htm (accessed 31 January 2016).

National Population and Family Planning Commission (2012) *China Population and Family Planning Yearbook 2012*, Beijing: China Population and Family Planning Yearbook Association.

Naughton, B. (1997) 'Danwei: The Economic Foundations of a Unique Institution' in X. Lü and E. J. Perry (eds.) *Danwei: The Changing Chinese Workplace in Historical and Comparative Perspective*, Armonk, NY: M. E. Sharpe, pp. 169–94.

New York State Division of Criminal Justice Services (2009) *Plan of Operation for Motor Vehicle Theft and Insurance Fraud Prevention Board*. Online. Available HTTP: http://www.criminaljustice.ny.gov/ofpa/pdfdocs/mvif09plan.pdf (accessed 1 February 2016).

Ngok, K. (2014) 'Bringing the State Back In: The Development of Chinese Social Policy in China in the Hu-Wen Era' in K. H. Mok and M. K. W. Lau (eds.) *Managing Social Change and Social Policy in Greater China: Welfare Regimes in Transition*, London: Routledge, pp. 96–110.

Ngorsuraches, S., Ma, W. M., Kim, B. and Kulsomboon, V. (2012) Drug Reimbursement Decision-Making in Thailand, China, and South Korea, *Value in Health*, 15 (1): S120–5.

Ni, K. and Yu, Z. (2012) The Research on Paying Inpatient Medical Expenses Out of Pocket Under the Basic Medical Insurance System for Urban Employees, Chinese Version, *Modern Business Trade Industry*, 7: 47–8.

Ningxia Hui Autonomous Region Public Resources Transaction and Management Bureau (2015) *Notice on Drug Procurement Office Handling Drug Manufacturers Which Did Not Supply Drugs After Winning the Bids*, Chinese Version, Online. Available HTTP: http://www.nxzfcg.gov.cn/article.aspx?type=6&index=20750 (accessed 14 June 2015).

Office of Inspector General's (2016a) *Medicare Fraud Strike Force*. Online. Available HTTP: http://oig.hhs.gov/fraud/strike-force/ (accessed 1 February 2016).

—— (2016b) *Medicaid Fraud Control Units*. Online. Available HTTP: http://oig.hhs.gov/fraud/medicaid-fraud-control-units-mfcu/ (accessed 1 February 2016).

Organisation for Economic Co-Operation and Development (2015) *OECD Economic Surveys: China 2015*. Online. Available HTTP: http://www.oecd.org/eco/surveys/China-2015-overview.pdf (accessed 12 August 2015).

Ouyang, J. T., Wang, Y. and Zhu, Y. B. (2012) An Analysis on Cognition Status of the Basic Medical Insurance System and Its Influencing Factors among University Students in Beijing City, Chinese Version, *Chinese Journal of School Health*, 33 (8): 958–60.

Pearson, V. (1995) 'Health and Responsibility; But Whose?' in L. Wong and S. Macpherson (eds.) *Social Change and Social Policy in Contemporary China*, Aldershot, England: Avebury, pp. 88–112.

The People's Government of Hainan Province (1995) *Implementation Details of Medical Insurance Ordinance for Urban Employees of the Hainan Special Economic Zone*, Chinese Version, Online. Available HTTP: http://www.law-lib.com/lawhtm/1995/60593.htm (accessed 23 July 2015).

Peters, B. G. (1999) *Institutional Theory in Political Science: The 'New Institutionalism'*, London: Pinter.

Pierson, P. and Skocpol, T. (2002) 'Historical Institutionalism in Contemporary Political Science' in I. Katznelson and H. V. Milner (eds.) *Political Science: State of the Discipline*, New York: Norton; Washington, DC: American Political Science Association, pp. 693–721.

Population Census Office and Department of Population and Employment Statistics (2012a) *Tabulation on the 2010 Population Census of the People's Republic of China (Book I)*, Chinese Version, Beijing: China Statistics Press.

—— (2012b) *Tabulation on the 2010 Population Census of the People's Republic of China (Book III)*, Chinese Version, Beijing: China Statistics Press.

Population Census Office and Department of Population, Social, Science and Technology Statistics (2002) *Tabulation on the 2000 Population Census of the People's Republic of China (Book I)*, Chinese Version, Beijing: China Statistics Press.

Population Census Office and Department of Population Statistics (1985) *1982 Population Census of China (Results of Computer Tabulation)*, Chinese Version, Beijing: The Statistical Publishing House.

Procuratorial Daily (2008) 'People Involved in the Purchase and Resale of Drugs Formed a Fixed Chains of Interests', Chinese Version, *Procuratorial Daily*, 20 December. Online. Available HTTP: http://finance.sina.com.cn/consume/puguangtai/20081220/14065664008.shtml (accessed 3 October 2015).

Public Network (2014 March 31) *The Zero-Markup Drug Policy Brought Happiness and Worries to Public Hospitals, Public Hospitals Find it Difficult to Hang On, Chinese Version*. Online. Available HTTP: http://www.ebnew.com/newsDetail-v-id-440675013.html (accessed 5 February 2016).

Qian, J. (2013) 'Reinventing China's Health System' in G. Wang and Y. Zheng (eds.) *China: Development and Governance*, Singapore; Hackensack, NJ: World Scientific Pub. Co., pp. 333–42.

Qingdao Municipal Bureau of Human Resources and Social Security (2015) *Methods of Assessing Designated Medical Institutions of Social Medical Insurance in Qingdao City*, Chinese Version. Online. Available HTTP: http://www.qingdao.gov.cn/n172/upload/150702153831588652/150702153831333431.pdf (accessed 5 February 2016).

Rawte, V. and Anuradha, G. (2015) *Fraud Detection in Health Insurance using Data Mining Techniques*. Online. Available HTTP: http://ieeexplore.ieee.org/ (accessed 5 February 2016).

Roberts, M. R. and Sufi, A. (2009) Financial Contracting: A Survey of Empirical Research and Future Directions, *Annual Review of Financial Economics*, 1: 207–26.

Rogers, Durin B. (1993) The Medicare and Medicaid Anti-Kickback Statute: Safe Harbors Eradicate Ambiguity, *Journal of Law and Health*, 8: 223–44.

Rosenthal, M. and Greiner, J. (1987) 'The Barefoot Doctors of China: From Political Creation to Professionalization' in M. M. Rosenthal (ed.) *Health Care in the People's Republic of China: Moving Toward Modernization*, Boulder, CO: Westview Press, pp. 5–34.

Rosenthal, M. and Pongor, P. (1987) 'Rural Health Care Delivery in the People's Republic of China: Is It Equitably Distributed?' in M. M. Rosenthal (ed.) *Health Care in the People's Republic of China: Moving Toward Modernization*, Boulder, CO: Westview Press, pp. 77–121.

Rösner, Hans-Jürgen (2004) China's Health Insurance System in Transformation: Preliminary Assessment, and Policy Suggestions, *International Social Security Review*, 57 (3): 65–90.

Saich, T. (2004) *Governance and Politics of China*, 2nd edn, Basingstoke, Hampshire, UK; New York: Palgrave Macmillian.

Scharping, T. (2003) *Birth Control in China, 1949–2000: Population Policy and Demographic Development*, London; New York: Routledge.

Scheid, V. (2002) *Chinese Medicine in Contemporary China: Plurality and Synthesis*, Durham, NC: Duke University Press.

Scheid, V. and Lei, S. (2014) 'The Institutionalization of Chinese Medicine' in B. Andrews and M. B. Bullock (eds.) *Medical Transitions in Twentieth Century China*, Bloomington, IN: Indiana University Press, pp. 244–66.

Sellers, D. (2015) *The Best Medicine for China's Ailing Tendering System*. Online. Available HTTP: http://www.eurobiz.com.cn/the-best-medicine-for-chinas-ailing-tendering-system (accessed 5 February 2016).

Shanghai Municipal Government (1996) *The Shanghai Provisional Regulations on Hospitalization Insurance for Urban Employees*, Chinese Version, Online. Available HTTP: http://www.cnnsr.com.cn/csfg/html/1996040900000019854.html (accessed 24 July 2015).

——— (1997) *The Shanghai Provisional Regulations on Partial Outpatient and Emergency Services Medical Insurances for Urban Employees*, Chinese Version, Online. Available HTTP: http://www.chinalawedu.com/news/1200/23051/23053/23065/2006/3/sh4715224027236002725–0.htm (accessed 24 July 2015).

——— (1998) *The Shanghai Provisional Regulations on Outpatient and Emergency Services Medical Insurances for Urban Retirees*, Chinese Version, Online. Available HTTP: http://www.chinalawedu.com/news/1200/23051/23053/23065/2006/3/sh8207153040272360021347 5–0.htm (accessed 24 July 2015).

——— (2011) *Methods on Supervising and Managing Shanghai Municipal Basic Medical Insurance*, Chinese Version. Online. Available HTTP: http://www.shanghai.gov.cn/nw2/nw2314/nw2319/nw2407/nw25451/u26aw24687.html (accessed 5 February 2016).

——— (2013) *Measures of Shanghai Basic Medical Insurance for Urban Employees*, Chinese Version. Online. Available HTTP: http://www.12333sh.gov.cn/201412333/xxgk/flfg/gfxwj/shbx/yilbx/201405/t20140523_1184269.shtml (accessed 21 September 2015).

Shen, H. (2014) 'The Challenges of Cancer in China' in S. M. Griffiths, J. L. Tang and E. K. Yeoh (eds.) *Routledge Handbook of Global Public Health in Asia*, New York: Routledge, pp. 148–66.

Shenzhen Municipal Government (1996) *The Shenzhen Provisional Regulations on Basic Medical Insurance*, Chinese Version, Online. Available HTTP: http://www.chinalawedu.com/falvfagui/fg23051/97572.shtml (accessed 22 July 2015).

Shi, J. X. (2003) *The Pattern and Development of Health Insurance in China*, Chinese Version, Beijing: China Price Press.

Sidel, V. W. and Sidel, R. (1979) 'Health Care Services as Part of China's Revolution and Development' in N. Maxwell (ed.) *China's Road to Development*, 2nd edn, Oxford, Eng.; New York: Pergamon Press, pp. 155–68

Skocpol, T. (1992) *Protecting Soldiers and Mothers: the Political Origins of Social Policy in the United States*, Cambridge, MA: Belknap Press of Harvard University Press.

Social Insurance Fund Management Center (2015) *Notice Concerning the Temporary Suspension of the Use of Health Insurance Card of Health Insurance Participants*, Chinese Version. Online. Available HTTP: http://www.kssbzx.net.cn/webPages/nry.aspx?id=473 (accessed 5 February 2016).

Song, S. G., Yang, J. H. and Chen, L. P. (2012) The Empirical Study on the Basic Medical Insurance for Urban Residents and the Problems of 'Being Difficult to See Doctors and Being Expensive to See Doctors': Analyzing the Survey Data of Huaihua City, Hunan Province in 2011, Chinese Version, *Social Security Studies*, 2: 70–76.

South China Morning Post (2015) *China's Workforce Shrinks by Nearly 4 Million Amid Greying Population. South China Morning Post*, 20 January. Online. Available HTTP: http://www.scmp.com/news/china/article/1683778/chinas-workforce-shrinks-nearly-4-million-amid-greying-population (accessed 12 August 2015).

Southern Metropolis Daily (2015) Floating Population Will Reach 300 Million within Five Years, the Average Age of Floating Population of Floating Population Continues to Increase, *Southern Metropolis Daily*, 12 November. Chinese Version. Online. Available HTTP: http://gd.sina.com.cn/finance/industry/2015–11–12/cj-ifxk nutf1715330.shtml (accessed 6 February 2016).

Stallone, M. N. (ed.) (2013) *Health Care Fraud and Questionable Costs: Select Investigations*, New York: Nova Science Publishers.

The Standing Committee of the People's Congress of Hainan Province (1995) *Medical Insurance Ordinance for Urban Employees of the Hainan Special Economic Zone*, Chinese Version, Online. Available HTTP: http://www.law-lib.com/lawhtm/1995/60579.htm (accessed 23 July 2015).

The State Commission for Restructuring the Economic Systems, Ministry of Finance, Ministry of Labor and Ministry of Health (1994) *Opinions on the Trial of Health Care System Reform for Urban Employees*, Chinese Version, Online. Available HTTP: http://www.law-lib.com/law/law_view.asp?id=10362 (accessed 26 July 2015).

The State Council (1992) *The Notification of the State Council on Further Doing a Good Job in Reforming the Urban Health Care System*, Chinese Version. Online. Available HTTP: http://law.lawtime.cn/d609273614367.html (accessed 17 February 2016).

——— (1998) *The Decision of the State Council Concerning the Establishment of the Urban Employee Basic Medical Insurance*, Chinese Version. Online. Available HTTP: http://www.gov.cn/banshi/2005–08/04/content_20256.htm (accessed 17 February 2016).

——— (2007) *The Guiding Opinions on Piloting Basic Medical Insurance for Urban Residents*, Chinese Version, Online. Available HTTP: http://www.gov.cn/zwgk/2007–07/24/content_695118.htm (accessed 29 May 2015).

——— (2008) *Guiding Opinions on Including University Students in the Pilot Basic Medical Insurance for Urban Residents*, Chinese Version, Online. Available HTTP: http://www.shanxigov.cn/n16/n8319541/n8319612/n8321663/n8322659/n8335963/n8338869/8686438.html (accessed 21 July 2015).

——— (2013) *The Opinions on Key Works in Deepening the Economic System Reform in 2013*, Chinese Version, Online. Available HTTP: http://www.miit.gov.cn/n11293472/n11293832/n13095885/15424320.html (accessed 16 October 2014).

——— (2015) *Guiding Opinions on Perfecting the Centralized Drug Procurement System of Public Hospitals*, Chinese Version. Online. Available HTTP: http://www.gov.cn/zhengce/content/2015–02/28/content_9502.htm (accessed 5 February 2016).

The State Council Information Office of the People's Republic of China (2015) *The 2015 Drug Administration Law of the People's Republic of China*, Chinese Version, Online. Available HTTP: http://www.scio.gov.cn/xwfbh/xwbfbh/xczb/xgzc/Document/1444596/1444596.htm (accessed 5 February 2016).

Steinmo, S. (2008) 'Historical Institutionalism' in D. D. Porta and M. Keating (eds.) *Approaches and Methodologies in the Social Sciences: A Pluralist Perspective*, Cambridge: Cambridge University Press, pp. 150–78.

Tang, S. and Meng, Q. (2004) 'Introduction to the Urban Health System and Review of Reform Initiatives' in G. Bloom and S. Tang (eds.) *Health Care Transition in Urban China*, Aldershot, Hants; England; Burlington, VT: Ashgate, pp. 17–37.

Tansey, O. (2007) Process Tracing and Elite Interviewing: A Case for Non-Probability Sampling, *PS: Political Science and Politics*, 40 (4): 765–72.

Tao, H. Y. (2009) The Current Status of New Rural Cooperative Medical System in More Developed Regions: A Survey Report on Rural Village in Wujiang City, Jiangsu Province, Chinese Version, *China Collective Economy*, 31: 14–5.

Thelen, K. (1999) Historical Institutionalism in Comparative Politics, *Annual Reviews of Political Science*, 2: 369–404.

———— (2003) 'How Institutions Evolve: Insights from Comparative Historical Analysis' in J. Mahoney and D. Rueschemeyer (eds.) *Comparative Historical Analysis in the Social Sciences*, Cambridge, UK; New York: Cambridge University Press, pp. 208–40.

Thelen, K. and Steinmo, S. (1992) 'Historical Institutionalism in Comparative Politics' in S. Steinmo, K. Thelen and F. Longstreth (eds.) *Structuring Politics: Historical Institutionalism in Comparative Analysis*, New York: Cambridge University Press, pp. 1–32.

Tian, Y., Gu, Y. and Ni, Y. (2011) 'China's Health Reform Cuts Drug Prices, But Still Fights Pain', *Xinhua News*, 23April. Online. Available HTTP: http://news.xinhuanet.com/english2010/china/2011–04/23/c_13842651.htm (accessed 18 February 2016).

Tisdell, C. (2009) Economic Reform and Openness in China: China's Development Policies in the Last 30 Years, *Economic Analysis & Policy*, 39 (2): 271–94.

Traub-Merz, R. (2011) *All China Federation of Trade Unions: Structure, Functions and the Challenge of Collective Bargaining*, Online. Available HTTP: http://www.global-labour-university.org/fileadmin/GLU_Working_Papers/GLU_WP_No.13.pdf (accessed 22 December 2015).

Tulchinsky, T. and Varavikova, E. (2014) *The New Public Health: An Introduction for the 21st Century*, San Diego, CA; London: Academic Press.

Tuohy, C. H. (1999) *Accidental Logics: The Dynamics of Change in the Health Care Arena in the United States, Britain, and Canada*, New York: Oxford University Press.

United Nations (2013) *World Population Ageing 2013*. Online. Available HTTP: http://www.un.org/en/development/desa/population/publications/pdf/ageing/WorldPopulationAgeing2013.pdf (accessed 7 August 2015).

———— (2015) *World Population Prospects: The 2015 Revision, Key Findings and Advance Tables*. Online. Available HTTP: http://esa.un.org/unpd/wpp/Publications/Files/Key_Findings_WPP_2015.pdf (accessed 7 August 2015).

Wang, C. F., Chang, W. and Deng, Y. M. (2011) Analysis on the Disease Pattern of Inpatients and their Use of Drugs in Township Health Centers Under the New Rural Cooperative Medical System, Chinese Version. *China Pharmacy*, 22 (16): 1448–50.

Wang, H. (2004) 'News Reporter Visit Xunyi, the Apple Growing Capital of China Today', *Chinese Business View*, 19 September. Online. Available HTTP: http://hsb.hsw.cn/gb/newsdzb/2004–09/19/content_1285162.htm (accessed 10 October 2014).

Wang, J. C. F. (2002) *Contemporary Chinese Politics: An Introduction*, 7th edn, Upper Saddle River, NJ: Prentice Hall.

Wang, J. W. (2014) 'The Payment Risk of Health Insurance Fund Begins to Show in Some Regions in Heilongjiang Province', Chinese Version, *Economic Information Daily*, 27 June, Online. Available HTTP: http://jjckb.xinhuanet.com/2014–06/27/content_510418.htm (accessed 22 October 2015).

Wang, S. (2009) Adapting by Learning: The Evolution of China's Rural Health Care Financing, *Modern China*, 35: 370–404.

Wang, Y. and Lu, S. (2011) 'Xunyi Took the Lead to Realize the Unification of Medical Insurance System for Urban and Rural Residents', Chinese Version. Online. Available HTTP: http://www.snxunyi.gov.cn/XuanChuanBu/contents/1965/404. html (accessed 10 October 2014).

Wang, Y., Ren, H. and Zhao, S. (2011) 'The Zhanjiang Model: An Innovative System', Chinese Version, *Nan Fang Magazine*, 7 April. Online. Available HTTP: http://www.nfyk.com/gg/ShowArticle.asp?ArticleID=3159 (accessed 10 October 2014).

Wang, Y., Wei, L., Liu, J., Li, S. and Wang, Q. (2012) Comparison of Cancer Incidence between China and the USA, *Cancer Biology & Medicine*, 9 (2): 128–32.

Weaver, R. K. (2010) Paths and Forks or Chutes and Ladders?; Negative Feedbacks and Policy Regime Change, *Journal of Public Policy*, 30 (2): 137–62.

Wei, C. (2013) 'Barefoot Doctors: The Legacy of Chairman Mao's Healthcare' in C. N. Wei and D. E. Brock (eds.) *Mr. Science and Chairman Mao's Cultural Revolution: Science and Technology in Modern China*, Lanham: Lexington Books, pp. 251–80.

Welch, E. and Wong, W. (1998) Public Administration in a Global Context: Bridging the Gaps of Theory and Practice between Western and Non-Western Nations, *Public Administration Review*, 58 (1): 40–9.

White, T. (2006) *China's Longest Campaign: Birth Planning in the People's Republic, 1949–2005*, Ithaca, NY: Cornell University Press.

Wilenski, P. (1976) *The Delivery of Health Services in the People's Republic of China*, Ottawa: International Development Research Centre.

Wilsford, D. (1994) Path Dependency, or Why History Makes It Difficult but Not Impossible to Reform Health Care Systems in a Big Way, *Journal of Public Policy*, 14 (3): 251–83.

Wong, C., Lo, V. I. and Tang, K. (2006) *China's Urban Health Care Reform: From State Protection to Individual Responsibility*, Lanham, MD: Lexington Books.

Wong, V. and Chiu, S. (1997) Health-Care Reforms in the People's Republic of China: Strategies and Social Implications, *International Journal of Public Sector Management*, 10 (1/2): 76–92.

World Bank (1997) *At China's Table: Food Security Options*, Washington, DC: World Bank.

—— (2010) *Fixing the Public Hospital System in China*. Online. Available HTTP: http://siteresources.worldbank.org/HEALTHNUTRITIONANDPOPULA TION/Resources/281627–1285186535266/FixingthePublicHospitalSystem. pdf (accessed 4 October 2015).

—— (2015) *GDP Per Capita (Current US$)*. Online. Available HTTP: http:// data.worldbank.org/indicator/NY.GDP.PCAP.CD (accessed 12 August 2015).

World Health Organization (2005) *Achieving Universal Health Coverage: Developing the Health Financing System*. Online. Available HTTP: http://www.who.int/ health_financing/documents/pb_e_05_1-universal_cov.pdf?ua=1 (accessed 18 February 2016).

—— (2008) *Primary Health Care: Now More Than Ever*. Online. Available HTTP: http://www.who.int/whr/2008/whr08_en.pdf (accessed 19 February 2016).

—— (2013a) *The World Health Report 2013: Research for Universal Health Coverage*. Online. Available HTTP: http://apps.who.int/iris/bitstream/10665/85761/ 2/9789240690837_eng.pdf?ua=1 (accessed 9 October 2014).

——— (2013b) *China-WHO Country Cooperation Strategy 2013–2015: Bridging the Past towards a New Era of Collaboration*. Online. Available HTTP: http://www.who.int/countryfocus/cooperation_strategy/ccs_chn_en.pdf (accessed 16 August 2015).

——— (2014) *World Health Statistics 2014*. Online. Available HTTP: http://apps.who.int/iris/bitstream/10665/112738/1/9789240692671_eng.pdf (accessed 17 August 2015).

——— (2015) *World Health Statistics 2015*. Online. Available HTTP: http://apps.who.int/iris/bitstream/10665/170250/1/9789240694439_eng.pdf?ua=1&ua=1 (accessed 6 February 2016).

Wu, N. (2013) 'Taicang Emerging As Modern City', *China Daily*, 22 April. Online. Available HTTP: http://www.chinadaily.com.cn/travel/2013–04/22/content_16430322.htm (accessed 11 October 2014).

Wuhan Evening Post (2014) 'Can the Practice of "*gua chuang zhu yuan*" Save Money?', Chinese Version, *Wuhan Evening Post*, 28 April. Online. Available HTTP: http://www.chinanews.com/jk/2014/04–28/6113657.shtml (accessed 23 September 2015).

Wuxi Daily (2006) 'Who Cares About the Problem of "Difficult to See the Doctor" Faced by the Floating Population', Chinese Version, *Wuxi Daily*, 17 January. Online. Available HTTP: http://news.sina.com.cn/c/2006–01–17/09118004262s.shtml (accessed 5 February 2016).

Xia, J. (2013) 'Performance Appraisal of Local Government was Pegged to the Participation Rate of New Rural Cooperative Medical System. Local Government Became Swindlers', Chinese Version, *China News*, 3 December. Online. Available HTTP: http://www.chinanews.com/sh/2013/12–03/5571975.shtml (accessed 30 October 2015).

Xia, Q. Y. and Wang, Z. Y. (2013) *The Mode of Setting Drug Prices Has Not Changed, Imposing Price Caps on Drugs for 31 Times Fails to Address High Drug Prices*, Chinese Version. Online. Available HTTP: http://www.yicai.com/news/2013/09/2983293.html (accessed 5 February 2016).

Xiang, Z. (2015) *The 'Double Envelope' Tendering System Will Continued to Be Used in the Centralized Drug Procurement System for Public Hospitals*, Chinese Version. Online. Available HTTP: http://digitalpaper.stdaily.com/http_www.kjrb.com/kjrb/html/2015–06/25/content_307650.htm?div=-1 (accessed 5 February 2016).

Xie, J. (2016) 'As Local Government Debt Balloons, So Do the Risks', *Global Times*, 1 February. Online. Available HTTP: http://www.globaltimes.cn/content/966775.shtml (accessed 5 February 2016).

Xinhua Net (2011) *The Common Program of the Chinese People's Political Consultative Conference*, Chinese Version. Online. Available HTTP: http://news.qq.com/a/20111116/000896_2.htm (accessed 12 December 2015).

Xinhua News (2004) 'From 35 Years to 72 Years: Life Expectancy in China Becomes Higher and Higher', Chinese Version, *Xinhua News*, 28 September. Online. Available HTTP: http://news.xinhuanet.com/newscenter/2004–09/28/content_2032154.htm (accessed 17 August 2015).

——— (2007) 'The Urban Resident Basic Medical Insurance Will Be Piloted in 79 Cities in China', Chinese Version, *Xinhua News*, 15 August. Online. Available HTTP: http://news.xinhuanet.com/newscenter/2007–08/15/content_6537661.htm (accessed 18 February 2016).

—— (2013) 'The Report Showed That Every Minute, Six People Were Diagnosed with Cancer in China', Chinese Version, *Xinhua News*, 10 January. Online. Available HTTP: http://news.xinhuanet.com/politics/2013–01/10/c_124211560. htm (accessed 21 August 2015).

—— (2015a) 'China Is Going to Conduct a Large-Scale National Survey on China's Ageing Population', Chinese Version, *Xinhua News*, 28 July. Online. Available HTTP: http://news.cnr.cn/native/gd/20150728/t20150728_519338966. shtml (accessed 7 August 2015).

—— (2015b) 'The Total Fertility Rate Was Somewhere between 1.5 and 1.65 per cent; China Has Yet to Fall into the Low Fertility Trap', Chinese Version, *Xinhua News*, 11 July. Online. Available HTTP: http://news.jxnews.com.cn/ system/2015/07/11/014035508.shtml (accessed 17 August 2015).

—— (2015c) 'Infant Mortality Rate Fell to 9.5 Per 1,000 Live Births in China in 2013', Chinese Version, *Xinhua News*, 4 February. Online. Available HTTP: http://news.xinhuanet.com/2015–02/04/c_1114254623.htm (accessed 17 August 2015).

—— (2015d) 'Some Hospitals in Anshun City, Guizhou Province Defraud New Rural Cooperative Medical System Fund of More than RMB 34 Million', Chinese Version, *Xinhua News*, 10 April. Online. Available HTTP: http://news. xinhuanet.com/mrdx/2015–04/10/c_134139977.htm (accessed 28 September 2015).

Xinjiang Daily News (2014) 'Why Can't the Practice of Using Medical Insurance Certificate to Buy Non-Drug Items Be Prohibited?' Chinese Version, *Xinjiang Daily News*, 16 July. Online. Available HTTP: http://news.163.com/14/0716/09/ A1915ESF00014AED.html (accessed 28 September 2015).

Xu, D., Sun, Z., Li, J. and Lei, Y. (2012) Dynamic Analysis of the New Rural Cooperative Medical System in Hunan Province from 2003 to 2009, Chinese Version, *Journal of Central South University (Medical Science)*, 37 (2): 147–51.

Xu, Y. H. and Zhang, C. P. (2012) An Analysis on the Current Status of the Medical Insurance System for University Students, Chinese Version, *Journal of Youjiang Medical University for Nationalities*, 5: 695–7.

Xu, Z. Y. (2010) Analysis on University Students Joining the Basic medical Insurance for Urban Residents in Enshi City, Chinese Version, *Journal of Hubei University for Nationalities (Medical Edition)*, 27 (4): 75–6.

Xue, X. D. and Liu, G. E. (2009) Study on the Willingness to Join the Basic Medical Insurance for Urban Residents and Its Influencing Factors, Chinese Version, *Northwest Population*, 30 (1): 62–6.

Xunyi County Cooperative Medical Website (2014a) *Xunyi in Shaanxi: Insurance for Critical Illnesses Let Chinese Peasants Get Cured*, Chinese Version. Online. Available HTTP: http://www.snxunyi.gov.cn/HeLiaoBan/contents/2715/296.html (accessed 14 December 2014).

—— (2014b) *The New Cooperative Medical System for Urban and Rural Residents in Xunyi County in 2015*, Chinese Version. Online. Available HTTP: http://www.snxunyi.gov.cn/HeLiaoBan/contents/2717/341.html (accessed 14 December 2014).

Xunyi County Government (2011) *Issuing the Notice about the Implementation of New Cooperative Medical System for Urban and Rural Residents in Xunyi County*, Chinese Version. Online. Available HTTP: http://www.snxunyi.gov.cn/ contents/372/10518.html (accessed 14 December 2014).

Yan, H. (2006) *China's One-Child Policy in Need of Change*, Singapore: East Asian Institute, National University of Singapore.

Yan, S., Li, B., Bai, Z., Wu, J., Xie, D., Ma, Y., Ma, X., Zhao, J. and Guo, X. (2014) Clinical Epidemiology of Gastric Cancer in Hehuang Valley of China: A 10-year Epidemiological Study of Gastric Cancer, *World Journal of Gastroenterol*, 20 (30): 10486–94.

Yang, L. (2006) Incidence and Mortality of Gastric Cancer in China, *World Journal of Gastroenterology*, 12 (1): 17–20.

Yang, Q. (2012) 'The Jiangyin Model: A Role Model for Commercial Health Insurance', Chinese Version, *The First Financial Daily*, 17 September. Online. Available HTTP: http://www.yicai.com/news/2012/09/2083802.html (accessed 10 October 2014).

Yang, Y. L., Zhou, L. Y. and Zheng, J. Z. (2009) Analysis on the Current Status of the Basic Medical Insurance for University Students in Taiyuan City, Chinese Version, *Chinese Rural Health Service Administration*, 29 (4): 259–61.

Ye, J., Gao, F. and Wu, J. (2015) Analysis on the Outcome of the Zero-Markup Drug Policy and Measures to It, Chinese Version, *Jiangsu Healthcare Administration*, 26: 116–7.

Yong, Li (2015) *Sichuan and Chongqing Province Starting from July 1 Implement Medical Insurance Settlement Service for Medical Expenses Incurred outside Home Territory*, Chinese Version. Online. Available HTTP: http://cq.qq.com/a/20150630/045571.htm (accessed 5 February 2016).

Yu, K. (2008) *Globalization and Changes in China's Governance*, Leiden; Boston: Brill.

Yu, M. (2005) *Learning from the Soviet Union: CPC Propaganda and Its Effects*. Online. Available HTTP: http://mercury.ethz.ch/serviceengine/Files/ISN/108649/ichaptersection_singledocument/f920403e-75b3–4719–966d-33b0f829b3d8/en/minling.pdf (accessed 29 November 2015).

Yuan, C. X., Wang, X. and Zhang, P. P. (2012) The Empirical Study on Medical Insurance for University Students in Hebei Province, Chinese Version, *Economic Research Guide*, 26: 61–67.

Zeng, Y. (2012a) 'Taicang Lead by Example', Chinese Version, *Chinese Hospital CEO*. Online. Available HTTP: http://www.h-ceo.com/article/read/4/419.html (accessed 9 October 2014).

—— (2012b) *Critical Illness Insurance Needs to be Implemented in Accordance with Local Conditions: A Survey on the Taicang, Zhanjiang and Xunyi Models*, Chinese Version. Online. Available HTTP: http://health.sohu.com/20121118/n357931791_4.shtml (accessed 11 October 2014).

—— (2015) The Analysis on New Mode of Essential Drug Procurement in Guangdong, Chinese Version, *China's Rural Health*, 8: 38–9.

Zhai, F., Wang, H., Du, S., He, Y., Wang, Z., Ge, K. and Popkin, B. (2007) 'Lifespan Nutrition and Changing Socio-Economic Conditions in China' in F. Di (ed.) *Essay Collections for China Health and Nutrition Survey*, Beijing: China Science Publishing & Media Ltd., pp. 869–78.

Zhang, J. and Zhang, J. (2014) *Why Do Inexpensive Essential Medicines Keep Disappearing from the Market?*, Chinese Version, Online. Available HTTP: http://paper.people.com.cn/smsb/html/2014–02/28/content_1396440.htm (accessed 5 February 2016).

Zhang, K. T. and Guo, P. (2010) *Blue Book on Population Ageing and Elderly Conditions in China*, Beijing: China Society Press.

Zhang, M. (2012) *The Impact of Declining Demographic Dividend and Socioeconomic Transformation*. Online. Available HTTP: http://www.chinausfocus.com/political-social-development/the-impact-of-declining-demographic-dividend-and-socioec onomic-transformation (accessed 12 August 2015).

Zhang, N. and Wu, J. (2011) Factor Analysis of Medical Expenses of the Inpatients of the Basic Medical Insurance for Urban Employees in Tianjin, Chinese Version, *China Journal of Pharmaceutical Economics*, 1: 27–31.

Zhang, P. (2014) 'The Concept of the International System and China's Foreign Policy' in J. Yang (ed.) *China's Diplomacy: Theory and Practice*, Hackensack, NJ: World Century Publishing Corporation, pp. 65–120.

Zhang, Q. A. (2001) The Medical and Health Work and the Construction of Medical Ethics in the Shaan-Gan-Ning Border Region, Chinese Version, *Chinese Journal of Medical Ethics*, 3 (77): 57–8.

Zhang, S., Liu, Z. and Gu, Z. (2002) Disease Control and Prevention in China in the 20th Century and Prospects for the New Millennium, *Environmental Health and Preventive Medicine*, 7: 132–37.

Zhang, S., Zhang, W., Zhou, H., Xu, H., Qu, Z., Guo, M., Wang, F., Zhong, Y., Gu, L., Liang, X., Sa, Z., Wang, X. and Tian, D. (2015) How China's New Health Reform Influences Village Doctors' Income Structure: Evidence from a Qualitative Study in Six Counties in China, *Human Resources for Health*, 13: 26.

Zhang, W. (2012) Ageing China: Changes and Challenges. Online. Available HTTP: http://www.bbc.com/news/world-asia-china-19572056 (accessed 7 August 2015).

Zhang, X. (2014) *Enterprise Management Control Systems in China*, Berlin; Heidelberg: Springer.

Zhang, X. X. (2015a) *The First Health Preservation Pharmaceutical Cooperative in the Shaan-Gan-Ning Border Region*, Chinese Version, Online. Available HTTP: http://www.aiweibang.com/yuedu/47669323.html (accessed 26 December 2015).

—— (2015b) *The First Cooperative Health Agency that United Chinese and Western Medicine in the Shaan-Gan-Ning Border Region*, Chinese Version, Online. Available HTTP: http://www.cntcm.com.cn/zywh/2015–10/15/content_7884.htm (accessed 26 December 2015).

Zhang, X. X. and Zhang, D. (2012) 'China's Average Life Expectancy Increase by Five Years of Age in Twenty Years', Chinese Version, *Remin Daily News (Overseas Edition)*, 8 August. Online. Available HTTP: http://paper.people.com.cn/rmrbhwb/html/2012–08/08/content_1093795.htm?div=-1 (accessed 17 August 2015).

Zhang, Y. (2012) 'Xunyi in Shanxi Explores New Rural Cooperative Medical Allowance System for Critical Illnesses', Chinese Version, *The Economic Post*. 24 September, Online. Available HTTP: http://paper.ce.cn/jjrb/html/2012–09/24/content_129827.htm (accessed 11 October 2014).

Zhang, Z. C. and Yan, J. (2015) *In Xia County, Shansi: Three Health Care Center Have the Practice of 'gua chuang zhu yuan'*, Chinese Version. Online. Available HTTP: http://mt.sohu.com/20150623/n415468358.shtml (accessed 28 September 2015).

Zhao, H. (2013) 'Zhanjiang Courting Industry, But Retains Passion for Nature', *Xinhua News*, 22 July. Online. Available HTTP: http://news.xinhuanet.com/english/china/2013–07/22/c_132562495.htm (accessed 11 October 2014).

Zhao, P., Dai, M., Chen, W. and Li, N. (2010) Cancer Trends in China, *Japanese Journal of Clinical Oncology*, 40 (4): 281–85.

Zheng, B. and Zhang, X. (2013) An Innovative System That Is Full of Life and Energy: The Analysis of 'Taicang Model' for Critical Illness Insurance, Chinese Version, *Administrative Management Reform*, 6: 21–29.

Zheng, G. C. (2009) *The Development of Social Security System with Chinese Characteristics*, Beijing: China Labour & Social Security Publishing House.

Zheng, Y. (2004) *Contemporary China: A History Since 1978*, West Sussex: John Wiley & Sons Inc.

—— (2011) 'Four Parties Gain from the Zhanjiang Model: It Is Worth Promoting the Zhanjiang Model', Chinese Version, *The 21st Century Economic Report*, 25 November. Online. Available HTTP: http://www.21cbh.com/HTML/2011–11–25/1MMDM2XzM4MzE1MQ.html (accessed 11 October 2014).

Zhong, W. J. and Tao, S. H. (2015) The Problems of the Medical Insurance Fund and Their Solutions, Chinese Version, *Management Observer*, 565 (2): 35–41.

Zhou, S. (2011) *Changes in the Official Ideology in Contemporary China*. Online. Available HTTP: https://www.griffith.edu.au/__data/assets/pdf_file/0011/333749/Zhou-Regional-Outlook-Paper-29.pdf (accessed 17 February 2016).

Zhou, Z., Su, Y., Zhou, Z., Gao, J., Yu, Q., Chen, J. and Pan, Y. (2013) The Impact of Zero-Markup Drug Policy on Inpatient Expenditure: Evidence from County Public Hospital in Shaanxi Province, Chinese Version, *Chinese Journal of Health Policy*, 6 (12): 25–32.

Zhu, L. J. and Han, L. (2014) *Getting Insurance Reimbursement by Borrowing Medical Insurance Certificate? Shangrao Xiehe Hospital Was Said to Be Involved in Health Insurance Fraud by Having 'gua chuang zhu yuan'*, Chinese Version. Online. Available HTTP: http://jxsr.jxnews.com.cn/system/2014/11/21/013449620.shtml (accessed 28 September 2015).

21st Century Business Herald (2015) 'The Chengdu Model Explores New Supervision Model on Health Insurance: Data Mining Facilitate Health Care Reform', Chinese Version, *21st Century Business Herald*, 29 January. Online. Available HTTP: http://finance.eastmoney.com/news/1355,20150129472963322.html (accessed 5 February 2016).

Interviews

Interview 10SH1, Shanghai health official, July 2010.

Interview 10SH4, a female citizen in Shanghai, July 2010.

Interview 14KM1, government official in China Food and Drug Administration, April 2014.

Interview 15KM3, a senior nurse in a municipal hospital, January 2015.

Interview 15KM4, a senior nurse in a municipal hospital, January 2015.

Interview 15KM5, a senior nurse in a municipal hospital, September 2015.

Interview 15KM6, a mainland scholar, December 2015.

Interview 15KM7, a senior nurse in a municipal hospital, December 2015.

Interview 15KM8, a civil servant in Social Security Bureau, December 2015.

Interview 15KM9, a Kunming citizen, December 2015.

Interview 15KM10, a Beijing citizen, December 2015.

Interview 16KM1, a junior nurse in a municipal hospital, January 2016.

Interview 16KM2, a junior nurse in a municipal hospital, January 2016.

Interview 16KM3, a mainland expert in law, January 2016.

Interview 16KM4, a junior nurse in a municipal hospital, January 2016.

Index

Italicized page numbers indicate tables.

accidental logic 6
adverse selection problem 87
ageing population: epidemiologic
  transitions and 19–25; financial
  sustainability of funds and 77–8;
  geographical differences 13–15;
  getting old before getting rich
  phenomenon 18–19; health financing
  and 25–6; scale of 12–13; speed
  of 11–12; urban-rural differences
  16–18, *17*
All-China Federation of Trade Unions
  (ACFTU) 38
anti-fraud measures: data mining
  technology 95–6; insurance card
  suspension 97–8; insurance fraud
  bureaus/control units 92–4; law
  enforcement/legislation 90–2; public
  fraud reporting system 94–5

barefoot doctor system 36
Basic Medical Insurance (BMI) fund:
  formation of 49; insurance card
  suspension 97–8; misuse of 82–3; for
  privileged groups 72; questionable
  sustainability of 77
Basic Medical Insurance for Urban and
  Rural Residents (BMIFURR) 65, 66
black clinics 75

cancer *21–3*, 21–5
central argument 9
Central Committee 48, 52, 63, 103
centralized drug procurement system
  100–2
Central Pricing Commission 33
cerebrovascular disease *21–3*, 21–4

*China Health and Family Planning
  Yearbook 2013* 24
China's Aging Statistics Compendium 12
China Statistical Yearbook 1986 21
Chinese Communist Party (CCP) 27–8,
  29–30, 52
*Circular on Several Questions
  Concerning the Improvement of the
  Labour Health Insurance System* 38
Cold War 28
Compartmental Model *see* Hainan
  model of health insurance
competing bureaucratic interests, in
  health insurance reform 51–2
conjunctures, historical institutionalism
  and 6
Cooperative Health Agency (CHA)
  39–40
cooperative medical system (CMS)
  39–41, 45
co-payment reform measure 47
Criminal Law of the People's Republic
  of China (CLPRC) 4, 91–2
Critical Illness Insurance Scheme
  (CIIS): implementation of 50–1, 64;
  Jiangyin model 66–7; Taicang model
  64–5; voluntary nature of 2; Xunyi
  model 67–8; Zhanjiang model 65–6

data collection methods 8–9
data mining technology 95–6
*Decision Concerning Health Reform and
  Development* 48
*Decision of the State Council Concerning
  the Establishment of the Urban
  Employee Basic Medical Insurance*
  (1998 Decree) 48–9

Decision on Further Strengthening Rural Health Work (2002 State Council Decision) 50
demographic dividend 19
Deng, Xiaoping 44, 54
discretionary power, of local governments 52–3
disparity in medical treatment 71–4
doctors: growing violence against 5, 79; health insurance fraud by 80–1
'double-envelope' tendering system 102
Drug Administration Law of the People's Republic of China 99–100
drug distribution system 3–4
drugs *see* pharmaceutical drugs

early retirement, financial sustainability and 77–8
employers, fraud by 85–6
environmental triggers 6–7, 54
epidemic prevention stations 30–1
epidemiologic transitions: causes of cancer-related mortality 24–5; causes of death *21–3*, 21–4; shift to NCDs 11, 19–21
Expanded Programme on Immunization (EPI) 31–2
experimental phase of health insurance reform (1993–7): Hainan model 58–9; overview of 48; Shanghai model 59–61; Shenzhen model 57–8; two-*jiang* model 57
exploration phase of health insurance reform (1984–92) 47–8
extension phase of health insurance reform (2002 to present) 49–51

financial sustainability measures: anti-fraud measures 90–6; drug pricing liberalization 98–100; establishing 12358 Price Reporting System 105–6; health insurance management appraisal 96–7; perfecting centralized drug procurement system 100–2; strengthen use of individual MSAs 98; suspension of medical insurance cards 97–8; zero-markup drug policy 103–5
First National Health Conference 30
first tier, in three-tiered medical institution network 33–4, 35–6
floating population, uninsured 74–5
fragmented risk pools 3

fraud *see* health insurance fraud
fraud control units 92–4

geographical differences, in ageing population 13–15
government drug price control policy 98–100
Government-Funded Health Care Scheme (GHS) 38–9, 45, 53
Great Leap Forward campaign 35
Green Book of Health Reform and Development 2014 84–5
Gross Domestic Product (GDP) per capita 18–19
Guiding Opinions on Further Improving Basic Medical Insurance Settlement Service for Medical Expenses Incurred outside Home Territory 76
Guiding Opinions on Further Strengthening the Management of the Basic Medical Insurance Fund 61
Guiding Opinions on Including University Students in the Pilot Basic Medical Insurance for Urban Residents (2008 Guiding Opinions) 63
Guiding Opinions on Perfecting the Centralized Drug Procurement System of Public Hospitals (2015 Guiding Opinions) 102
Guiding Opinions on Piloting Basic Medical Insurance for Urban Residents (State Council 2007) 50
Guiding Opinions on the Launch of the Work on Critical Illness Insurance for Urban and Rural Residents (Guiding Opinions) 51

Hainan model of health insurance 58–9
health care providers, insurance fraud and 4, 78–80
health financing: ageing population and 25–6, 77–8; increasing expenditures 44–6; *see also* financial sustainability measures
Health Insurance Bureau 76
health insurance fraud: immature legal system and 4–5; insurance card suspension 97–8; measures to combat 90–6; by patients 81–4; by providers/physicians 80–1
health insurance management appraisal 96–7
health insurance reform phases: background/context of 43–6;

complex interplay of forces in 51–5; four phases overview 46–51; overview of 2–5, 8–9, 43; regulation/guiding opinions *46*
Health Insurance Reforms in Asia (Luk) 5
health insurance settlements 76–7
health insurance system, discriminatory 3
health insurance system financial sustainability *see* financial sustainability measures
Health Preservation Pharmaceutical Cooperative (HPPC) 39–40
heart disease *21–3*, 21–4
historical institutionalism 5–8
hospital system: cost recovery policy 44; fake hospitalization 80–1; financial contracting with 47; flaws in 4; health insurance management appraisal 96–7; profit-seeking behavior of 78–80; zero-markup drug policy for 103–5
household registration system 74–5
Hu, Jintao 55

ideational forces, shaping health insurance reforms 7–8, 54–5
implementation phase of health insurance reform (1998–2001) 48–9
incentive reward scheme 94–5
individual medical savings accounts (MSAs): BMI formed from 49; individual responsibility and 55; poor transferability of 86–7; role of 9; SPF combined with 48; strengthen use of 98
individual responsibility, health insurance plans and 53–5
inequality in medical treatment 71–4
infectious diseases 19–21, 30–2
Insurance Fraud Bureau (IFB) 92–4
iron rice bowl 29, 54

Jiang, Zemin 54
Jiangyin model of CIIS 66–7

Khrushchev, Nikita 34–5
Knowledge Discovery in Databases (KDD) 95

Labor Insurance Scheme (LIS) 37–8, 45, 53
law enforcement measures, for health insurance fraud 90–2
legal system, immature 4–5

life expectancy, increased 12–13, 20, 41
local governments' discretionary power 52–3

Management of Designated Medical Institutions of Social Medical Insurance 96
Mao, Zedong 27–9, 34–5, 35, 54
Mao's era *see* pre-reform era
market economy 44
mass vaccination programmes 31
Medicaid Fraud Control Units (MFCUs) 94
medical expenses, rising 78–80
Medical Financial Assistance (MFA) System 2, 68–70
medical insurance see *health insurance entries*
Medical Insurance Ordinance for Urban Employees of the Hainan Special Economic Zone (1995 Hainan Medical Insurance Ordinance) 58–9
medical savings account (MSA) *see* individual medical savings accounts (MSAs)
Medicare Fraud Strike Force (MFSF) Teams 94
Methods of Assessing Designated Medical Institutions of Social Medical Insurance in Qingdao City (2015 Assessment Method) 96
Minimum Livelihood Guarantee Scheme 69–70
Ministry of Health (MOH) 35, 47
Ministry of Labor and Social Security (MOLSS) 49
multi-layered social health insurance system: CIIS representative models 64–8; as discriminatory 3; four experimental phase models 56–61; MFA System and 68–70; NRCMS 62–3; overview of 56; UEBMI 61; URBMI 63–4; *see also* problems in current health system

National Basic Medical Insurance Drug Formulary List (Drug Formulary) 49
National Health and Family Commission of the People's Republic of China 13
negative policy-feedback effects 53
New Rural Cooperative Medical Allowance System for Critical Illnesses (Medical Allowance System) 67–8

New Rural Cooperative Medical Handling Center 68

New Rural Cooperative Medical System (NRCMS): features of 62–3; implementation of 49–50; lack of benefits from 72–4; lack of understanding about 89; merger with URBMI 67–8; treated as compulsory 87–8; voluntary nature of 2

non-communicable diseases (NCDs) 11, 19–21, 26

Notice Concerning the Temporary Suspension of the Use of Health Insurance Card of Health Insurance Participants 98

Notice on Accelerating Pilot Work of the New Rural Cooperative Medical System 62

Notice on Accomplishing the Task of New Rural Cooperative Medical System 62

Notice on Regulating the Task of the Centralized Drug Procurement System for Medical Institutions 100

old-age dependency ratio, rising 18

12358 Price Reporting System 105–6

Opinions on Basic Medical Insurance Settlement Service for Medical Expenses Incurred outside Home Territory 76

Opinions on Deepening the Health Care System Reform, 63, 103

Opinions on Establishing Pilot Urban Medical Financial Assistance System 68–9

Opinions on Further Improving Medical Financial Assistance System and Implementing Medical Financial Assistance System for Catastrophic Illnesses in Full Swing (2015 Opinions) 70

Opinions on Further Improving Urban and Rural Medical Financial Assistance Systems (2009 Opinions) 69

Opinions on Implementing Drug Price Reform (2015 Opinions) 100

Opinions on Implementing Pilot Medical Financial Assistance System for Catastrophic Illnesses (2012 Opinions) 69

Opinions on the Implementation of Rural Medical Financial Assistance 68

Opinions on the Trial of Health Care System Reform for Urban Employees (1994 Opinions) 48, 57

Pathway Model *see* two-*jiang* health insurance model

patients, and health insurance fraud 81–4

People's Republic of China (PRC) 19–20, 27–9

performance appraisal, of public hospitals 96–7

pharmaceutical drugs: centralized bidding/procurement system 100–2; illegal purchase/resale of 83–4; pricing liberalization 98–100; zero-markup drug policy 103–5

policy actors 7

policy paradigms 7

political institutions 8

portability of health insurance schemes 75–7

positive policy-feedback effects 53

pre-reform era: background/context of 27–9; health care delivery system 32–7; health care financing system 37–41; health care principles in 29–30; public health system 30–2; summary remarks 42

prescription drugs 83–4; *see also* pharmaceutical drugs

preventive medicine, in pre-reform era 30–2

problems in current health system: additional BMI problems 85–9; floating population/migrant workers 74–5; inequality/disparity in treatment 71–4; overview of 71; portability of insurance schemes 75–7; sustainability of funds 77–85

programmatic ideas, policy change and 7

public fraud reporting system 94–5

public health campaigns 32

public health education 31

public health system, in pre-reform era 30–2

public hospitals *see* hospital system

Public Security Bureau 93

punctuated equilibrium 6

refined theory of historical institutionalism 5–8

Report Concerning a Number of Policy Issues Connected with the Health Service Reforms, 47

Report on China's Migrant Population Development 2015 14

Research Group on Health Care Reform 47

respiratory disease *21–3*, 21–4
risk pools, fragmented 3
rural areas: ageing population in
16–18, *17*; forced participation in
NRCMS 87–8; leading causes of
death *21–3*, 21–4; MFA System for
68; three-tiered medical institution
network in 35–7; uninsured migrant
workers 74–5

second tier, in three-tiered medical
institution network 34, 36
Shanghai model of health insurance
59–61
Shenzhen model of health insurance
57–8
*Shenzhen Provisional Regulations on
Basic Medical Insurance* (1996
Provisional Regulations) 57
Sino-Soviet relationship 27–8, 34–5
Social Insurance Law of the People's
Republic of China (SILPRC) 4, 91–2
social pooling fund (SPF): BMI formed
from 49; MSAs combined with 48;
role of 9; social solidarity and 55
social solidarity, health insurance and
53, 54–5
societal beliefs 7
Soviet Union 28, 30–1, 34
State Council, shaping health insurance
reforms 52
state laws, health insurance fraud and
90–2
state-owned enterprises (SOEs),
uninsured 45
*Statistical Reports on National Economic
and Social Development* 18
supplier-induced demand (SID) 44–5,
78–80
sustainability of health insurance funds
77–80; *see also* financial sustainability
measures

*Tabulation on the 2010 Population
Census of the People's Republic of
China (Book I)* 12
Taicang model of CIIS 64–5
third tier, in three-tiered medical
institution network 34, 37
three-tiered medical institution network:
in pre-reform era 32–3; in rural areas
35–7; in urban areas 33–5

top-down decision-making model
51–2
total fertility rate (TFR) 12–13, 18
transferability of individual MSAs 86–7
*Trial Implementation of Basic Medical
Insurance for Urban and Rural
Residents* 66
*Trial Implementation of Methods
of Assessing Designated Medical
Institutions of New Rural Cooperative
Medical System* 96–7
two-*jiang* health insurance model 48,
53, 57
2000 Population Census of China
14, *15*
*2010 Population Census of the People's
Republic of China* 14, *16*, 17

universal health coverage (UHC)
1–5, 90
urban areas: ageing population in
16–18, *17*; leading causes of death
21–3, 21–4; MFA System for 68–9;
three-tiered medical institution
network in 33–5
Urban Employee Basic Medical
Insurance (UEBMI): accumulated
deficit in 84–5; compulsory nature
of 2; discriminatory nature of 72;
enterprise-level non-compliance
85–6; implementation of 49;
questionable sustainability of funds
78; unique features of 61
urban *hukou* status 74–5
Urban Resident Basic Medical Insurance
(URBMI): adverse selection problem
87; features of 63–4; implementation
of 50; lack of benefits from 72–3; lack
of understanding about 88–9; merger
with NRCMS 67–8

working-age population, shrinking
18–19
work units 29, 47, 85–6
World Health Organization (WHO) 1,
2, 24

Xi, Jinping, President 5, 71
Xunyi model of CIIS 67–8

zero-markup drug policy 103–5
Zhanjiang model of CIIS 65–6